Exploring the New Horizons of International Law Concerning Globalization of Economy

Jamil Afzal

Exploring the New Horizons of International Law Concerning Globalization of Economy

Springer

Jamil Afzal
School of International Law
Southwest University of Political Science
and Law
Chongqing, China

ISBN 978-981-95-1311-6 ISBN 978-981-95-1312-3 (eBook)
https://doi.org/10.1007/978-981-95-1312-3

This Springer imprint is published by the registered company Springer Nature Singapore Pte Ltd.
The registered company address is: 152 Beach Road, #21-01/04 Gateway East, Singapore 189721, Singapore

Dedication goes to my father, my mentor Mian Muhammad Afzal (Advocate High Court Lahore) for his patience and guidance during the long hours spent immersed in academic pursuit. I am also thankful to the dedicated editorial staff at Springer Nature, particularly Lydia Wang. Finally, my most sincere thanks go to my family, especially; my mother Bushra Bibi, and my wife Asma Batool.

Foreword

It is a token of honor for me to write the foreword for this book *Exploring the New Horizons of International Law Concerning Globalization of Economy*. As a practitioner of Economic Law and WTO, for the novelty of this book, I would like to extend my heartfelt congratulations to author Dr. Jamil Afzal and the publishers for their initiative in compiling this wealth of information and expertise. The author briefly discussed the globalization of the economy and the digitalization phenomenon in the context of international law.

The digital economy is an international system in which digital technologies support business, financial exchange, and professional collaboration. This includes e-commerce sites that offer different types of goods and services, along with digital financial solutions such as online banking, digital currencies, and mobile payments. Digital economy platforms also benefit from applying AI to streamline processes and derive insights while working with (the Internet of Things (IoT), invigorating device connectivity and enabling better performance and data collection. Such innovations greatly support international commerce because they make transactions easier, expand the market, and provide personalized solutions. The success stories of powerhouses like Amazon and Alibaba have enabled firms to enter abroad markets without barriers of locality. Also, the development in digital finance has ensured easy cross-border dealings, which has prompted expansion amongst firms in both sectors. The fusion of AI and IoT massively maximizes efficiency via workflow optimization, predicting movements in the market, and automating operations. International trade has been greatly adjusted through the adoption of digital technologies, simplifying operations and reducing expenses. Due to e-commerce, markets have crossed national boundaries to allow small entrepreneurs to participate in global trade. New opportunities for international investment and funding are emerging on the digital finance platforms, while the improved AI and IoT have already revolutionized core industries, including logistics, manufacturing, and customer services. For instance, they use artificial intelligence to provide customized recommendations, adaptive pricing, and improved customer service to facilitate the establishment of more flexible and responsive global trade networks. Finally, these technological innovations have led to new business strategies and enabled a more united, flexible, and borderless trade and commerce.

The statistics of the digital economy have not only transformed traditional industries but also created new barriers for international legal frameworks. There is a complicated relationship between international law and the digital economy, with legal structures often lagging behind the advancement of technologies. Even though there are such agreements as the WTO's GATS that are concerned with digital trade, the processes of defining common global norms in digital services, data border regulations, privacy, and intellectual property are still developing. Businesses and consumers cannot operate peacefully without clear, universally agreed-upon rules, calling for international law to follow the digital era. The development of the digital economy plays a central role in globalization, which brings many advantages and new challenges. The rise in global data transfers, digital commerce, and internet-driven services has radically changed cross-border business and consumer activities. The increased flow of data is driving innovations, but also incredible debates about privacy, security, and the governance of data. Being a researcher, and practitioner, I feel this book is a valuable resource for researchers, students, and policymakers interested in the field of digital economy.

Yongmei Chen

June 2025

Prof. Chen Yongmei
Southwest University of Political Science and Law
Chongqing, China

Preface

This book studies how international law is evolving to meet the challenges of the digital era. We are discussing how the global economy is changing and how WTO and the UN are trying to set up the stage for cooperation, regulation, and order. As we stand on the brink of a fully globalized digital economy, we must ask: Can international law truly keep pace with technological advancements? This book tries to answer this question by presenting a detailed analysis of how international law is responding or failing to respond to the digital economy.

To get a proper sense of this global shift, we had to look at actual systems of law and real-life applications. That is why the qualitative research approach based on case law, legal analysis, and comparative analysis of various national and international legal systems has been chosen. The author investigates how leading countries with advanced digital economic systems, including the regulation of cryptocurrencies or digital trade and E-commerce in the European Union, China, and the USA have approached these issues. How do countries with differing legal traditions find common grounds, and where do they clash? By studying how these systems function in practice, the author not only highlights successes but also uncovers the gaps that remain. Now, countries are still struggling with their domestic laws on regulation while international treaties, and conventions, regulate the world economy and trading rules. But do these frameworks offer a sufficiently stable and adaptable foundation to regulate the complexities of the digital economy? Taking the WTO and the UN as examples, the book examines the efforts made by these international institutions to retrofit traditional legal structures for a world increasingly defined by the internet. Can global trade rules designed for physical goods be applied to digital products and services? How can global institutions facilitate cooperation between countries with drastically different levels of technological development? These questions shape the discussion. For digitalization, the author discussed the Contemporary Theory of Digitalization (CToD); the Contemporary Theory of Digitalization (CToD) provides and logical framework, through which organizations, institutes, and states may be digitalized. The author presents three levels of the Contemporary Theory of Digitalization; the first level consists of 3Ds, the second level consists of 5Ds, and the third level consists of 7Ds. This also provides a framework for organization-to-organization or state-to-state digital linkage.

The approach used in this book does not only focus on the laws but also the growing technological world. The digital world is more dynamic than it is possible to regulate it through laws that may take a lot of time to be adopted and enforced. Some laws were drafted many years ago and may now be incomplete and full of loopholes and ambiguities. By mixing legal research with real-world examples, this book aims to provide practical insights into how international law can progress to address these issues at the front. This book provides the reader with a valuable understanding of the digital economy and its relationship with international law by integrating comparative legal analysis with insights regarding contemporary global economic conditions. The author has looked at laws and regulations, examined case studies, and critically assessed how international law might (or might not) be the solution to the challenges of globalization in the digital age.

Chongqing, China Jamil Afzal

Acknowledgments My sincere appreciation goes to my following fellows, whose guidance and expertise were instrumental in shaping the research direction of this book.

- Prof. Chen Yongmei, from Southwest University of Political Science China.
- Prof. Yang Guohua from Tsinghua University, China.
- Dr. Aftab Haider, from Southwest University of Political Science China.
- Prof. Zheng Yun, from Southwest University of Political Science China.
- Prof. Yuqun Meng, from Southwest University of Political Science China.
- Mr. Ibrar Ahmad, Southwest University of Political Science China.
- Dr. Yasir Munir Leghari, Editor in Chief, International Journal of Law and Legal Advancement (IJLLA).
- Mst. Balqees Amjad, Advocate High Court, Lahore.
- Mst. Anza Fatima, Department of IR, Bahauddin Zakariya University, Multan.

Competing Interests The author has no competing interests to declare that are relevant to the content of this manuscript.

Contents

Abbreviations

ADA	American with Disabilities Act
ADB	Asian Development Bank
AfCFTA	African Continental Free Trade Area
AIIB	Asian Infrastructure Investment Bank
AML	Anti Money Laundering
APTs	Advance Precisistent Threats
B2B	Business to Business
B2C	Business to Consumer
BEPS	Base Erosion and Profit Shifting
BIS	Bank for International Settlements
BITs	Bilateral Investment Treaties
BRI	Belt and Road Initiative
C2B	Consumer to Business
CAC	Collective Action Clause
CBAM	Carbon Border Adjustment Mechanism
CBDCs	Central Bank Digital Currencies
CC	Criminal Code
CCPA	California Consumer Privacy Act
CFPB	Consumer Financial Protection Bureau
CFT	Combating the Financing of Terrorism
CISA	Cybersecurity and Infrastructure Security Agency
CJEU	Court of Justice of European Union
CMPI	Committee on Payments and Market Infrastructure
CPC	Criminal Procedure Code
CPTPP	Comprehensive and Progressive Agreement for Trans-Pacific Partnership
CTF	Counter Terrorist Financing
Defi	Decentralized Finance
DMA	Digital Markets Act
DSA	Digital Services Act
DSB	Dispute Settlement Body

DSM	Digital Single Market
DST	Digital Service Tax
EIOs	European Investigation Orders
ESF	Environmental and Social Framework
ESG	Environmental, Social and Governance
ESMF	Environment and Social Management Framework
FATF	Financial Action Task Force
FDI	Foreign Direct Investment
FinCEN	Financial Crimes Enforcement Network
FIUs	Financial Intelligence Units
FSB	Financial Stability Board
FTX	Futures Exchange
GATS	General Agreement on Trade in Service
GATT	General Agreement on Tariffs and Trade
GDPR	General Data Protection Regulation
IBRD	International Bank for Reconstruction and Development
ICC	International Criminal Court
ICCPR	International Convenant on Civilian and Political Rights
ICESCR	International Convnant Economic Social and Cultural Rights
ICJ	International Court of Justice
ICOs	Initial Coin Offerings
ICSID	International Centre for the Settlement of Investment Disputes
IDA	International Development Association
IDB	Inter- American Development Bank
IEEPA	International Emergency Economic Power Act
ILO	International Labour Organisation
IMF	International Monetary Fund
INTERPOL	International Criminal Police Organization
IOSCo	International Organisation of Security Commissions
IP	Intellectual Property
IRS	Internal Revenue Service
ISDS	Investor- State Dispute Settlement
ITA	Information Technology Agreement
ITU	International Telecommunication Union
KYC	Know Your Customer
MEAS	Multilateral Environmental Agreements
MFN	Most Favored Nation
MiCA	Market inCrypto Assets
MOOCs	Massive Open Online Courses
NAFTA	North American Free Trade Agreement
NFTs	Non-Fungible Tokens
NGOs	Non Governmental Organisations
OECD	Organization for Economic Cooperation and Development
PBOC	People's Bank of China
PDPA	Personal Data Protection Act

RCEP	Regional Comprehensive Economic Partnership
REACH	Registration, Evaluation, Authorisation and restriction of Chemicals
SAPs	Structural Adjustment Programs
SSC	South South Corporation
TCFD	Task Force on Climate Related Financial Disclosure
TFA	Trade Facilitation Agreement
TRIPS	Trade Related Aspects of Intellectual Property Rights
UDHR	Universal Declaration of Human Rights
UN	United Nations
UNCTAD	United Nations Conference on Trade and Development
UNFCCC	United Nations Framework Convention on Climate Change
UNGPs	United Nations Guiding Principles on Business and Human Rights
USMCA	United States-Mexico-Canada Agreement
VASPs	Virtual Asset Service Providers
WIPO	Word Intellectual Property Organisation
WTO	World Trade Organisation

International Law and the Globalization of the Economy

1 Introduction

International law is a set of rules, modes, and standards that give order to how states, international organizations, and in some instances, even individuals interact [1]. International law is universal or applies to all countries, unlike domestic law, which applies only within a specific country. It is concerned with or ranges across several subjects, such as trade, human rights, environmental protection, conflict resolution, and criminal law [2]. Treaties, conventions, customary practice, judicial decisions, and generally accepted legal principles form a part of international law, as they respectively exist at the time of the destruction or damage [3]. Its main objective is to develop a framework in which countries and all other actors internationally can peacefully work together, resolve conflicts using diplomacy, and deal with global issues. It creates a context of how nations communicate, behave, and uphold norms through which nations interact with each other and agree upon norms, paying more attention to cooperation, violations, and inclusive peaceful resolution of disputes rather than violence or aggression. For instance, trade law regulates trade among countries, which is administered by the World Trade Organization (WTO) and resolves such conflicts [4]. Documents like the Universal Declaration of Human Rights set out to protect the rights of people worldwide, irrespective of their nationality, under international human rights law [5]. International environmental law deals with challenges for the planet like climate change and pollution, and international agreements like the Paris Agreement, to reduce greenhouse gas emissions globally [6]. As an international humanitarian law, the conduct that occurs during armed conflict is moderated to protect noncombatants (civilians and prisoners of war) [7]. In today's world, international law is instrumental in shaping the relations among states, but the legal framework for cooperation and interaction. A key area in which international law matters is global trade and business [8]. A world of interconnected economies requires stability of law that supports cross-border transactions, the international law provides such stability [9]. In other words, WTO helps to remove trade barriers,

J. Afzal, *Exploring the New Horizons of International Law Concerning Globalization of Economy*, https://doi.org/10.1007/978-981-95-1312-3_1

resolves disputes between countries, and ensures that both countries abide by agreed-upon rules. Without such legal frameworks, international trade could become disorderly as states may make unilateral decisions that might give rise to trade wars and other conflicts. International law regulates trade, promoting collaboration and development of the economy between nations to decrease the instability of an unregulated, non-competitive market [10].

Besides economic cooperation, international law plays a key role in maintaining global peace and security [11]. It prevents violence by establishing what should and should not be done if there is a dispute and providing what mechanisms to be used if problems do arise. The use of force to stabilize or prevent conflicts may be authorized by bodies like the UN Security Council, which can decide even the use of force against whom [12]. However, the International Court of Justice (ICJ) is a body to which states resort to settling their disputes with each other [13]. International law provides protocols in times of conflict that encourage peace, and order, and eliminate the risk of war over the recourse to the use of force. International law thus contributes to the status of peace, cooperation, and dialogue before the aggressive status. An important part of international law, human rights concern the discipline of protecting the individual from abuses worldwide [14]. The Universal Declaration of Human Rights (UDHR) and other international treaties define the fundamental principles about how people must be treated: freedom of expression, right to life, prohibition of torture, and others. However, if those rights are violated, international law offers an instrument to deal with such violations by making the state responsible for the mistreatment of people. For example, the International Criminal Court (ICC) investigates and prosecutes individuals responsible for war crimes, genocide, and crimes against humanity [15]. Human rights law manages to achieve this through legal penalties and actions on the international level, as abuses beyond national borders require global intervention.

International law also covers environmental protection, in view that matters such as climate change, pollution, and depletion of resources concern the whole world [16]. Many environmental issues go beyond the scope of action of a single country and are thus governed by international environmental law. Without international legal frameworks, countries can act without considering the global interest and damage the environment, and, in some cases, might lead to long-term damage or conflict. International law obliges nations to come to the aid of the environment without jeopardizing the concerns of national interest or the requirement of collective compromise for the preservation of resources for future generations [17].

The role of international law in settling disputes between states is especially important in the preservation of peace. Even seemingly simple issues such as border disputes, allocation of resources, or trade disagreements can escalate into conflict. Peaceful means of dealing with such problems are available under international law. In practice, legal actions may include resolving legal disputes between countries to prevent war, interpreting a treaty or making a ruling in arbitration, similar to ICJ, and pronouncing a tribunal to serve as a jury. It provides a structured way in which the states could manage the conflicts and the relations between the nations, with a clear procedure to resolve the differences between the nations. International law works to prevent conflicts by forcing countries to obey rules of fairness and justice and to prevent states from undertaking actions that they are not to take. Furthermore, it is an impartial platform for arbitrating disputes, thus maintaining the deterioration of international relations. ICC endows individuals subject to no status whatsoever with the possibility of being punished for grave crimes. This system also serves as a deterrent, as bad men of prey know they can be brought to the bar and thus will be punished. The legal framework thus makes individuals liable for actions that jeopardize global peace and security.

2 Concept of Globalization

Globalization is a term that has been used to describe or refer to the interconnection and interdependence of global markets, societies, and cultures [18]. This is the process by which nations interconnect their economies through trade, investments, technology, information, and people. It refers to the movement of goods, services, capital, and ideas across states. It is driven by improved technology, communication, and transport. Globalization is a phenomenon that has had profound impacts on the nature of interrelations between countries, and its influence manifests itself in almost all spheres of contemporary life, including business, political, cultural, and social spheres [19]. The rise of multinational corporations, the global spread of Western cultural products, and entertainment, and the spreading exchange of knowledge and education are demonstrated by this. In addition to disseminating rapidly, cultural trends, social transformations, and ideologies affect how people all around the world live and transact business. The history of globalization shows that globalization's roots are found in the prehistoric era [20]. Goods and cultures could move along the early trade route, the Silk Road, and the Mediterranean Sea [21, 22]. Although these initial exchanges would ultimately lead to the cultural, technological, and trade ties between people on very different continents, on a scale hundreds of times greater than today, they were nothing close to what modern society involves. The first great wave of globalization was in the Age of Exploration in the fifteenth and sixteenth centuries, when European countries started colonizing all over the world [23]. In this era, European culture, religion, and political systems spread, and exchanges of goods like spices, textiles, and silver occurred. However, it was in the nineteenth century that globalization in its present state started to be seen. The global economy had a major transformation from the beginning of the Industrial Revolution in Britain, in the late eighteenth century [24, 25]. Steam-powered ships and trains, and the telegraph made it possible to move goods faster and to communicate through much faster channels. As a result of these advancements, trade between nations was permitted to become more extensive and even allowed for capital to be allowed to flow across borders. The 19th Century also saw the rise of multinational corporations that would operate in many countries using an intercontinental supply chain. The second wave of globalization started in the middle of the twentieth century as global players started to look at the world in terms of reconstruction after the destructive effects of the Second World

War [26]. This period also saw the advancement of globalization due to the creation of institutions such as the International Monetary Fund (IMF), the World Bank, and WTO that provided for international cooperation on trade, investment, and finance. It marked the beginning of globalization based on the policies that encouraged free trade and international markets. The developed countries liberalized their economies and deregulated, making the environment more conducive to international business and MNCs. A second significant change appeared in the 1990s and the early years of the 2000s, due to the dynamic development of the Internet and digital technologies [27]. These changes facilitated the efficient transfer of information and ideas across borders, raising efficient supply chain management for businesses and individuals. The liberalization of economies like Eastern Europe and China in terms of trade and investment after the Cold War intensified the speed of international business and increased the extent of integration [28, 29].

Globalization played a strong role in the economic growth of countries across Asia, North America, and Europe by facilitating the increase in international trade on a large scale. In many regions, it is linked with great economic development, high living standards, and poverty reduction. Globalization has also allowed technology, innovation, and ideas to spread across sectors, such as manufacturing, agriculture, and services, to improve production [30]. It also presents new opportunities to businesses for penetrating foreign markets, outsourcing and offshoring, as well as diversifying their supply chains. Yet, for globalization not to be beneficial for all equally, this might be true. Developing nations have not managed well as developed nations get free rein of the benefits of increased trade, investment, and innovation without an iota of change. Rising economic inequality has been one of the most difficult challenges. Wealth is becoming concentrated in the hands of multinational corporations and economic elites. Globalization is also another cause of moving industries to countries where workers are cheap, especially in Asia, which has led to the loss of jobs in developed countries [31]. The speed of trade liberalization has added to the environmental problems as it has accelerated the exploitation of natural resources in countries that have begun globalization to improve productivity. As for the environmental problems, including climate change, deforestation, and ocean pollution, which are global concerns, they need international cooperation to be solved, but in many cases, countries cannot come to a consensus. Another important aspect is the cultural aspect of globalization, because of which cultural imperialism has become a major issue. The globalization of consumerism, media, and entertainment has caused a shift to a more globalized culture where local cultures are often replaced with those of the West [32]. This has led to discussions on the destruction of culture and the effects of globalization or consumerism on traditional communities. On the positive side, globalization has helped to share knowledge and cultural practices, promote the value of cultural differences, and increase cultural interrelation.

3 International Law and Globalization

3.1 Role of International Law in the Globalized Economy

International law acts as a framework for the regulation of global commerce because it provides stability and predictability to relationships among states and other players in the economy [33]. As the world becomes a global village, where barriers to international cooperation are coming down, international law lays down rules for its members to regulate cross-border transactions or relations, giving an equal platform for foreign business. International law is more specifically important in two main areas: these areas include trade and commerce across borders and the protection of international investments.

One of the crucial roles of international law in the globalized economy is to regulate international commerce [34]. Since the world economy has integrated and the process of globalization has been facilitated by removing trade barriers and liberalizing trade across borders, international law has been developed to support this integration by allowing the free flow of goods, services, and capital across national borders without experiencing unfair trade barriers or practices. Two of the most distinguished global organizations managing international trade is the GATT, which was succeeded by the WTO in 1995 [35]. Today, the WTO acts as the rule maker, negotiator, and referee of the global trade system and a venue for resolving trade disputes among the member countries [36]. It aims at dismantling barriers to trade, including tariffs, quotas, and any other barriers that impede the flow of goods and services across borders. Besides, the WTO also oversees other areas of concern, such as intellectual property, agriculture, and dispute settlement, hence, it plays an important role in international trade. The WTO thus promotes freer trade and economic liberalization by providing legal, enforceable rules and regulations for members. Apart from the WTO, there are bilateral and regional trade agreements, for instance, NAFTA of North America or the Single European Market SEM of the EU, which also facilitate trade among members by removing barriers. Such arrangements might involve legal aspects such as tariffs, market access, environmentalism, and labor relations. By prescribing the legal ways that cross-border trade can be conducted, these frameworks help minimize risk and improve the efficiency of international trade between countries and firms.

The protection of international investments is one of the important facets of today's international law [37]. The dynamic global economy is such a case that individuals and businesses endeavor to invest in something other than their own country. International law arranges these investments safely and guarantees the investor while, of course, ensuring the sovereign immunity of the state. Bilateral Investment Treaties (BITs) are agreements between two countries aimed at protecting investments made by nationals or companies from each country in the other [38]. They are the primary instrument to guarantee international investment. The most general of these treaties contain provisions barring discrimination, protection from abuses, as well as the prohibition of the uncompensated taking of an investor's property. Besides providing

BIT mechanisms for resolving investment disputes, investors can bring cases to international courts or ICSID arbitration forums. These legal measures reduce the vulnerability of foreign investment and thus promote capital and economic growth in both developed and developing countries. They also support the stability of the multinational companies that undertake operations in numerous countries because they will do so legally. Without such conventions, investors may be discouraged from investing in countries that they deem to be politically or economically volatile, thus constraining the potential for investment and growth.

3.2 *How Globalization Affects the Development of International Law*

Globalization not only has reinforced the significance of international law in the world economy but also played a crucial role in the formation and changes in international legal standards. The need for international instruments and new laws also grows with the sharp increase in countries' economic interconnections [39]. Globalization has brought about problems that cannot be resolved at the national level and hence has led to the emergence of new international law and improvement in the international legal order.

Issues such as climate change, transnational terrorism, and financial regulation are not issues that can be solved individually by a country [40, 41]. These are issues that concern the international community, and international law is the forum through which countries can negotiate and formulate covenants that give rise to legal rights and duties between nations. One good example of such a need is the Paris Agreement on climate change, which was signed in 2015 [42]. The agreement proves that people all over the world have come to realize that the environment is interrelated and that it is high time for concerted action against global warming. It also contains legal obligations that prescribe the emission reduction goals and climate change policies and measures. The significance of this treaty can be viewed in the fact that this is yet another example of the growing tendency to use legal tools in the regulation of international relations, crossing beyond the state level. Likewise, the Financial Action Task Force (FATF), formed in 1989, has been the driving force behind the standards necessary to curb money laundering and financing of terrorism [43]. Consequently, FATF has developed global enforceable measures for funding operations to ensure that all countries work together to fight financial crimes that affect other countries. There is the emergence of new threats and challenges with increased globalization, and the need for legal systems that can address these global issues. This is why legal agreements and treaties are more important in the contemporary world as globalization is advancing.

One of the most evident realities of the contemporary world is the increasing legal convergence that is happening all over the world [44]. These are international guidelines that assist nations in coming up with laws that are acceptable to the global society in areas such as trade, human rights, as well as the environment. An excellent example is the evolution into a complex and formal system of international human rights law based on the notion of the existence of human rights regardless of the country of the world. For instance, the Universal Declaration of Human Rights (UDHR) and the International Covenant on Civil and Political Rights (ICCPR) provide basic rights like the right to a fair trial, freedom from torture, and the right to vote that all countries should adhere to regardless of the legal systems in place [45, 46]. Most of these are now accepted as basic international standards. Similarly, in international trade, legal frameworks have been attempted to establish internationally on such matters as intellectual property, labor, and environmental protection. The field of protection of different types of inventions and ideas is another example of one such thing, namely Trade-Related Aspects of Intellectual Property Rights (TRIPS) created by the WTO for the protection of countries of origin of inventions and ideas [47]. I would commend these international legal norms because they offer simple and clear guidelines to lower confusion and prevent conflicts among businesses, individuals, and states in the area of transnational relations. Therefore, the development of the international legal system is expected to remain on the rise as people of the world seek to address international issues and maintain good relations among states.

4 The Rise of Global Economic Institutions

Globalization has also precipitated the formation and growth of global bodies whose function is to regulate, facilitate, and monitor production and commerce across borders. These institutions play a crucial role in formulating the legal environment that governs IBI, financial systems, and development [48]. Some of the most popular of these institutions are the WTO, the IMF, the World Bank, and their regional counterparts. The structure and function of each of these organizations are different, but they are all involved in international economic law.

The WTO was set up in 1995 following the GATT, which was formed in 1947 [49]. The main objective of the WTO is to liberalize trade by lowering trade barriers and to make sure the trading environment is as stable and open as possible. While GATT was primarily established to govern the trade of goods, the WTO broadened its coverage to services, Intellectual property, and Investment, apart from goods. The WTO sets the rules of trade among its very large membership, developing rules among multilateral trade relations through a series of agreements. It has a clear governing structure with the Ministerial Conference as the body to make decisions at the highest level, meeting every two years, and the General Council as a forum for the continued operations of the organization. The WTO also has specially constituted bodies and committees dealing with such areas as agriculture, services, trade and development, and trade-related aspects of intellectual property rights. The activities undertaken by the WTO are to ensure adherence to trade agreements and facilitate the negotiation of new trade rules, rules that include tariffs, subsidies, anti-dumping measures, intellectual property rights, and services, among others. Its job is to protect international trade from unfair practices and restrictive measures and prevent trade wars; thus, it helps to mitigate the risk of economic crises. The Dispute Settlement System is one of the essential components of the WTO that grants the member countries the opportunity to file a complaint with the WTO if they believe that the other country violates the agreed-upon rules of trade. The main goal is to guarantee that all members of the WTO abide by the rules and regulations of the organization. In case one country believes that the other has violated these rules, it can form a complaint and report it to the Dispute Settlement Body (DSB) [50]. This is followed by the formation of a panel that is tasked with the responsibility of assessing the case and making recommendations on how the problem can be solved. In case the panel determines that there was a violation, it normally demands that the violating country change its policies to be in line with WTO regulations. If the country does not do so, the injured country may seek authorization from the DSB to retaliate, for example by placing trade restrictions. This system also serves to prevent anarchy in world trade by ensuring that countries do not resort to protectionism or take retaliatory measures against other nations.

The IMF was created in 1944 as an international financial institution that has aimed to promote global monetary cooperation and assist in the responsible management of the international financial system, especially when member countries have balance of payment problems [51]. The main goals of the IMF are to encourage cooperation in international monetary relations, maintain exchange rate stability, and achieve better international economic relations. The IMF is an important institution in the global monetary system because it offers emergency short-term loans to countries, which means that a country cannot meet its balance of payment requirements. Such problems can be mainly attributed to political instability, poor economic policies, or external factors. The IMF offers funds for the balance of payments support and stabilizations to implement structural changes to put the microeconomic fundamentals back in place. They can also incorporate measures such as fiscal adjustment, devaluation of currency, and other measures aimed at economic growth. In addition to disbursing funds, the IMF also has an aspect known as Economic Surveillance. It tracks the state of the global economy and reassesses the economic position of the member countries periodically. In this way, the IMF informs its members about potential threats and provides necessary recommendations to deal with threats to financial stability. It also offers technical cooperation in the sectors of taxation, public expenditure, and the financial sector, which builds the human and institutional capital of a country. In this way, the IMF plays a role in maintaining financial stability by providing financial assistance during the crisis, at the same time, suggesting the proper policies to be followed. The IMF conducts its operations based on legal provisions and standards that define its lending policies, surveillance functions, and decision-making procedures. The framework of rules that govern the IMF is formally known as the Articles of Agreement, they provide the IMF with its structure, membership, and main function [52]. Conditions include the stand that IMF borrowers are required to maintain sound fiscal and structural policies for their economies, in addition to the standard financial and operational policies for the institution. Conditionality can be defined as the policy reforms a borrowing country has to undertake as a prerequisite for receiving funds. The transparency and accountability of its actions are secured through provisions of the IMF legal charter. Having discussed the nature of the IMF loans, its lending policies and practices often draw criticism, especially when the organization demands austerity measures from borrowing countries. Some people believe that conditions agreed with the IMF should be detrimental to the citizens of the borrowing nations, while others opine that reforms foster sustainable economic growth.

The World Bank is currently one of the largest and oldest organizations, whose mission is to fight poverty and contribute to the economic development of countries [53]. It has five affiliates, of which the largest are the IBRD and the IDA. These institutions give loans and/or grants to the nations depending on the level of development of such countries. The World Bank primarily contributes to the development of international economic law as a financier for major development projects in the developing world, mainly in the sectors of transportation, education, health, and energy. The legal environment in which the WB works is the principles of environmental protection, social policies, and openness. One of the most important tools applied in the framework of the World Bank is the Environmental and Social Management Framework (ESMF), aimed at reducing social and environmental risks of the projects carried out. The Environmental and Social Framework (ESF) is a set of policies that have to be fulfilled before a country is approved to borrow funds for developmental purposes without compromising the environment and people's lives. Other sources of funding include the regional development banks, including the Asian Development Bank (ADB), the African Development Bank (AfDB), and the Inter-American Development Bank (IDB), which offer funding and technical assistance to member countries. As mentioned earlier, these regional banks sometimes work with the World Bank to address regional development needs, and they are also involved in the formulation of rules of law for development within their regions, policies and standard operating procedures, and measures to promote safe and sound operations. These institutions' legal documents and operational arrangements enhance the integration of development objectives into the framework of international law. By setting standards for financing, environmental protection, and social responsibility, the World Bank and regional development banks help to shape the way international economic law addresses global development challenges.

5 Key Areas of International Economic Law

With the growth of global economic integration, there has been a dire need of global rules governing the flow of products and services, capital, and information across borders. The main branches of International economic law are International Trade Law, International Investment Law, and International Financial Law.

5.1 Trade Law

What role do international trade agreements like GATT and WTO play in regulating global trade? International trade agreements are at the center of trade law, and they set the terms in which trading partners can trade in goods, services, and intellectual property. The General Agreement on Tariffs and Trade (GATT), formed in 1947, and the World Trade Organization (WTO), founded in 1995, are the legal systems that govern global trade. The GATT mainly aimed at the reduction of tariffs and other barriers to trade to open world trade and commerce. It instituted several phases of negotiation where countries bargained over tariffs and trade liberalization. They wanted to bring trade negotiations to a higher level and to fill gaps that existed as trade and commerce developed new characteristics and grew more intricate. The WTO also brought a new dimension to International Trade Law by expanding the areas of services, intellectual property, and trade-related investment measures. It plays a role in supervising trade relationships and making certain that nations stick to the promises they make in their negotiation sessions. The WTO works to promote trade liberalization by establishing new trade agreements, reviewing members' trade policies, and mediating trade disputes. The existence of the WTO sets up the environment for its members to engage in international trade through a set of rules, which facilitates international trade relations. How are trade disputes addressed in international trade law? Trade disputes constitute an integral part of the global trading system, and some are unavoidable. If a country feels that another nation is breaching the rules of trade or the treaty, it can go to the WTO. The WTO Dispute Settlement Mechanism (DSM) contains a set of rules that govern the resolution of disputes. Disputes can be resolved by a dispute settlement body, which investigates the matter and makes its ruling by WTO regulations. If a violation has been committed, then the panel usually recommends that the errant country adhere to correct policies. In the case where the violating country does not confirm to the recommendations of the panel, the WTO enables the complaining country to seek permission to retaliate by placing barriers to trade. It aids in the protection of international trade agreements, hence preventing trade wars and disruptions of the economic system.

5.2 Investment Law

What are Bilateral Investment Treaties (BITs), and why are they important? BITs are treaties concluded between two nations protecting the investments made in a foreign country by individuals of the treaty partner country [54]. These treaties lay down certain legal rights enjoyed by foreign investors, such as protection against unfair treatment, expropriation, and discrimination. BITs are usually expected to afford the investor a legal redress right in the event the host country breaches the treaty provisions. These are important because they offer legal assurance to investors by offering a legal framework to investors to curb the risks as they invest in other countries. BITs have emerged to be essential in facilitating globalization because they act as the conduct through which capital flows across borders, which has been a key determinant in economic growth. They assure investors that their investments will be secure, thus encouraging foreign investment, especially in countries where the legal or political climate is volatile. What are dispute resolution mechanisms like ICSID, and how do they function in investment law? It is a contractual relationship that arises between an investor and a host country when the latter is accused of breaching the provisions of a BIT or any other investment treaty. To tackle such issues, international law offers remedial measures in the form of instruments of redress. The most famous is the International Centre for the Settlement of Investment Disputes (ICSID), which was created in 1966 by the World Bank [55]. ICSID offers a platform for arbitration between investors and host states. In the case of a dispute, the investor can submit the case to ICSID's arbitral panels, which consists of impartial arbitrators who assess the facts of the case and determine which legal provisions were violated. The awards given by ICSID are final, and the center also looks into the enforcement of the awards. ICSID arbitration is especially valuable because it provides for third-party intervention in the case of investment disputes so that domestic courts do not appear prejudiced against international investors. ICSID arbitration promotes fairness, transparency, and justice in the resolution of investment disputes originating from international investments. It also opens up the possibility for the investors to claim recompense in the event their investments are negatively affected by the government of the host country, supporting the legal guarantees afforded by BITs.

5.3 *Financial Law*

What role does financial law play in regulating cross-border banking and financial transactions? International banking and financial flows are critical components of the global economy, enabling the mobilization of funds and the funding of cross-border business and investment [56]. Financial law refers to the set of rules that are applied to financial activities to ensure compliance, the lack of fraud, and ensure security [57, 58]. One area of financial law is the international banking law that regulates various banking activities that span across countries [59]. In its operation, any business that operates in a particular country has to adhere to the laws of that country. This includes meeting legal requirements that govern the running of businesses, consumer protection standards, and laws against fraud and money laundering. Another feature of international financial law is the process of harmonization of the domestic legislation of different countries for the convenience of the operation of financial companies. To avoid financial crisis, there are institutions such as the Bank for International Settlements (BIS) and the International Monetary Fund (IMF). For instance, the BIS's Basel Accords provide the guidelines and minimum standards for banks and the ways that they are supposed to approach risk. The purpose of these rules is to maintain the stability of the financial system and minimize fluctuations in the markets, thus providing a positive impact on the world economy. To address some of the problems, such as money laundering, fraud, and terrorism financing that are prevalent in the modern world, there are sound legal measures that have been put in place. The Anti-Money Laundering (AML) laws are a set of legislations that have been put in place in the global markets to counter these threats and strengthen the structures of the financial systems. The FATF is an intergovernmental organization established in 1989 that develops policies to prevent money laundering and financing of terrorism [60]. It assists member countries in drafting domestic laws and obliges banking institutions to perform CDD, report suspicious transactions, and cooperate with the authorities. However, every country has its laws, and there are general rules for the functioning of FATF. For example, in the United States, there are the BSA and the Patriot Act that require financial institutions to fight against illicit financial transactions. Combined, these frameworks provide the foundation of the strategies for the identification, prevention, and management of financial crime and the protection of the international financial environment.

International economic law regulates the relations between states and deals with various issues of contemporary international concerns, such as inequality, protection of the environment, and the rivalry between the superpowers. These have remained as some of the prevalent issues in the process of globalization and have influenced the formation and implementation of international law. The major issues include sovereignty and globalization, the inequality gap, and the effects of economic globalization on the environment. Let us discuss these challenges in detail.

5.3.1 Sovereignty vs. Global Governance

National sovereignty means the right of a nation to control its affairs without the influence of other nations in the global community [61]. The principle of sovereignty, which is a cornerstone of the international system, states that no state can interfere in the internal affairs of another country within the borders of this country [62]. Nevertheless, in the sphere of globalization and international economic law, this principle is opposed to the creation of norms, rules, and institutions operating on a global level, such as the United Nations or the World Trade Organization, aimed at regulating transnational activities. Global governance is defined as the setting up of rules, treaties, and institutions at the international level aimed at dealing with global issues, including trade, human rights, security, and sustainability. Although these frameworks encourage countries to work together to accomplish shared objectives, they may involve relinquishing some national sovereignty in the process. This conflict is best illustrated in the realms of trade, human rights, and the environment. For instance, the domestic laws of the countries may be changed to suit international treaties or conventions, regardless of the effect they may have on the national interests or policies. Issues emerge when states are reluctant to be pressured or feel that they are constrained by international laws and regulations that are not compatible with their domestic law systems or political and cultural values. One of the most notable examples of such a clash is in the area of trade law. The rules of the WTO involve commitments that were set by the member countries within areas such as tariffs, subsidies, and the protection of intellectual property rights. However, domestic policies in areas of trade protectionism, development of domestic industries, or national security policies may violate these international commitments. One such case was the American Steel tariffs in 2002, which were considered to violate WTO rules and thus became a cause of a trade dispute between the United States and the European Union, thus showing the clash between national policies and international trade laws [63]. An example of such tension exists in human rights law, whereby domestic laws may conflict with international human rights law, posing a problem in determining sovereignty and global responsibilities. National governments may reject global human rights standards, saying that such standards encroach on their sovereignty and culture. For instance, some countries have opted out of provisions in international human rights instruments, particularly concerning the rights of women, children, or homosexuals, due to cultural differences or legal systems. It is seen as a struggle between national sovereignty and humanity's global responsibility to uphold human rights. This tension is also reflected in the Paris Agreement on climate change because people have to balance internal energy politics with global climate goals. Several countries have made efforts to reduce their emissions as agreed within the Paris Agreement; however, some countries find it difficult to achieve these goals because they rely upon the sale of fossil fuels or because of political factors.

5.3.2 Global Inequality

International law is a tool that can help to reduce and mitigate inequality, and it is also a process that reproduces inequality in the world. On the one hand, international legal frameworks, and laws can facilitate development, human rights, and social justice, striving to bring equality on the global level. On the other hand, the very principles and frameworks that foster economic development and international commerce and trade have differential effects on developing countries, thereby widening the divide between the developed and the developing world. Speaking of inequality, international human rights law has played a critical role in setting the benchmark on the guarantees of social and economic rights such as the rights to education, health, and shelter. For example, the International Covenant on Economic, Social, and Cultural Rights (ICESCR) aims to minimize inequalities because it holds that everyone in the world, irrespective of his or her nationality or assets, should gain certain rights [64, 65]. Also, development agencies the United Nations (UN), and other international organizations engage in development by initiating programs to eliminate poverty and provide resources for the needy populations in the developing world. However, there is agreement that globalization through trade mechanisms and trade policies leads to global inequality. Globalization has been accused of favoring the developed countries and the big MNEs at the expense of the developing world. For instance, the WTO rules for trade are unbalanced, in that they tend to protect the developed nations more, which have more capital, better technologies, and better access to international markets. Therefore, trade liberalization hampers the growth of developing nations because their economies may be inclined to rely on the export of natural resources or cheap labor. This dependency perpetuates poverty and underdevelopment and thus cements the existing world poverty map.

Globalization has had its advantages and disadvantages in the developing economies of the world [66, 67]. On the positive side, globalization has opened international markets, investment opportunities, and new technology that have helped some developing nations attain high rates of economic growth. For instance, China and India are some of the countries that have experienced relatively rapid economic growth in the last few decades, mainly because of globalization. International trade has made it possible for these countries to develop their manufacturing industries and infrastructure eradicate poverty and provide job opportunities for millions of people. However, there are also negative effects of globalization on developing economies. Some of the problems associated with globalization include the fact that many developing nations fail to reap some of the benefits that come with globalization, mainly because of competition and lack of adequate infrastructure in some sectors of the economy. But often, globalization has widened the income gap within countries rather than bringing about equitable development, as wealth is only accumulated in the hands of individuals or ‘global’ corporate entities. Multinational corporations can take advantage of low wages in developing nations to reap profits at the expense of local employees and their suppressed economic development. In addition, globalization has also been associated with negative impacts, such as the subordination of domestic businesses in some developing nations by TNCs and IFIs. It has been noted that imports place a lot of pressure on domestic players by flooding the market with low-cost goods, which in the long run, acts as a thorn in the side of home-grown enterprises.

5.3.3 Environmental Concerns

International environmental agreements have played an important role in addressing the global environmental issues, including climate change, biological diversity, and cross-boundary pollution [68]. The Paris Agreement on Climate Change is another important global treaty that was signed in 2015 under the UNFCCC. The Paris Agreement aimed at limiting the global temperature to below 2 °C above pre-industrial levels; the more ambitious level was proposed at 1.5 °C [69]. This legally binding instrument calls for countries to submit their nationally determined contributions (NDCs) on how they plan to cut emissions of greenhouse gases. It has led to the emergence of renewable energy, sustainable practices, and climate change adaptation around the world. Other important international environmental conventions include the Convention on Biological Diversity, which focuses on the conservation of biological diversity and the maintenance of natural resources, and the Kyoto Protocol, which set legal obligations for developed state parties for reducing their emissions of greenhouse gases (though it has been withdrawn from by the United States of America). Another example of effective international environmental legislation is the Montreal Protocol – an agreement on the phase-out of ozone-depleting substances [70]. These international treaties and agreements show an increased understanding that environmental issues are international and should therefore be addressed in unison. However, the implementation of such agreements and the balance between economic growth and environmental conservation is still questionable as various countries have different levels of commitment and capacity for implementing such polices.

Economic globalization has brought about several changes to global environmental policies in the world, these are some good and some bad. On the positive side, globalization has enhanced environmentalism since it allows the sharing of information and technology on the environment. For instance, advancements in renewable energy technologies, equipment for waste disposal, and efficient food production through sustainable means are currently evident across the world due to increasing globalization and the global market for green technologies. On the negative side, however, economic globalization has been found to have promoted environmental degradation. Globalization of supply chains and trade has accelerated the rate at which societies use up resources and generate pollution. The low demand for expensive but environmental friendly products forces manufacturers to take advantage of the poor regulations in developing countries. The forests are cut down, mines are opened, and industrial pollution rises as societies and governments seek to respond to market demands. Another negative impact of globalization is that the pursuit of economic growth can work at the expense of the environment. A lot of nations, especially those in the third world, place economic growth and eradicating poverty above environmental conservation. It creates conflict between the short-term economic benefits and the attainment of sustainable environmental objectives.

6 Case Studies of International Law in Action

The following case studies provide practical knowledge of how international law is applied with a focus on trade disputes, investment disputes, and financial regulation.

6.1 Trade Disputes

The American-European Union case on subsidies granted to the European Airbus company is perhaps one of the most well-known and significant cases in WTO history [71]. This case, which commenced in 2004, concerned the EU's alleged provision of prohibited subsidies to Airbus, a leading European aerospace company [72]. The United States accused these subsidies in the form of grants, loans, and other financial assistance extended by individual members of the EU to Airbus of violating the principle of nondiscrimination and distorting the competitive landscape in favor of Airbus against its American counterpart, Boeing. The case was particularly important as it provided a conflict between two of the world's largest economies, and it explored the way WTO rules could be applied to the issue of government subsidies of large sectors of industry. The WTO dispute settlement body provided its verdict in favor of the United States in 2011 regarding the European Union's subsidies to Airbus, as these were determined to violate WTO agreements. The ruling meant the EU had to remove such subsidies and also provided compensation for the harm it was causing to the United States through unfair competition. Nevertheless, the case did not end there because the EU filed counter allegations of subsidy distortions within the aerospace industry, specifically against Boeing Company, and thus the onset of the parallel legal showdown showed that challenges regarding subsidies and fair competition, and their control, persisted in global industries. This case shows why the WTO's Dispute Settlement Network is necessary for preventing trade violations or conflicts and ensuring fairness in the international market. It also reveals how the WTO tends to make decisions that may affect the economics and politics of the countries involved.

6.2 Investment Disputes

Another outstanding example of the ICSID investment arbitration is the CMS Gas Transmission Company claiming against Argentina [73, 74]. This case started back in 2003 as a result of the Argentine economic crisis that occurred in the early 2000s decade where Argentina experienced a lot of instability in its economy and was forced to devalue its currency from the US dollar. Some of the measures that the Argentine government took in emergency measures include the freezing of utility tariffs and the renegotiation of contracts with foreign investors in the gas and electricity sector, including CMS Gas Transmission Company from the United States. CMS, which was involved in the pipeline construction of natural gas in Argentina, sued Argentina under the US-Argentina BIT, claiming that the latter breached the treaty by expropriating its investment and failing to give it fair treatment. The ICSID in 2005 awarded $133m in compensation to CMS, demanding that Argentina pay up for the breach of the bilateral investment treaty. The tribunal pointed out that indeed Argentina had breached its duties under the BIT, especially regarding the treatment of foreign investors as well as the protection of investments from arbitrary or discriminatory conduct. This case shows that through ICSID, foreign investors can seek protection in case of disputes with the host state and shows the role BITs play in guaranteeing protection to investments. It also shows how ICSID arbitration can contribute to ensuring that states are held responsible for actions that violate the rights of investors, no matter the situation in the country or changes in government policies.

6.3 *Financial Regulation*

International law was particularly relevant during the 2007/2008 financial crisis, which was characterized by economic collapse and required a collective international response [75, 76]. It started with the failure of leading banks and other financial institutions in the United States and soon engulfed the financial systems, banks, and economy of the world. To address the problem, both global organizations and the legal system responded by trying to stabilize the financial markets. One of the main responses was the intervention of one of the giant global institutions, the International Monetary Fund (IMF). To prevent the situation in the global financial system from worsening during the crisis, the IMF gave some of the worst-affected countries, such as Iceland, Ireland, and Greece, emergency funding. However, these bailouts were not given freely, they required policy changes such as reduction of government spending, containing budgets, and undertaking long-term reforms. Consequently, the issue of regulating international financial transactions turned into one of the most sensitive and closely monitored fields of world relations. To mitigate these risks and avoid future occurrences of crisis, international organizations such as the Bank for International Settlements (BIS) and the Financial Stability Board (FSB) were put in place to lead the process of ensuring the stability of the banking systems.

Another major shift that was put in place after the financial crisis was the Basel III capital adequacy standard, which affected the enhancement of regulation, supervision, and management of risks in the banking sector. Basel III increased the leverage ratio, introduced new measures of liquidity, and greatly improved stress testing [77]. The G20 was also involved in coordinating the response to the crisis. The G20 countries are among the largest economies globally, and they provide goals and directions on how to remodel the financial structures to avoid such disasters in the future. Such measures involved improving the legal environment, enlarging the constraints on the financial sector, and addressing systematic risks. The financial crisis also brought into light the significance of international law and regulators in managing cross-border risks and emphasized the need for collaboration between the governments, individual, states and international institutions in formulating and implementing policies for managing the impact of financial and other economic shocks.

7 Conclusion

This chapter has presented general information concerning the connection between international law and the international economy. In the current world that is transforming into a global village, international laws are very important in the conduct of business and order in the global market. Trade and investment between countries are protected by international law, while any issues arising from the breach of these laws are handled by institutions such as the WTO and ICSID. Apart from settling trade disputes, the WTO plays a role in reducing risks in trade relations between the two countries. BITs and ICSID prevent and safeguard investors if countries that invested in them encounter political or economic difficulties. Nonetheless, there are some challenges; one challenge is the struggle between nationalism and internationalism, where countries are reluctant to be bound by international laws that are not favorable to their national legislation. Another issue is inequality, as many developing countries suffer from globalization and get unfair treatment and poverty, though they trade and invest.

Step Towards Globalization of Economy: Regional Treaties and WTO Convention for Digital Economy

1 Introduction

Digitalization of the economy is undoubtedly one of the most significant trends that has impacted the global economy in the past few decades [78, 79]. But, what can be said about the '*digital economy*'? In its basic form, the digital economy can be defined in terms of an economy that is reinforced by digital computing technologies [80]. It is not limited to the sale of goods and services or online business but is inclusive of all the digital technologies that influence commerce, business, and society. Some of these are cloud computing, big data, artificial intelligence, blockchain, and the Internet of Things. Social media, banking, and educational platforms have become part of the lives of most individuals as they have brought changes to the way people interact, transact, and even perceive economic activities [81].

Just imagine how this has changed the entire landscape of the economy; the digital economy has become an important part of the global economy and has surpassed traditional industries in many ways [82]. Software, electronic business, and digital content have become a critical focus of both trade and economic development [83]. Indeed, it is almost impossible to think of an industry that does not have a connection with the digital world. E-commerce alone is expected to contribute to a considerable amount of the total international trade in the future, and this is only one of the numerous components of the digital world [84]. But how did we arrive at this point, where digital trade has become not just a trend, but an economic necessity? The growth of the digital economy is due to several factors including technological progress, globalization, and the extensiveness of the internet [85]. The availability of broadband internet, the emergence of smartphones, and the spread of technology have made it possible for people, businesses, and even nations to engage in the digital economy as they have never done before [86]. Such changes have brought about the following effects: (a) business people are now able to access their customers around the world, (b) governments are in a position to put into practice digital policies for

J. Afzal, *Exploring the New Horizons of International Law Concerning Globalization of Economy*, https://doi.org/10.1007/978-981-95-1312-3_2

economic transformation and, (c) people are in a position to access services that they had no access to in many parts of the world.

But as it is with any fast-growing entity, there are new problems that have emerged. The digital economy has introduced more unconventional methods of commerce, different kinds of goods, and issues about security, privacy, and legislation [87]. Governments all around the world are in a dilemma on how they will control this almost boundary-less environment [88]. Modern trading systems that have been developed by the World Trade Organization (WTO) are struggling to adapt to the current technological advancement [89]. However, Regional Trade Agreements (RTAs) have emerged to try and take up the slack where global governance structures have been insufficient [90, 91].

This chapter will discuss how these regional treaties and the WTO are influencing the future of the digital economy. RTAs may be a useful addition to the global trade regulation system, but they could also lead to fragmented digital markets. Can the WTO adapt to the needs of the contemporary world and respond to the demands of the digital economy, or are there separate and unrelated systems developing? These are some of the important questions we will seek to answer.

2 Role of Regional Treaties and the WTO in the Digital Economy

With the development of the digital economy, it is evident that the existing approaches to trade do not meet the requirements of the modern world in terms of regulating digital trade [92]. Technological advancement and the fact that digital trade is not restrained by geographical boundaries demand a new and innovative approach to trade that is adaptive, progressive, and keen in its understanding of the challenges posed by e-commerce, data flows, and the digital gap [93, 94]. But why do we need new frameworks? What areas are still lacking in the current global governance structures that should be addressed? First, look at the digital gap, which is one of the most important problems that concerns both the economic and social divisions. On the one hand, the expansion of the digital economy has brought immense opportunities and growth to many regions of the world [95], on the other hand, it intensified existing unfairness [96]. While the developed nations enjoy state-of-the-art technology such as internet access, infrastructure, and modern platforms, many developing nations lag. This means that, unlike the technological divide that only refers to the availability of gadgets, it goes further to embrace the availability of opportunities, education, and markets. For countries that are already on the edge of the global economy, the digital division is a wake-up call that liberalization of digital trade is not fair [86]. Thus, how can new frameworks help to overcome this division and build a more inclusive digital economy? It is in this context that we find regional trade agreements (RTAs) and the World Trade Organization (WTO), which are among the current structures that define digital trade. Regional agreements are, by definition, generally more flexible and better suited to the particular circumstances of those who are members of the agreements. RTAs can have particular conditions on digital trade that may encompass data protection, cross-border data transfer, and e-commerce. The United States-Mexico-Canada Agreement (USMCA), for instance, includes strong digital trade sections that address these very issues, attempting to create a common framework for digital commerce within the region [97, 98]. These regional frameworks allow for more localized solutions that respond to specific regional challenges while fostering greater cooperation between member states. However, as a global organization, WTO has the advantage of setting up international trade rules that are general and effective for all parties [99].

2.1 Digital Data and Digital Trade

The role of RTAs and WTO in this regard is further highlighted by the fact that data underpins digital trade. Data is the lifeblood of the digital economy and is used in various applications such as cloud services, e-commerce, artificial intelligence, and data analysis [100, 101]. International data flows are essential for businesses to conduct operations in the global market, but countries are gradually becoming more protective of data and imposing policies and measures that form barriers to these flows. Thus, both RTAs and the WTO have their parts to play in regulating the flow of free data while seeking to protect privacy and security. Regional treaties can respond to data flows in a manner that is consistent with the needs of the regional members [102]. For instance, the General Data Protection Regulation (GDPR) is a regulation that addresses data protection in the European Union member countries. This regulation not only defined the level of privacy protection for the European region but also shaped how countries from other parts of the world manage data protection. Currently, the WTO has not developed a clear set of rules governing the data flows. There were general discussions on e-commerce in WTO, but these negotiations have been stuck mainly because of different priorities among the members, most especially the developed and the developing countries. The WTO's moratorium on electronic commerce tariffs enacted in 1998 was a good start, but it is evident that much more needs to be done to address the whole range of concerns regarding digital trade [103, 104]. Therefore, what are the implications for the future? Can RTAs effectively manage the digital economy or is a global, multilateral solution through the WTO needed? It is probably in between a combination of the two. RTAs are a practical approach to responding to the particular demand of areas, promoting cooperation, and developing new approaches to digital trade. Yet, it is imperative to point out that if no global solutions are implemented there will be a fragmentation of the digital economy, and every region will have its rules and standards that could become a barrier to digital trade across borders. In this respect, the WTO's function in setting rules for digital trade at a global level has not lost its relevance.

2.2 Research Gap and Concerns

How can RTAs and the WTO work together for the advancement of digital accessibility? It is therefore important to know what can be done to make sure that the positive impact of digital trade is spread out to these countries, especially the ones with the growing digital environment. These questions can be answered best when there is a clear understanding of how the regional framework and the global policies will be harmonized so as not to exclude the developing countries in the digital economy. Another important factor is related to data movements and national sovereignty [105]. While data has emerged as the most essential commodity in the digital economy, the growing concerns over privacy, security, and sovereignty of data have led to the introduction of protectionist measures such as data localization and higher regulatory standards. This raises several questions: How can the RTAs and the WTO balance their recognition of the sovereignty of countries and the open flow of data? To what extent is it possible to harmonize these agreements to ensure compliance with different data protection laws for cross-border electronic business? To answer these questions, it is necessary to look at the current trends and the concepts that offer sufficient protection of personal data and the freedom of data transfers across borders. However, this is not to say that RTAs and the WTO have not made a significant effort in the regulation of digital trade because, despite all their efforts, some challenges are still present. An example is the WTO's Trade Facilitation Agreement (TFA) and the Information Technology Agreement (ITA) since they seek to liberalize trade in information technology products by reducing tariffs [106, 107]. Still, the question is: Are these agreements up to date to meet the current technological changes, or are they irrelevant in addressing new issues like artificial intelligence, cybersecurity, and digital taxation? An evaluation of the existing frameworks in these areas will reveal the deficiencies in the existing governance structures and indicate where change might be required. But there are clear prospects for the development of cooperation between regional and global governance systems. With the increased level of digitalization in the economy, the need to have a harmonized set of trade policies has also emerged. Then the question arises, how can RTAs and the WTO work jointly to develop such a framework? What good practices can be promoted to ensure that nations are in a position to mutually agree on the regulations governing digital trade? This chapter will examine several best practices, and these strategies will be transferable to the broader digital trade context.

3 The Rise and New Trends of Digital Economy

3.1 Historical Evolution of the Digital Economy

Today's digital economy has evolved over the years with technology, especially the internet, being the main driver of the change. Which was once a tool for communication has evolved into the world economy's backbone and the main platform for social connections and the exchange of information. With the availability of broadband internet, cloud computing came into the picture, which made it possible for the companies to store and process data offsite, which reduced operational costs significantly and made it possible to scale globally; at the same time, the concept of big data also emerged as a phenomenon. Through computing and analyzing large volumes of data, businesses were able to gather insights that enhanced decision making and customer profiling. AI took this revolution to the next level by automating many processes and bringing about innovations that were once inconceivable [108]. The last emerging technology is blockchain, which presented decentralized and secured systems for the management of transactions and expanded digital trade in areas such as finance and supply chain. These innovations played a very important role in the formation of the digital economy and a time when the physical barriers faded and new forms of doing business emerged [109].

This technological revolution transformed the face of commerce from physical shop-based business to online-based business. E-business became a leading phenomenon and created new opportunities for selling products and services across borders [110]. Traditional industries, which earlier were operating locally, now could see the potential of expanding internationally. One of the most significant changes is the globalization of trade, which means that commodities and services no longer need to physically move across borders since digital products, services or content can easily travel through the internet. This transition to the digital market not only expanded the business reach, but also changed the foundation of the business models, where subscription-based models, digital products, and virtual services became common.

3.2 Key Drivers of Digital Trade

Several factors have contributed to the growth of the digital economy and the most influential ones are platforms and technologies. Marketplaces like Amazon, Alibaba, and eBay have enabled businesses to reach customers around the world and get rid of the barriers that used to exist in terms of geographical location [111]. These are crucial to e-commerce as they help in the completion of transactions and also in the sharing of information on products between buyers and sellers in different parts of the world. On the same note, the availability of online payment methods such as PayPal, mobile money, and cryptocurrencies has also made it convenient for consumers to buy products and services without being constrained by banks or the exchange rate of currencies.

Technology has played a significant role in changing the landscape of various industries in the marketplace [112]. The advancements in the finance industry through the use of technology have brought mobile banking, peer-to-peer lending, and blockchain transactions that are cheaper, faster, and transparent. The entertainment industry has also changed drastically with the introduction of Netflix and Spotify, where a consumer has access to media from across the world through a few clicks. Education (edtech) has also changed with the use of online platforms and the opportunity to learn online or with the help of MOOCs for learners regardless of their location. Even healthcare has embraced new technologies through health technologies such as telemedicine, electronic health records, and health monitoring apps that make the services more accessible to millions of people around the globe. The industries that were strongly related to physical infrastructure have also embraced digital methods and have grown, produced, and reached new heights like never before [113]. All these innovations contribute to the creation of the digital economy, which is steadily expanding at the moment.

3.3 Challenges in Managing Digital Trade

Despite its many advantages, the digital economy also brings with it several challenges, particularly in the areas of data privacy, intellectual property, and sovereignty. Data privacy and cyber-security are perhaps the most imminent issues when it come in the digital environment [114]. Since more and more people share their personal and financial information through the Internet, the protection of such information is essential. Malicious activities like data leakage or hacking have already exposed the fragility of the digital economy and have impacted both consumers as well as businesses. The question is whether current security can protect the systems from all these latest technologies that are developing faster and faster. As highlighted in the previous section, the current and future threats to cybersecurity are complex and require the development of better and stronger measures to secure digital transactions and consumer information.

It has also emerged that the protection of intellectual property rights in the realm of cyberspace has its complications too. While in the physical realm, it is more straightforward to implement IP laws, the digital environment makes it challenging to enforce them due to the ease of copying and distribution of content. The advancement of digital piracy, sharing of content, and illegal copying of software leave businesses and creators with this pertinent question: How do businesses and creators protect their ideas, products, and content in a world where copying is almost as easy as a child's play? One more issue arises due to the global use of the Internet, which has different laws in different countries, making the protection of those goods in question often inadequate due to patchwork enforcement. Another drastic problem of the digital economy is sovereignty and jurisdiction [115]. In contrast to conventional export and import of goods, which involve the movement of physical goods across borders, digital transactions encompass information that is easily transferable across countries. This leads to another even more complex issue of which laws of the countries are applicable in cyberspace. To whom does the conflict of laws apply when the contract was entered into electronically and the parties are from different states? How are conflicts of laws resolved in cases where the laws of two or more nations conflict? The current increased use of the Internet for commercial purposes presents legal ambiguities that make it challenging to address regulation and enforcement.

4 Regional Trade Agreements (RTAs) and the Digital Economy

Regional Trade Agreements (RTAs) are defined as agreements between two or more countries that are aimed at liberalizing and promoting trade within a particular geographical area. Some of the RTAs have been formed in the context of the digital economy, and some of the objectives they have implemented include digital trade liberalization [116, 117]. For instance, the Digital Single Market strategy is a policy framework of the European Union that addresses the free movement of goods, services, capital, and people within the EU specifically in the digital space. Similarly, for the CPTPP, there are provisions for the member nations to engage in joint efforts on the creation of a single digital market with aspects like the transfer of data across borders, the imposition of restrictions on digital trade, and the formulation of policies on e-commerce. The United States–Mexico–Canada Agreement (USMCA) includes new provisions on digital trade, which might be of interest to modern international trade, including data localization and source code protection [118].

These agreements have e-commerce sections that contain provisions that regulate the conduct of business over the Internet such as consumer protection, formation of electronic contracts, and means of resolving disputes. These provisions are very important in making sure that digital trade is secure, safe, and credible for both the traders and the buyers. Data protection and privacy regulation also form part of RTAs to ensure that personal data is processed in a way that complies with the laws of the respective countries and international best practices [119]. With the increasing awareness of the protection of data, RTAs are faced with the challenge of protecting the privacy of the data as well as promoting the free flow of data across borders. Furthermore, it is also necessary to note that rules regulating international data transfers are crucial for the proper functioning of digital services like cloud solutions and online marketplaces. These provisions assist in eliminating any hurdles that may hinder digital trade across the globe while at the same time not neglecting sovereignty issues on data. Another important element of RTAs is competition provisions that are aimed at limiting anti-competitive behaviors in digital markets [120]. These provisions are intended to ensure that online platforms and service providers compete fairly, and that monopolization is discouraged. Furthermore, RTAs cover issues of taxation and regulation of new digital business models, such as market platforms and cryptocurrencies. One of the ways through which RTAs facilitate this is by coming up with clear policies on taxation and regulation so that digital businesses are not exploited by the government. Another significant effect of RTAs in the digital economy is that they have led to the elimination of trade barriers. This also involves the removal of barriers such as tariffs on digital products and services to promote innovation and market access. In this way, RTAs contribute to eliminate barriers in the global digital market, which in turn, is advantageous to businesses and consumers in the member countries.

The emergence of RTAs with digital provisions has greatly influenced the global governance of digital matters. The EU Digital Single Market and Association of Southeast Asian Nations (ASEAN)'s digital policies are among the most influential regional digital policies in the world today [121, 122]. These measures not only facilitate digital trade within their regions but also establish the best practices for global digital trade. These frameworks are being adopted as countries seek to align with regional powerhouses shaping policies within the global digital trade. Nevertheless, the development of regional digital governance frameworks also poses the threat of fragmentation of international trade regulation. Although RTAs enable regions to lead in the formulation of digital policies, this leads to the formation of multiple standards that may hinder international business. For instance, the General Data Protection Regulation (GDPR) laws in the EU are much stricter than those in other parts of the world, thus limiting data transfer and making cross-border digital trade challenging [123]. This has the effect of potentially splintering the digital economy, and it becomes more difficult for companies to conduct their operations across countries that have different rules and standards. Another important point of discussion is the conflict between regional leadership and global governance. On the one hand, regional governance is beneficial as it permits member countries to establish policies that are most suitable for their context; on the other hand, this type of governance hinders the global digital governance process. If every region sets its rules independently and without international coordination, the world may find itself with an array of different rules that may slow down the growth of the digital economy. This fragmentation could also lead to higher compliance costs for organizations that may be required to address different legal requirements for each region or country. Finally, there is the problem of division in international trade rules, which may act as an interruption. Frankly, as all countries and regions advance their digital trade strategies, the lack of global governance is quickly becoming apparent. This is because if there is no proper digital trade governance, the digital trade may be hampered by barriers that may hinder the free flow of goods, services, and data. Digital trade will have a future only if countries can find a balance between regional and global needs to make Digital trade easier and more effective while protecting the interests of all the countries involved [124].

5 The WTO and the Digital Economy

Since its creation in 1995, WTO succeeded GATT, and its coverage extended to services by resorting to the General Agreement on Trade in Services (GATS) [125, 126]. This was important as services, especially the service needs of the world, increasingly started to become a vital component of trade in the global market. However, the WTO is limited in its efforts to adapt to the digital economy due to its initial structure, which was particularly optimized for physical products. With advancements in the application of digital technologies in the commerce sector, new modes of trade were created that were not captured in the earlier theories. The inclusion of the digital economy into the WTO negotiations is an effort towards the modernization of the global trade rules given the current importance of digital services, data, and e-commerce [127, 128]. However, this has not been easy to achieve as the WTO has experienced challenges in integrating these new issues in a fast-changing digital world. There are no general laws for the digital economy, so there are a large number of regional and national laws that create tensions between global trade rules and internal legislation.

5.1 WTO's Role in Facilitating Digital Trade

GATS has played a significant role in the creation of the digital services trade by laying down the framework for electronic services, including e-commerce and cloud services [129]. The agreement's provisions, however, are very general and very much out of touch with the current fast-evolving trends in technology. For instance, the GATS structures did not capture the essence of data flows and cross-border digital service delivery when it was drafted and the applicability of GATS to modern digital services is still a matter of debate. The e-commerce moratorium, which began in the late 1990s, remains one of the key measures to develop digital trade within the WTO environment [130]. Since the moratorium applies to digital goods and services, it supports free and open digital markets by avoiding the imposition of tariffs. However, it is not without its critics, especially in the developing world, which feel the moratorium will favor the developed countries that have strong internet connections. Opponents of tariff elimination in digital goods say that it widens the digital division since developed markets will benefit from digital trade more than developing markets. The third aspect of the WTO's digital trade policies is the regulation of cross-border data flows. The organization has been seeking to enhance the liberalization processes of the flows of data, which is essential for cloud computing, online platforms, and international digital services. However, the WTO has not established a clear framework for data flows, and therefore, this has conflicted with national data sovereignty laws such as that of the EU, which has strict data protection measures like GDPR. Nevertheless, the WTO's efforts to develop international consensus on such matters have not been successful and have instead resulted in fragmented global governance of digital space. The TFA, effective in 2021, serves a major function in easing the complexity of digital trade through the simplification of customs measures that are charged on trade [131]. Even though the TFA mainly concerns traditional trade, it is also relevant to the digital economy to some extent, particularly concerning the digitalization of customs and the availability of trade-related information. However, it does not address the more nuanced aspects of the digital economy such as data management and online platform rules, which means that it only provides a partial solution to the problems of an integrated digital trade environment.

5.2 Challenges in Frameworks of the Digital Economy

The issues related to the WTO and its ability to adapt to the digital economy are complex; another major issue is the absence of a coherent and comprehensive digital trade policy. The current WTO rules were set in an era when the digital economy was not very relevant in the global market, and hence they do not capture the modern digital economy trade relations. Although digital services have been classified under GATS, there is no single framework to address the digital economy issues such as cross-border data flows, digital taxation as well as cybersecurity. Technological advancement also becomes a major factor that needs to be handled carefully. The WTO's multilateral negotiation processes cannot keep up with the speed of growth of the digital economy [132]. These new technologies such as artificial intelligence, blockchain, and cloud computing are disrupting these existing markets at a very fast pace, and the WTO's multilateral system of negotiations is slow in responding to such changes. This slow pace of adaptation has been a source of concern for the stakeholders in the digital economy, especially the businesses that are operating in an environment that is characterized by a lot of uncertainties.

The last problem, which should not be left unaddressed, is the developed/ developing countries divide. Most of the developed countries, or the ones with technology integrated in their economies, are the ones that support the liberalization of data flow and trade policies. On the other hand, developing countries are more inclined to policies that enable them to regulate data and promote their digital markets. This has given rise to a split in the WTO especially on key issues such as localization of data, privacy and the protection of property rights in the information age. That is why the WTO has faced difficulties in establishing global rules that would be fair and suitable for all the member countries, especially when issues of economic justice and the digital divide have emerged. However, issues to do with cybersecurity, privacy, and intellectual property rights remain complex in the WTO. The WTO has chosen the trade-related intellectual property system provided by the Trade-Related Aspects of Intellectual Property Rights (TRIPS) agreement, which was designed for the analog world and does not adequately address such challenges as digital piracy and the protection of intangible assets in a digital environment [133]. Similarly, issues of privacy, especially those relating to the transfer of data across borders, have created friction between countries with strict privacy laws and those that support the free movement of data. As these concerns arise, the WTO's current regime on IPR and data protection has been described as wanting and out of touch with these pertinent matters.

5.3 Prospective Reform in the WTO for Digital Economy

WTO persisted in responding to these challenges through work program on e-commerce intended for the negotiation of new rules for e-commerce [134]. This topic encompasses various aspects like electronic contracts, cross-border data transfer, and e-business in international trade. However, the scope of the work program has been defined in a more limited manner, and the outcomes are still vague, as the member countries cannot come to terms on certain issues. Some have proposed a WTO Digital Trade Agreement, a treaty that is more committed and far-reaching and is meant to address digital trade challenges [135, 136]. This could give direction on matters such as data transfers, taxation of digital business, protection of user data, and regulation of online marketplaces. However, this proposal has been objected to by some developing countries fearing that such an agreement will weaken their authority to control their digital markets.

The interaction between WTO rules and domestic digital regulations is another issue that needs change. Most members of the WTO have established domestic digital regulations to deal with the emerging issues in the digital economy but these are against the WTO regulations therefore creating tension and hindrances. Perhaps a better synchronization in domestic and international regulations is needed to make the entire international trade process less cumbersome for the companies engaged in multiple jurisdictions. When we look at the relationship between regional treaties and the World Trade Organization (WTO), we start to see a significant tension between local and global approaches to regulating the digital economy. One of the most obvious questions, which can be posed here, is the following: Do regional agreements provide more suitable conditions for some groups of countries, or do they harm the world trade system by establishing conflicting rules? Existing regional treaties like the EU General Data Protection Regulation demonstrate how local treaties can provide rules that are in direct opposition to global frameworks. The GDPR is regarded as one of the most comprehensive frameworks of rules regarding the protection of personal data that protects citizens. However, this framework is not entirely consistent with the WTO's more liberal, trade-focused terms that were not built with such restrictions on data protection in mind. The worry here is that these regional laws could be so stringent as to diminish the freedom of information crossing borders, which would make it difficult for enterprises in one region to adhere to the regulations of another. If the WTO does not elaborate more concrete rules concerning digital trade, we may expect more such controversies in the future that may cause some complications in the manner in which business is conducted across borders. For example, the United States-Mexico-Canada Agreement (USMCA) included a new digital trade chapter. Despite addressing many of the deficiencies in digital trade,

USMCA poses a challenge to the WTO because it formulates its rules, which are sometimes in opposition to the global ones. Thus, although RTAs are very useful and efficient for cooperation in specific regions, they may become an issue in WTO negotiations due to the presence of many competing standards.

Another question that arises as one tries to understand regional treaties in the context of digital trade is the issue of the digital divide. As seen in the example of the RTAs such as the CPTPP or the EU Digital Single Market, there is a benefit to the economically developed countries while a disadvantage to the developing countries. These nations may lack the necessary infrastructure, technologies, or institutions that enable full participation in the digital economy under such agreements. The WTO as a more flexible global organization, in theory, has provided the best opportunity for bargaining; however, it has not been able to address the various needs of different economies effectively. Here is why the global consensus has been difficult to achieve: while some countries like the U.S. and those in the EU are insisting on liberal open data flows and least restriction, others like India and Brazil are advocating for data protection and development of local digital industries. Thus, the WTO might have to find ways to provide a platform for such approaches and create frameworks that take into consideration the differences in connectivity and economic status of the countries. Moreover, the fragmentation of digital trade rules has emerged as a serious risk to the global digital economy. The current trend of autonomous number setting by RTAs has largely made it challenging for organizations with operations across various regions as they are forced to adhere to different standards hence increasing the cost of operation. For example, a digital company based in the U.S. that buys and sells products with both the EU and China would be faced with different rules on data privacy, digital taxation, and the transfer of data across borders. This leads to another pertinent question: How will firms continue to operate profitably when they are faced with various and sometimes competing regulations across different countries? This fragmentation may not only be disadvantageous to the business entities but also be a detriment to the global economy. It puts in place obstacles where they should not be, thereby limiting the possibility for digital trade to grow in the world. Moreover, such fragmentation of the global regulatory landscape could complicate the process of coordinating international trade policies as every region would have its agendas and regulations. The worry is that the fragmentation of the current global system could lead to a situation where countries start caring more about regional arrangements than global ones, thereby bringing about a situation where the world is full of incompatible rules that could slow down the growth of digital trade.

The WTO, along with other regional organizations, will have to look for a way forward in driving the integration of national and international interests in the best manner in the context of the development of a coherent digital market. We need collective work so that digital trade is not only just but also effective for all economies and not only for the leading ones.

6 Case Studies

6.1 The EU Digital Single Market (DSM)

The DSM of the European Union is one of the most significant regional attempt to liberalize digital trade across borders [137]. In its essence, the DSM seeks to establish a single digital environment in the EU for goods, services, and persons and their products to circulate as freely as they do in the traditional internal market [138]. One of its core objectives is to reduce restrictions on digital trade, especially in electronic commerce, digital services, and data. However, to what extent has the DSM been successful in this goal, and what can be learned from its application? This has probably contributed to the fact that the DSM has undoubtedly had many accomplishments. The GDPR is now a worldwide reference for data protection and has changed the way companies manage personal information and affected laws outside the EU. In addition, the removal of digital frontiers, which include the differences in the rules regarding data protection and those concerning electronic commerce among member states, has facilitated free trade in the EU region by enhancing the operations of commerce as well as making it easier for the consumers to access the services and goods. For instance, while engaging in e-commerce, firms had to deal with the complex and overlapping legal framework of the member states, they now have a better-defined legal framework that regulates digital transactions. However, implementing the provisions of the DSM has not been without some hitches; one of the most important concerns is the question of data ownership. While the DSM helps in the free flow of data, some countries outside the EU especially those with weak data protection laws feel that Europe is too protective about data and hinders free international trade. The conflict arising from the GDPR, for instance, has precipitated tensions with other areas that consider their digital goods and services constrained by Europe's regulations. Furthermore, the DSM's objective of dismantling barriers to digital trade within the EU poses new challenges because nations such as the UK, which left the EU after concluding the study, are no longer part of the fold. In this regard, the DSM despite its success on a regional level, is limited in its applicability to the global context where countries with different regulatory systems and digital access negotiate their respective digital trade agreements.

6.2 Comprehensive and Progressive Agreement for Trans-Pacific Partnership (CPTPP)

The CPTPP is a contemporary trade agreement signed between the countries of the Pacific region, and its focus on the digital economy brought much attention [139]. In contrast to previous trade agreements, CPTPP contains provisions for digital trade, commitments to ease restrictions on the flow of data across borders, streamline measures for e-commerce, and safeguard consumers' rights [140]. But how has this agreement affected the digital economy of its member countries and the globalization of trade? Among the most notable dynamics of the CPTPP is the fact that the parties have agreed to open digital trade without tariffs or unjustified limitations on data transfer. For instance, the agreement prohibits data localization, which are laws that seek to compel data to be stored within the country or region, thus promoting free information flow. This provision is essential because it goes against developments in some countries, especially Asian and European ones, which have passed data sovereignty laws to protect their interests. In this way, the CPTPP reduces the likelihood of these kinds of barriers to digital trade and makes it easier for members involved to innovate and operate more efficiently. Nevertheless, it is imperative to question whether the CPTPP's provisions enhance the balance between protecting privacy and facilitating data flows. Although the agreement encourages digital trade, it does not address some of the concerns such as data protection and cybersecurity. Some of the nations that emerged uncomfortable with the agreement's perspective on free data flow include the United States and Japan with strong privacy laws similar to Australia. Also, the various mechanisms for settling disputes about the CPTPP digital trade have been exercised in the last few years. While the agreement has provisions in the form of clauses for the settlement of digital trade disputes, it remains to be seen on their effectiveness when the regulations of member countries differ. The key issues of concern, including an ever-evolving focus on data flows across borders, including data protection and privacy, indicate that the effectiveness of the CPTPP in terms of dispute settlement may be dependent on the capacity of its members to work in concordance in the future.

6.3 The WTO's Role in Resolving Digital Trade Disputes

The WTO has historically played a central role in resolving trade disputes related to goods and services. Nevertheless, the WTO has faced several challenges in settling disputes that arise within the framework of digital trade which has emerged as the new frontier of international trade [92]. While the WTO has been involved in digital trade disputes; for example, in the trade dispute between the US and China, the WTO dispute settlement procedures were used to solve issues concerning the protection of digital assets' intellectual property rights and excessive restrictions on cross-border data transfer [103, 141]. However, the critics opine that the WTO is slow to adapt to the rapidly evolving digital economy. The existing frameworks of the WTO were established at a time when trade was mainly physical, and it has been challenging to adapt them to the digital economy. For instance, in digital trade disputes, the WTO's approach to IP, which was created for material goods, can be relatively unsuitable in dealing with digital products like software and online services. It is however important to note that the WTO has also faced criticism in areas such as the slow time taken to make decisions. The process of Dispute resolution under the WTO can take years and this can be unhelpful, especially given the fact that technological advancement is fast. In the context of the digital economy, it is unviable for businesses to wait for years to receive a verdict on any digital goods or services, data privacy, or digital content-related issue. To remain relevant, the WTO needs to reform its approach to digital trade disputes, possibly by creating specialized panels or mechanisms that can handle these cases more efficiently. RTAs are an integral component of the global trade system as countries seek more specific, regional approaches to digital trade challenges. New-generation RTAs such as the EU's DSM and CPTPP have specific policies addressing digital challenges, including data regulation and e-commerce standards. On the one hand, RTAs can be used as a laboratory for potential provisions of the digital trade that could be implemented on a global level, but in reality, they can contribute to the emergence of various competing sets of rules that businesses must follow. This is indeed a nightmare for companies that are operating in different jurisdictions, as they are confronted with the possibility of running into different legal requirements. Ideally, the WTO should be able to mimic the best features of RTAs and implement them on a global level. The digital economy is by its nature borderless as information, services, and goods can be transmitted at the speed of light. On that note, for digital trade to be a success on an international level it must be supported by international organizations to develop transparent digital trade rules. A handful of countries especially in the global north have been able to establish themselves in the new digital economy while the majority of countries in the global south are lagging. The issue here is whether these countries will be able to participate in the determination of the rules governing digital trade or be left out. There is a real possibility that the digital economy will be controlled by the few hence developing countries will be locked out. This is because in today's world, even if the rules govern data flows, digital taxation, or intellectual property, they may have a greater impact on developing countries.

7 Summary

The fact is that the WTO has been facing many problems in governing the area of digital trade. Conceived as an organization that was aimed at regulating the traditional physical trade in physical goods, the WTO has not been capable of adequately addressing issues to do with data flows, digital services, and e-commerce. The WTO has failed to meet the expectations, therefore RTAs have emerged to undertake the roles left by the WTO. But this tends to see RTAs emerging as the main players in the regulation of digital trade the WTO is likely to play a reactive role. The WTO is trying to adapt, to the e-commerce work program and others, but it is uncertain whether these endeavors will be enough to keep the WTO afloat in the age of the digital economy.

The position of emerging technologies like AI and blockchain is another factor that makes it challenging. Information technologies are increasingly revolutionizing industries and forging the future of digital trade. For instance, AI is revolutionizing financial services, while blockchain is presenting solutions for secure and transparent transactions. But how will these technologies fit into the existing trade laws that were developed in an era when these technologies were unknown? The truth of the matter is that both the WTO and RTA are lagging behind the change. The advance of innovative technologies further enhances the possibilities of digital trade but at the same time creates new legal challenges. For example, AI can be used for decision making leading to problems of intangible ownership as well as the data used in the process and blockchain, which can revolutionize the current financial systems by decentralizing the transaction process. International trade law will need to evolve rapidly to incorporate these technologies if it hopes to remain relevant in the digital age. The prospect of digital economy governance depends on the countries' capacity to cooperate and respond to the dynamics of technological development. Even though there are specific regional agreements that have been effective in tackling some aspects of digital trade, there is a need for multilateral reform. This can only be done through international collaboration, multilateral organizations, and new approaches to dealing with the issues that arise from the development of newer technologies. If WTO, RTAs, and developing countries can come to a consensus and collaborate then the digital economy can be a source of inclusive development. The digital world has continued to evolve at an unprecedented rate and this has raised questions on how best to manage these emerging technologies. It is about guaranteeing that trade is sustained beyond the present and that digital economies are open, equitable, and inclusive for everyone. The relations between RTAs and WTO have emerged as an important issue in this new world. Although RTAs have the advantage of catering to the needs of the regions, they also pose the danger of developing a situation whereby different parts of the world are subjected to different sets of rules that may be contradictory to each other. Whereas the WTO is a more universal organization, it is still lagging in addressing the digitalization of global trade. The increasing rate of innovation is putting pressure on the current system and calling for a more adaptive approach to the regulation of trade.

Legal Framework of Globalization of the Economy and Digital Trade

1 Introduction

The core elements of today's global economic system emerged in 1944 through the Bretton Woods system. This event created a formal system to manage international economic relations [142]. 44 allied nations convened at the Bretton Woods Conference in 1944 to establish our present-day framework for resolving international economic affairs [143]. These institutions established the IMF and the World Bank, which maintain their dominant roles in international financial regulation today [144]. According to economic metrics, these institutions helped rebuild the world economy, which shrank by more than 15% between 1939 and 1945 because development needs legal systems and administrative rules [145]. To manage currency stability and money teamwork IMF stepped forward while the World Bank concentrated on financial development assistance. The Bank for International Settlements gained new importance in 1930 as a central banking center to help international monetary stability [146]. BIS financial records show banks have more than $33 trillion of international financial claims now because these institutions connect global banking markets and maintain stability under control.

Following World War II, the General Agreement on Tariffs and Trade (GATT), created in 1947, started formalizing international trade regulations. Between 1947 and 1994, average global tariffs dropped from 22% to under 5%, a shift driven by multilateral negotiations under GATT's successive "rounds" [147, 148]. The General Agreement on Tariffs and Trade evolved into the World Trade Organization foundation through its legal framework. Since its start, the DSB has processed more than 600 trade disputes through the WTO's official dispute resolution system, which makes trade law enforceable [149]. The World Trade Organization was formed in 1995 with its 164 member states now overseeing 98% of global trade, which makes it a major foundational legal system for the international economic union [150]. During the early years of global economic law, states led negotiations and signed agreements. But today, the twenty-first century marks a shift toward global management. The

J. Afzal, *Exploring the New Horizons of International Law Concerning Globalization of Economy*, https://doi.org/10.1007/978-981-95-1312-3_3

number of bilateral investment treaties has surged from 400 in 1989 to more than 2500 today, and ISDS mechanisms have emerged as a new way to settle disputes [151, 152]. Under this model, foreign investors can take host states to international arbitration panels outside of regular court proceedings. Over 1,200 ISDS cases filed by 2022 show that corporate entities increasingly shape global economic law through their involvement in dispute settlements [153].

Private businesses work with the OECD and UN to create soft law rules, and they establish ESG requirements for their respective sectors [154]. Under national rights authority, countries move apart through "centrifugal" rules, yet common trade connections establish "centripetal" connections between them. More than 17,000 business owners from 160 nations across the world joined the UN Global Compact to confirm their shared values in this informal agreement [155]. Business standards now shape law more than ever before. Stronger economies and multinational organizations participate actively in talks, but developing countries have little influence in these events. UNCTAD research shows that developed countries write 60% of the clauses in trade deals with developing partners, which makes developing nations feel disrespected in their legal jurisdiction [156].

From a unique perspective, the evolution of global economic law can be seen as a response to two opposing forces: The global economy's legal framework now consists of multiple overlapping public and private actors instead of its post-war nation-centric basis. Organizations like the WTO and IMF combine national rules with common standards through compromised frameworks. Yet, the evolution is incomplete; new challenges in digital money and platform business require faster legal action because the existing rules process globalization very gradually. The legal framework that controls international trade has transitioned from a post-World War II nation-focused system to a hybrid system run by public agencies and private players. It enables significant business connections between countries but also creates new safety concerns and different legal systems across the globe. The future of global economic law depends equally on improving both official institutions and creating a fair system that gives equal power and influence on everyone involved.

2 Key Legal Instruments in the Global Economy

Each type of legal arrangement creates a specific business framework with distinct rules and capabilities. The legal instruments that guide the global economy include treaties and agreements with binding powers and non-binding standards and guidelines [157]. These systems create distinct economic rules through combinations of official and unofficial standards across many areas. Our analysis reveals that different legal systems operate jointly but need universal approval to sustain their power.

Multilateral Agreements: Law with Universal Ambitions

WTO Agreements – GATT, GATS, TRIPS

The GATT, GATS, and TRIPS agreements, which fall under the WTO framework, set strict and broad rules for international trade [158]. These agreements fight discrimination by using MFN and National Treatment rules together with a Dispute Settlement Body (DSB) to solve disputes. These agreements create the basics but still face critical evaluation. The TRIPS agreement prioritizes pharmaceutical companies, which leads to significant criticism for harming global health. This concern is especially important as the world addresses COVID-19 vaccine inequality. GATS forces governments to open public services to international competition, which can weaken their authority to set sector rules.

UNCTAD (United Nations Conference on Trade and Development)

Despite lacking legal power, like the WTO, UNCTAD functions as a balance by showing what developing nations want [159]. The organization stands for equal trade terms alongside environmental and technological advancement. The organization's opinions carry limited weight in important trade discussions. The differences between UNCTAD's development platform and WTO's market freedom system show that trade law has important political beliefs behind it.

Bilateral and Regional Agreements: Fragmented Power, Unequal Outcomes

NAFTA/USMCA, AfCFTA, RCEP, EU Trade Law

Multiple trade deals between two nations and in regional areas grow faster than the WTO updates [160]. These agreements, including USMCA and AfCFTA, no longer function as balanced platforms for trade. The deals commonly show a mismatch between the negotiating strength of states. China and ASEAN member states pushed for investment and e-commerce policies that support business interests, although these rules make governments cautious about regulatory interference [161]. Through its trade regulations, the EU enforces high standards on environmental protection and data privacy, which other nations typically must adopt. The added consumer protections through regulation reduce the competitiveness of trading partners who lack effective oversight systems.

Investor-State Dispute Settlement (ISDS)

People mostly challenge the ISDS system in modern trade deals because businesses can use it to sue countries that damage their investments [162]. People who disagree claim this approach grants business investors authority ahead of public control of government decisions. Under ISDS regulations, Philip Morris challenged healthcare policies in Uruguay at the international level. People across the globe push for the elimination of ISDS because investors have limited legal options, and the tribunal maintains undisclosed contradictory decisions.

Soft Law Instruments: Governance Without Legal Teeth?

OECD Guidelines for Multinational Enterprises

These rules help companies practice ethical business conduct when dealing with human rights, labor, and environmental issues [163]. Companies and investors often use these standards when preparing their ESG reports and due diligence evaluations. Because multinationals run these programs voluntarily, their implementation remains dependent only on corporate willingness.

Basel Accords

The Basel Committee on Banking Supervision sets standards to direct how banks use their funds and avoid potential dangers. Although Basel III rules showed results following the 2008 crisis, many banks failed to follow them, while emerging nations struggled to reach compliance, generating arguments about inappropriate rules for developing markets [164]. The Basel Accords receive limited global support because they emerge from discussions among a small number of central bank representatives.

UN Guiding Principles on Business and Human Rights (UNGPs)

The UNGPs created a new framework known as Protect, Respect, and Remedy, which asks states to create laws for businesses to abide by and for victims to act [165]. They do not have legal force, which restricts their effectiveness. Many companies include ESG principles in their actions, but they follow these rules inconsistently. Rights advocates across many states and civil organizations call for a new UN treaty forcing companies to respect human rights because self-regulation does not work.

3 Legal Dimensions of Trade Liberalization and Market Access

International laws control global trade operations by setting both trade partner choices and other essential rules, plus benefits and risks [166]. Trade liberalization serves as both a political and economic process that reshapes how businesses can transport their products globally [167]. International legal platforms, particularly the WTO standards, present consistent trade rules for economic systems of different nations. The promised open markets of trade liberalization usually break down due to existing power differentials and disagreements about rules and authority.

3.1 Tariff and Non-Tariff Barriers

WTO made significant progress in limiting duties through international trade law; during these decades, global trade agreements brought down average import duties internationally from 20% to under 5% [168, 169]. Despite tariff decline, current trade policies now rely heavily on more sophisticated non-tariff measures as barriers.

NTBs take the form of regulatory tools like import permits and technical standards, which limit trading opportunities indirectly. NTBs are hard to challenge under trade rules because governments disguise them as regular domestic regulations for safety and health protection. Countries use these methods to disguise trade limits in their economic activities, which later result in WTO dispute settlement. Establishing the difference between laws created for protection and those put in place for valid reasons is what makes this legal matter so hard to solve. The EU's ban on US hormones in beef triggered a WTO trade conflict because US officials believed it masked a trade barrier. Liberalization rhetoric targets tariffs, yet NTB regulations have become the major trade war field because different countries apply their own protectionist rules here.

3.2 *Most-Favoured-Nation (MFN) and National Treatment*

Trade liberalization within the WTO system depends on its two core principles of Most-Favoured-Nation (MFN) and National Treatment [170]. WTO members have to grant all other WTO members the same trade benefits as another country receives. The principle protects all trading nations from unfair treatment and establishes a common ground for fair trade practices. Under National Treatment regulations, each imported product must enjoy equal market opportunities as home-made products from the moment it enters the market. These equality-building trade rules struggle to work in actual international trade settings. Many nations now join regional trading blocs like the EU or USMCA that give better trade terms only to their members instead of applying them to all WTO members [171]. National Treatment faces repeated challenges from domestic rules that appear neutral but unfairly affect trade from outside countries. The WTO rules forbid countries from offering trade advantages to their local solar manufacturer even if the subsidies meet their legal requirements. WTO disputes about market entry show fundamental conflicts between countries trying to balance their domestic freedom to set rules against market opportunities for international trade. People strongly disagree about how to enforce these principles because the WTO struggles to maintain fairness across multiple economic systems.

3.3 *Customs Procedures and Technical Barriers to Trade*

The actual workings of international trade depend on customs operations and technical trade barriers to trade [172]. Having an effective customs system ensures faster border crossings without additional expenses or corruption problems. The development of new customs technology remains out of reach for basic institutions in developing countries, which forces them to impose trade limits. The WTO Trade Facilitation Agreement TFA started operating in 2017 to create global customs standards and promote trade transparency [173]. The WTO expects lower-income nations to cut trade expenses by more than 14% after following all TFA regulations [174]. As a special agreement, the TFA combines mandatory trade rules with technical help and adaptable implementation dates for least-developed countries. The WTO now accepts that legal rights do not automatically create fair conditions for its members.

When it comes to technical barriers to trade, the legal system features extensive complexity. TBTs use product specifications, testing requirements, and labeling rules to make trade challenges invisible. Under WTO principles, member states must develop trading rules that follow international norms while being as free trade-friendly and fair as possible. People disagree on how to define the exact requirements for dealing with necessary and reasonable situations. Developing country exporters criticize REACH (Registration, Evaluation, Authorisation and Restriction of Chemicals) because the European Union's chemical regulation is too strict and expensive for their products to enter the EU markets [175]. This situation confirms an essential issue between different legal systems. Governments must determine how they can maintain public safety goals during trade openness policies despite their different legal frameworks. Multiple private sustainability labels contribute to market entry difficulties when national authorities do not make these standards.

3.4 Trade Facilitation Measures and E-Commerce Protocols

International trade simplification efforts now extend from border crossings to online business. The rapid rise of online shopping created new trade patterns that need updated customs legislation to regulate them [176]. Digital items like software, music, and online services move across borders digitally, which questions the basic function of customs control [177]. The WTO talks about creating global e-commerce rules, but member countries cannot agree on major topics like data movement rules and taxes, plus regional product requirements. EU members enforce strict data security rules, but other nations support unhindered online commerce. A scattered legal system for online trade leads businesses to have incomplete online trade knowledge, especially small merchants in developing nations who lack technical support for different digital trade rules. Officials now recognize electronic documentation and single-window systems with digital signatures as necessary trade facilitation tools to cut administrative burdens. Many organizations do not fully use these tools today. Advanced digital trade systems operate in Singapore and Estonia, whereas basic paper records govern commerce in low-income nations. Legal systems now have two different trading approaches operating side by side: digital and streamlined trade versus manual procedures. To make the systems work better, companies and governments need to spend money on standardizing cybersecurity and interoperability rules.

4 Regulation of Transnational Corporations (TNCs)

4.1 Jurisdictional Challenges of TNCs

Because Transnational Corporations (TNCs) operate through separate legal entities across multiple countries, they create difficult legal enforcement issues for authorities [178]. The law maintains each business unit as an independent entity regardless of parent company control. Under the separate entity doctrine, parent companies stay immune from legal responsibility for their international subsidiaries, especially when operating in nations with weak rule of law systems. During the legal action against Shell in the Niger Delta environmental lawsuit Nigerian courts refused to make the parent company pay for damages [179]. The courts in the UK started to accept cases under tort law only in recent times. The practice of shielding parent companies from their foreign subsidiary actions happens less often than regular corporate operations. Through this fragmented legal identity, TNCs enjoy global market benefits without facing national oversight regulations. The legal separation weakens governments' power to uphold safety regulations at work and protect nature. Companies use multiple locations to run their business in places that give tax breaks, pay lower wages, and have weaker environmental rules. Restricting fair competition and limiting the government's ability to protect people are the harmful effects of this practice.

4.2 Corporate Accountability in a Global Legal Vacuum

The main issue today is the lack of enforceable international rules that hold companies responsible for their actions. Under public international law, corporations do not have legal rights that states must obey. Every business within these states must follow their domestic legal requirements. When local governments cannot enforce their business rules because of corruption or inadequate resources, corporations find easy ways to do what they want. The global power of TNCs exceeds the legal boundaries of individual nations, which results in a management problem [180]. Both legal suits based on tort law and consumer campaigns provide remedies, but they take too long and cost too much to work well in most situations. Few countries outside the United States have legal mechanisms available to handle class action suits despite the lack of effective justice systems. Companies find it tough to prove their innocence due to expensive legal services and unfair information advantages that make it hard to hold them responsible. The lack of proper laws affects transboundary issues like climate change the most because crimes originate from multiple sources, and companies easily pass responsibility to others.

4.3 International Efforts

Organizations from around the world push for soft law tools to help companies make better decisions. In 2000, the UN Global Compact started working with businesses to support their adoption of ten principles covering human rights, labor, environmental, and anti-corruption standards [181]. The UN Global Compact offers its services to over 25,493 participants from 165+ countries and ranks as the world's largest corporate sustainability initiative [182]. The Compact does not include specific ways to ensure companies follow its standards. The standards represent a moral code that companies can use to share values, yet lack the power to enforce actions. Besides this, the OECD Guidelines for Multinational Enterprises provide voluntary guidelines about environmental protection and anti-bribery activities, along with operational requirements. Companies can take allegations to the National Contact Points when they experience harm under this system. The system works with no formal rules and no required actions, which leads to unsatisfying advice for participants. These instruments support corporate responsibility, but they lack the power to force companies to obey rules. Businesses must choose to support these standards through goodwill because there is no legal requirement for them in profit-driven international markets.

Many Global South nations and civil society groups support the creation of mandatory UN regulations for business and human rights. The Human Rights Council's Open-ended Intergovernmental Working Group started talks about a business and human rights treaty, yet powerful corporate groups and certain developed nations block progress. The disagreement between parties emphasizes the need for a fresh law structure that views TNCs as international responsibility holders alongside their operational roles across countries.

4.4 Home vs. Host Country Legal Obligations

Regulators face a major weakness because they cannot fully control parent companies that operate subsidiaries outside their own country [183]. Home countries control behavior that takes place on their national soil, while host countries cannot enforce rules against foreign investors. When global companies divide legal tasks between their home and host countries, they can easily avoid full accountability; certain states now adjust their practices. French companies with worldwide operations must track and stop human rights and environmental risks under their 2017 Duty of Vigilance Law. Both Germany and Norway set new rules through their laws that make companies responsible for monitoring their global impact. These actions show that companies must now follow rules that extend beyond their home borders. Though progress is happening in a few places today, these actions remain rare compared to the general business landscape. Governments do not want to stop their firms from operating internationally because it threatens their business advantages and foreign business relationships. The current global investment system furnishes foreign investors with strong protections yet provides minimal means to enforce compliance with environmental and social standards. Host states can take legal action against excessive regulation, but investors cannot face legal consequences for failing to meet social expectations. The existing law structure gives foreign investors special protection yet does not hold them accountable for their actions.

5 Global Financial Regulation and Capital Mobility

Global financial integration has turned capital into the most mobile economic force worldwide [184]. Global capital movements between nations through FDI, portfolio investments, and speculative transactions can boost economic growth and technological advancement [185]. Standardized laws need to catch up quickly with the fast pace of international finance operations to work effectively. Legal oversight of global finance exists to handle multiple risks involving countries that send and receive finances and deal with state authority versus financial entities and open markets versus tax evasion.

The movement of capital affects both financial systems and requires appropriate legal protection. Unrestricted or weakly managed cross-border investments caused financial system problems that led to the economic failures of 1997 in Asia and 2008 internationally [186]. The speedy entry of money into the economy then followed by rapid money departures, triggered currency failures and debt traps, combined with severe societal unrest; the legal problems in this situation are major. Financial borders limit the actions of national governments despite quick-money capital movements that happen in a split second. When investment rules differ between nations, investors exploit these differences to make money while hurting global financial stability.

The International Monetary Fund leads global financial governance activities when crises occur. Under the Articles of Agreement, the IMF monitors exchange rate systems and provides emergency funds to support international financial cooperation [187]. Many people oppose the IMF rule that requires countries to adopt reforms before receiving financial aid. The system aims to stabilize economies yet brings strict economic changes that mainly hurt poor people and weaken government control. People in Greece, Argentina, and Pakistan strongly opposed the reforms the IMF made them follow. According to critics, the IMF's consent-based authority becomes coercive when a country needs financial aid desperately.

The OECD-G20 Base Erosion and Profit Shifting (BEPS) project took a significant step forward with its adoption of the global minimum corporate tax agreement in 2021 [188]. The system targets companies that move profits to tax-friendly locations to stop them from evading taxes. The international tax agreements with their bilateral treaties and multilateral instruments create a system that requires corporations to pay at least 15% tax no matter where they do business. The world now moving away from national tax competition and moves towards a united international tax regulation. The tax model shows weak, consistent execution across nations, yet developing countries maintain that its design unfairly benefits OECD states because it misses source tax requirements.

Financial tracking approaches both help and hurt us as a society. Financial transparency tools are vital for fighting money laundering but create problems when they affect our rights to privacy and the nation's independence. Global anti-money laundering bodies, including the FATF and CRS networks, have built advanced systems to monitor financial activity [189]. Experts point out that agencies that block transactions need to make their activities more open while choosing which countries to target. Whistleblowers in Panama Papers and Pandora Papers have shown that high-compliance countries can help hide criminal money [190]. The world is moving toward better financial transparency rules but continues to balance privacy concerns against accountability needs. Sovereign debt refers to the funds governments borrow to manage their national affairs. Governments use these loans to construct infrastructure projects and fund essential services. Every nation needs to borrow money to operate its government, and developing countries especially seek these funds to expand their economic growth. Debt issues emerge whenever governments cannot repay their borrowed funds. Governments avoid bankruptcy court procedures since they operate differently from private entities. Global authorities do not provide guidelines or procedures to handle unpaid debts. Treating this problem proves challenging, particularly for developing nations. Different organizations and groups have taken steps to assist countries with their debt management issues. Both the Paris Club and the London Club represent examples of international debt management organizations [191]. These are not recognized courts but instead represent groups of lenders who work to create repayment terms for nations facing financial distress. The Paris Club consists primarily of Western nations; the London Club consists of leading private banking establishments. These groups determine which debts a nation needs to pay back and when it should make these payments, but they are not neutral. Their goal primarily serves to benefit lending institutions rather than fulfill debt obligations for developing nations. Nations do not influence how private lenders structure their debt deals. Borrowing procedures have undergone significant updates throughout history. Many countries today sell bonds to investors worldwide to raise funds; these are called Eurobonds. Nations obtain funding from private investors internationally instead of being limited to government and bank loans. Many bond contracts include legal terms that follow New York or English law standards [192]. When legal conflicts arise, the parties agree to have the court in the U.S., or the U.K. make the final decision instead of their home country. The lenders receive substantial benefits through this arrangement. Major concerns exist regarding both credit rating agencies, like Moody's and Standard & Poor's [193]. Private entities rank countries based on their payment reliability for borrowed funds. A poor credit rating causes more financial challenges for nations when trying to secure loans. Investors often withdraw their funds when this happens, which creates an even bigger financial crisis. These organizations control significant power, yet their actions remain dubious and unclear. They do not face legal consequences when their rating decisions harm people.

Loan agreements now incorporate Collective Action Clauses (CACs) to manage debt repayment challenges [194]. A Collective Action Clause enables a majority bondholder group to decide about debt repayment terms and make them mandatory for all investors. The accepted plan from 75% of bondholders becomes mandatory for every investor in the deal, including dissenters [195]. CACs protect deals from holdout investors who try to block them through total payment demands. Despite their benefits, Collective Action Clauses appear in only certain agreements, and many nations do not employ them. The system provides relief but still has its flaws. The absence of an international standard for debt management during payment difficulties becomes evident through these diverse difficulties. When businesses face bankruptcy, they must adhere to well-defined legal procedures. In times of national difficulties, the decision-making system remains uncertain, leading to political influence determining the outcome. When countries get in debt, they need to reduce their expenses while increasing taxes and following loan agreements established by the IMF and other financial organizations. When governments make these spending cuts, they harm their citizens, especially people from lower economic backgrounds who need assistance from these services. Developing nations experience greater injustice because of this unequal system. They take loans to help their citizens but have no protection when unexpected events such as wars or economic crises occur. Most lenders stay free from legal punishment when they approve dangerous loans. Many people and organizations now push for a universal and equal procedure to help nations facing financial crises. This setup matches bankruptcy court procedures but applies to nations instead of individual companies. This proposed solution would assist both lenders and borrowers in resolving their challenges while shortening the time needed for recovery. The system requires defined standards for its operation. An impartial organization must supervise this system while remaining independent from global powers and financial institutions. The UN and Jubilee Debt Campaign support this debt relief approach, yet powerful nations reject its implementation. Present circumstances support an appropriate time to implement new policies. Several nations, particularly in Africa and Asia, endure severe debt burdens due to COVID-19 impacts and international market instabilities [196, 197]; these countries need fair solutions. Governments must avoid placing blame on citizens for uncontrollable circumstances. Many professionals now recognize that debt's effects extend beyond finance into individual human struggles. The need to remedy our system becomes urgent when human suffering results from distant legal or business choices.

6 Labor, Environment, and Human Rights in Global Legal Regimes

Other areas of international economic law, such as trade, human rights, and environmental protection, typically do not coordinate well with each other. As globalization grew, trade and investment rules moved ahead rapidly, but social and environmental protection progressed only [198]. This gulf is intrinsically based on more fundamental structural distinctions. Trade systems are therefore mostly used to stimulate the growth of the economy, while Labor and human rights frameworks are used to protect people and the environment. Due to these differences, contradictions emerge, for instance, when trade rules dilute attempts to protect workers or the environment. The World Trade Organization (WTO) is a clear manifestation of such contradictions. Although the WTO is fiercely opposed to protectionism, it does not mandate that countries respect labor rights or environmental standards. Attempts to introduce environmental issues (whether through "green box" subsidies or non-violation complaints) have been met with political blows. Many developing countries do not want to add International Labor Organization (ILO) standards to WTO rules, but they consider this a means for rich countries to protect their industries [199]. Arguments over carbon taxes or eco-labels demonstrate the clash between WTO trade rules and what global climate goals require under the Paris Agreement. This indicates how outdated the WTO's approach is in terms of linking trade with social /environmental policies. Lately, trade and investment agreements have also incorporated the Environmental, Social, and Governance (ESG) parameters [200]. They are soft law tools to make businesses consider their effects on people and the planet. However, ESG clauses are typically non-binding, and companies are left to police themselves. Critics contend that ESG is largely a means to protect corporate reputations and is powerless without actual legal authority or responsibility. The condition in the countries of the Global South is even worse. These countries tend to be pushed into opening their markets, but without having the legal power to hold foreign investors to be answerable for harmful practices. Many also find it difficult to fulfill complex ESG requirements. Consequently, they fear these standards may become new obstacles to growth rather than real help in achieving sustainable development.

7 Legal Pluralism and the Fragmentation of Global Economic Governance

The world's global economy is regulated by a combination of overlapping legal systems that instruct how international trade works. Although globalization provides the advantage of more open markets, it introduces legal confusion. These various legal frameworks support different policy goals, but they combine to make it difficult to keep the system organized. Sometimes trade rules conflict with environmental protection law, labor rights, and human rights commitments, and this results in inconsistency in the application and enforcement of the global economic rules. These various legal systems, with their structures, objectives, and modes of dispute resolution, coexist with each other but are not always in harmony. The World Trade Organization (WTO) deals with the removal of trade barriers and market opening. On the contrary, the Paris Agreement and the Convention on Biological Diversity advance the issue of environmental sustainability and preservation of natural ecosystems [42, 201]. Meanwhile, in human rights law, states are supposed to adhere to such principles as fairness and equality, as provided in the International Covenant on Economic, Social, and Cultural Rights. Such frameworks usually operate separately, and since they do not coordinate well, problems occur when countries or companies are supposed to follow diverse, and at times conflicting, rules. This legal diversity, often referred to as legal pluralism, refers to the fact that one issue can be addressed in various forums, depending on the legal system that is applied. For instance, a disagreement on food safety could be submitted to the WTO or addressed under human rights law or laws about health. This enables countries and firms to select the legal environment that is most advantageous to them in winning, forum shopping. Although it is permitted now under international law, it can cause concern. Critics argue that it allows powerful players to abuse the system, rather than the provision of fair and equal justice for all.

The different legal systems work in isolation because they do not engage with each other. WTO tribunals tend to dismiss human rights and environmental protections as separate from trade law issues during their judicial decisions. During the EC–Hormones case, the WTO maintained strict scientific trade standards while ignoring ethical ramifications and related public health impacts [202]. The Appellate Body prefers to uphold trade agreements without bringing in relevant international environmental treaties to make meaningful changes to its judgments. The refusal of different legal systems to work together creates an order of legal rules that puts trade rules first ahead of social and ecological concerns. Trade liberalization and climate action create clear conflicts that everyone can see. When nations place taxes on carbon emissions while also supporting green products and limiting fossil fuels through trade regulations, they receive more objections from trade law systems. The EU and Japan challenged Canada's renewable energy subsidies under WTO regulations, which found the program violated trade rules between member states. When trade law decisions support international agreements, they do not help countries meet their climate objectives, thus showing us how separate legal systems can fight against each other. The challenge goes beyond specific rules because it also includes organizational resistance and repeated existing policies. During COVID-19, global health challenges showed that TRIPS intellectual property protection rules do not fully match essential disease prevention responsibilities. The process of obtaining vaccine licenses stalled due to legal proceedings, which showed how hard it is to balance public health needs with TRIPS trade protections [203]. When legal systems operate independently without coordination, they create practical problems that block people from getting basic needs like essential services and public resources. Legal fragmentation particularly burdens developing countries since they need to handle multiple legal frameworks that they cannot easily understand. Wealthy nations with their legal teams hold overwhelming advantages in international negotiations compared to Global South states, which lack enough experts to defend their interests. Developing countries must follow rules that sustain power differences and reduce their ability to create new policies or advance public welfare. One legal system's requirements place restrictions on what another system can achieve within its mandates.

Despite its hurdles, legal pluralism still brings benefits to society. The system enables multiple legal systems to exist side by side while allowing people to test different rules and challenging standards to strengthen the global order's legitimacy. When institutions fail to create system-wide connections between regulatory environments, the risk of functional breakdown rises. That led to the creation of different organizations, including the WTO's Committee on Trade and Environment, plus the UN Guiding Principles on Business and Human Rights. These mechanisms struggle to enforce their decisions and usually disappear when conflict becomes intense. The global economy requires a system of coordination standards that help separate entities communicate while preserving legal autonomy. An integrated system could combine mutual recognition rules with shared witness contributions and joint dispute resolution processes that merge different legal views. A change to this system needs both new legal ideas and strong support from major global economic powers. Our global economic governance system shows how diverse interests and legal systems interact across different national contexts. A properly managed approach to legal pluralism enhances international law, but without governance, it turns into a source of legal confusion and misconduct. Scholars need to work with policymakers and international organizations to organize different economic systems properly and create fair practices in our linked global society.

7.1 Digital Economy and Cyber Regulation

Our digital economy is expanding at breakneck speed, which pushes traditional legal systems to change while proving how well international law can adjust to new demands [128]. The digital transformation between countries and their digital independence creates an important conflict. Data should move freely between countries to support all major online business sectors such as e-commerce, cloud services, and AI development. The nations across the world now control digital platforms in their territory and want foreign services to abide by national regulations. Several nations, such as China and Russia, have put data localization rules in place for security reasons, while nations across the EU want to keep the internet borderless for economic and technological advancement. International organizations are now working to develop standards that control digital development. Since 2019, the WTO Joint Initiative on E-Commerce has worked to develop basic rules for digital commerce across all nations [130]. It strives to solve practical problems with digital information movement, digital agreements, software asset defense, and tax operations through electronic means. The attempts to advance have taken lengthy periods and created disagreements. Developing nations fear that early digital market liberalization will strengthen the control of Big Tech companies from developed nations, while some nations deny international commitments unless they know their local control systems work well. The current lack of agreement shows that the international community faces major problems. Digital opportunities face challenges between open internet access and fair business control.

Local data protection laws like GDPR in the EU and CCPA in California have become general international standards that help guide other nations when they write their data privacy rules. GDPR demands explicit user consent for data collection while reducing data quantity and sets large punishment rates for any violation by businesses working with EU citizens. Despite defending personal privacy, these laws make it hard for smaller businesses internationally to run their operations because of weak internet systems. The different abilities of businesses to follow digital rules create worries about rules limiting digital trade. International law needs to create rules for new technologies like AI systems and virtual payment systems, plus online platforms. The UN and regional organizations released ethical standards, yet international regulatory structures haven't been established. The legal gaps in AI fairness regulations and digital platform control create new global inequalities. As digital trade develops as our international economic base, international law needs to change to both support new technologies and keep digital rights safe in an equal environment.

7.2 *The Role of Emerging Economies in Rewriting Global Economic Law*

Over a century, governments from Western developed nations have guided global economic rules and regulations in trade, business, and investment markets. After World War II, the WTO, IMF, and World Bank emerged through frameworks shaped primarily by the US and Western European economic systems. Multiple BRICS nations, including China and India, now challenge traditional Western economic rule while expanding their global influence. These nations refuse to just obey rules made by others when they have no say in creating them. They push for changes to global law to match their needs and expertise. The most success has been by the BRICS nations, which have transformed global institutions to suit their interests better [204]. They've frequently criticized the IMF and World Bank for being dominated by the United States and Europe, which reduces the influence of BRICS nations on decisions that influence their economies. In reaction, there has been the development of financial affiliates by the BRICS, including the New Development Bank (NDB) and the Contingent Reserve Arrangement, providing development funding with fewer political strings than Western lenders have been known to enforce [205]. The increasing role of these new institutions speaks volumes for the fact that developing nations are stepping into the shoes of controlling international economic and legal policies. Also arisen are new methods of handling disputes that are appropriate for diverse legal cultures and economies. The NDB, for example, has its mechanism to settle disputes in case of conflict that may arise in its project. China's Belt and Road Initiative (BRI) is setting up its own set of laws, such as China's International Commercial Courts, that are mandated to address cross-border trade disputes along the BRI routes [206, 207]. These courts do not adopt the rigid, adversarial approach typical of the Western type of law but rather a more flexible and locally sensitive approach.

At the same time, several countries, especially from the Global South increasingly pushing the envelope on the trade and investment rules imposed by the Western powers. An example is their increasing resistance to investor-state dispute settlement (ISDS) clauses in investment treaties, enabling multinational corporations to challenge governments over public-interest policies. These countries state that such clauses override their right to regulate in fields of health, environment, or labor protections. The African Union works on legal reforms through the African Continental Free Trade Area, which develops regional trade systems that benefit development and are fairer. The past legal system continues to function, but signs show that multiple legal systems from different regions now exist. Legal advancements now emerge from multiple regions across the globe. Legal systems and economic frameworks across different nations now influence the development of global rules and regulations. As emerging economies take a more active role in international law, they help to create guidelines that better represent different world regions. The upcoming era of globalization will see different belief systems influence its development through collective meetings.

7.3 Challenges and Critiques

The promise of global economic development and legal systems failed to eliminate existing unfair legal powers between countries and corporations. Powerful businesses in wealthy states use their influence to create rules and settle disputes while developing countries must follow rules set for them. The unequal distribution of power within our economic system shows more than just administrative problems because it creates lasting economic injustice across all countries. Free trade deals encourage market access without considering how developing nations should compete in those markets. Transnational corporations use forum shopping and legal arbitrage to take advantage of existing economic inequalities between nations. Big companies create subsidiaries in places where tax rates are low, and labor rules are easy to break while making storage locations away from their headquarters. These practices decrease state control over their legal systems and fiscal resources, particularly in developing nations. The IMF reports that countries in development suffer $200 billion a year from tax avoidance actions like BEPS, which show how corporations exploit legal opportunities for profit.

Many developed nations control economic policy decisions across the entire planet. Most international institutions, including the WTO, the IMF, and the OECD, allow Western and G7 nations to control their operations. The evidence appears clearly in WTO trade negotiations and IP regulations, along with conditions attached to IMF loans. Under US and European pharmaceutical industry influence, TRIPS developed IP rules that block the Global South from getting cost-effective medicine. The fact that many countries adopt these standards not through democratic debate but through external pressure or necessity highlights the undemocratic nature of global legal ordering. Critics believe that international economic law helps colonial-style power relationships continue. After decolonization, former colonial rulers and current economic superpowers use trade policies and debt practices to extract value from and control developing nations through international agreements. Today's economic control methods, including loans with conditions and investor-state dispute settlements, echo past colonial methods but operate inside valid economic partnerships. The global code needs changes to bring equal participation and better match today's suffering with past effects to stop becoming a legal system that helps powerful groups.

8 Conclusion

Different types of law influenced globalization, including international agreements by the WTO and the IMF alongside regional trade treaties and regulations for digital trade and corporate responsibility. International laws establish basic rules for international commercial exchanges between nations and enterprises. The present system has not treated all people fairly. Big corporations and wealthy nations led the rule creation, yet developing countries lacked influence, causing them to benefit less from these rules. People now demand a transformation of our international economic law system. To build a fairer world, technology, and economic law systems need to give equal representation to nations and communities. Our decisions today will determine what direction we take in our future. Our current difunctional system stays open, or we establish a united platform to protect everyone involved in international business. People can achieve better tax rules, better worker safety, and environmental protection, plus international data and digital rights, through new agreements. Real change demands active support from political leaders, international organizations, and private sector companies. The legal system needs to guide the movement of globalization towards justice and equality.

Developing countries struggle to match international law standards since they lack basic legal enforcement abilities and bargaining power. Digital marketplaces and digital currencies develop too quickly for current legal frameworks to regulate them properly. The challenges posed by globalization have evolved alongside its development, particularly affecting domestic legal systems. National authorities find it hard to control multinational companies that conduct business in several countries. Developing countries suffer from poor legal defense as their limited financial resources cannot support international law protection. New economic zones, including online marketplaces and cryptocurrencies, expand so fast that legal systems cannot keep up, leading to gaps in oversight.

Digital Security Legislation Trends to Facilitate Digital Economy

1 Introduction

The advancement in the society through adoption of the internet and digital platforms has not only granted us with a possible higher level of connection and productivity but also made a way forward for all types of unlawful deeds [208]. This is where the issue lies for the Police force because they must work their way through a myriad of legal frameworks in order to arrest and charge offenders [209]. There is a dire need to implement international cooperation in response to cyber threats [210]. Legal systems need to change so that there can be a convergence of laws and regulations to allow countries to develop synergism to the fight against cybercriminals [211]. Without an international effort, cybercriminals will always be quick to shift through legal jurisdictions to avoid getting caught [212]. Innovations like AI-based attacks, frauds through blockchain, and activities on the Dark Web cannot be effectively counteracted using the approaches of traditional legal measures; so the need to evolve legal instruments to these developments is necessary [213]. All sort of cybercrime requires unique legal treatment, which explains why cyberspace legal systems should distinguish one crime from another in order to ensure proper punishment of offenders [214]. Criminals in digital space using the internet for their illicit activities hide behind proxy servers and can only rarely be tracked down to provide tangible evidence that will stand up in court [215]. This is the reason why there is a need for digital forensics that will go hand in hand with the help of different countries to make a better solution to identify the people behind this and have them arrested. Sharing of digital evidence is problematic from a privacy point of view due to various data collection practices [216]. The measures that protect from threats have to be designed to exclude the possibility of abusing rights and freedoms, that is why legal acts are also supposed to ensure security without violating civil liberties and rights [217].

Advanced technologies, despite their promise to revolutionize everything, have evolved to be a ban; AI and the dark web provide cybercriminals with tools that make their work easier to conduct, and hard to detect [218]. This has created a new

J. Afzal, *Exploring the New Horizons of International Law Concerning Globalization of Economy*, https://doi.org/10.1007/978-981-95-1312-3_4

technological arms race that needs sound legal and technology protocols that can be able to avoid cyber threats [87]. Cybercrime chose the boundary-less environment and this poses a challenge to the traditional judicial systems' legal responses since they fail to deal with jurisdictional realities [219]. To successfully prosecute cyber criminals across borders, it is essential to prosecute international laws regarding cybercrime [220]. This has a global approach with the aim of enhancing cooperation between nations in the prosecution process of cyberspace offenders [221]. If we are to rightly fight cybercrime, it needs to be done comprehensively; since global threats act in cyberspace, cooperation is crucial [222]. This is particularly important in making threats known, implementing benchmarks, and aligning legal systems an example being the adoption of an integrated approach in the fight against cybercrime [223]. As technology emerges with the ever-growing technologies, the threats related to cybercrime will also proceed [224]. The need for future trends, investment, and development studies is critical to today's practices, and the revision of existing laws to address the new challenges of tomorrow's cyber threats makes preparing for tomorrow's threat landscape a fundamental ingredient [225].

This chapter aims to review the legal issues in the fight against cybercrime to facilitate the digital economy environment, which has become critical due to rapidly increasing interactions between crime and technology.

- Recognizing the different legal factors of cybercrimes, this chapter aims to provide knowledge on how to protect society in the increasingly digital era, to ensure the growth of the digital economy.
- The focus of this chapter is on collaboration, international law, privacy, and individual rights to ensure that the judicial system can adapt to the ever-changing threats of the digital economy.

2 Scrutiny of Legal Framework Challenges

Cybercrimes have emerged as a phenomenon via the Internet adding to the problem of jurisdictions that do not fall within a single country [226]. Unlike traditional offenses which are restricted by space, cybercrime takes place with little hindrance in an environment that is non-territorial [227]. This therefore makes it difficult for the agencies to investigate and pinpoint the culprits [228]. Due to the big size and the increasing complexity of the cyber threats, no country is ready to face and fight them alone [229]. This means that the forces, knowledge, and savvy of many nations are necessary to create a strong defence against cybercriminals [230]. Such agencies like INTERPOL have vital functions in this collaboration because they act as communication centres/forums for information sharing, formation of another shared platform to conduct advanced interdisciplinary investigations, coordination, and formulation of procedures that may enhance inter-connectivity. Working on the basis of collaborative work and supporting the exchange of information and mutual cooperation in criminal investigations, Europol plays a major role in guaranteeing cyber security to states and around the globe [231].

The integration of new technology in computer systems indicates that the problems of cybercrime will worsen in the future [232]. For these new challenges, there is a need to build resilient and forward-looking legal arrangements and international cooperation arrangements [233]. National legal systems are also in the process of responding to an evolving along with applied technologies as well as to future legal issues, and cooperative undertakings, such as joint strategic working groups and joint threat monitoring centers, will increasingly assume significance. Analyzing technological innovations, cybersecurity is a dynamic field where technology can represent all chances and threats [234]. As these technologies continuously integrate and enhance numerous segments of society, they sometimes proceed at a higher pace than the legal mechanisms intended for combating emergent types of cyber threats [235]. Due to the emergence of new technologies in society, legal developments are faced with challenges in responding to such change. New advanced technologies including artificial intelligence, block chain, and internet of Things among other innovations present new risks and difficulties to handle by the current legal frameworks [236]. Acknowledging the necessity of flexible legal instruments is an important part of establishing the connection between technological progress and the construction of a legal framework. Dynamic legal solutions include legal frameworks that are crafted in a way that ensures that they can meet the dynamic and ever-changing cybersecurity environment [237]. This flexibility is crucial to counter cyber threats as laws in this field must be continuously effective against such threats so that law enforcement agencies have proper tools to fight new crimes without violating constitutional guarantees of citizens' rights and liberties.

As for the current legislation concerning IT security, it is necessary to carry out systematic revisions and amendments as well as updates on the new technologies have appeared and new threats have emerged [238]. This meant that lawmakers had to work in close consultation with technologists and cybersecurity professionals to enact legislation that is both all-encompassing and would cease to be rendered ineffectual in a relatively short period. Legal systems have to promote technological advancement while adopting measures that will prevent the negative use of the same [239]. To maintain this balance the legislators, technologists, legal advisers, and IT security professionals must work together to develop legislation that does not inhibit the creativity of developers while creating strong legislation which is capable of being enforced. Due to the globalization of threats to cyberspace, legislative innovations are possible only with cooperation with foreign states [240]. For the countries to find an effective way of addressing the cross-border cyber threats they need to join forces, benchmark, and align their legal frameworks. International organizations i.e. United Nations and other related bodies may serve as a venue for these cooperative legislative policies.

3 Cyber Space and Cybercrimes

Cyber threats do not fit into a simple category of unlawful activities; the spectrum is quite broad [241]. These include garden variety of criminal activities involving identity theft, credit card fraud, paraphernalia, etc. through advanced and complex threats including ransomware attacks, cyber espionage, and attacks on critical infrastructure. Different types of cybercrimes also imply different legal concerns, which is why the classification ought to proceed within the legal framework to properly fit responses and corresponding sanctions [242, 243]. Legislators and legal analysts should remain abreast with technology advancement and the new emerging cyber threats in society and make necessary changes to the law as perhaps required [244]. The distinction made between various types of cyber offenses should reflect the distinctions between these types as far as their modus operandi and consequences are concerned. This differentiation also assists law enforcement agencies in formulating an exclusive approach to assigning resources to fight various types of cybercrime. Legal systems therefore need to be ready to deal with all sorts of crimes that are now including fake online activities, theft of identity, and financial hackers [244]. Further, cyber espionage sponsored by states and matters related to cyber terrorism and attacks on infrastructure demand specific legal consideration.

Since ransomware attacks are becoming more common, legal definitions should include unauthorized data encryption with associated threats of extortion [245]. The legislation should prescribe measures for both first-degree criminals and those who offer services that enable such crimes to be committed. As the threats are global thus it is crucial to have consistency in the definitions of the laws all over the world [246]. Cooperation with international counterparts assures the world is fighting cybercrime in unison, also facilitates extradition, and fights cross-border offenses at one front [247]. To police cyberspace and prosecute cybercriminals, the problem of balancing efficient law enforcement with respect for people's rights has emerged as paramount in the process. With each progressive day, cyberspace stains, raise question marks over the ability to prey into the personal lives of individuals during cybercrime investigations. In contemporary societies, people conduct their business and store or transmit personal data through the internet, with concerns about unauthorized observation and likely abuse of data [248]. Law enforcement agencies have to adopt high technology within their working times to conduct investigations more efficiently to transform the means into ends hence aiming at an unjustified invasion of people's privacy thus the need to consider the balance between the security needs the rights of individuals. As a result of these problems, Data protection laws have become popular in the modern world. Global legal instruments such as the General Data Protection Regulation (GDPR) in the EU are another scheme that seeks to enfranchise individuals on their data [249]. They set standards on how one can legally gather, handle, and store personal data and therefore form the framework on how police want to investigate while respecting the rights of citizens to their privacy.

This means that in order to alter this equilibrium there is a need to create structures that uphold the privacy provisions while at the same time allowing access under the law when necessary. The cooperation of IT firms, authorities, and lawyers, is essential for developing clear action plans that allow this type of access but reduce the opportunities for abuses significantly [250]. Moreover, the relevant content that has to do with maintaining this balance can be supported by new technologies; these technologies in the legal system improve the efficiency of cybercrime investigations and comply with privacy laws. Another important element that refers to striking the balance is public awareness [251]. These types of awareness-creating efforts serve the public well by alerting the community to the significance of privacy, the legal protections afforded by Constitution, and difficulties that law enforcement agents have in investigations [252]. Publicity of laws having to do with cybercrime investigation fosters public confidence in the legal process while recognizing the legal privacy of all citizens. Stakeholder conversation, changes in legislation, and accustoming the public to privacy-preserving technologies will be crucial in considering the role of the right to privacy aiming to address the complexities of cyberspace [253]. This system needs tangible privacy protection and a flexible technological environment to be incorporated into the legal instruments, which would strengthen the system both in terms of security needs and human rights.

4 Common Legal Framework and Global Trade

Transnational issues arising in law do not respect national jurisdictions this has led to increased aspects of international cooperation and synchronization of the laws [254, 255]. Among countries, cooperation provides a more coordinated approach for addressing such complex legal questions. Different states becoming more mutually dependent and hence require the same multitude to address issues such as cybercrime, climate change, or the existing global pandemic. The equalization of laws creates less risk and brings legal systems to promote equitable treatment throughout an area. Harmonization of this kind not only enhances cross-border commerce and relations but also lays down rules and regulations. The WTO is an indispensable actor in the global trade system and it serves as the legal procedures setter [256]. By way of bargaining and bargaining cooperation, the WTO provides guidelines that regulate international business, solving matters such as tariffs, subsidies, and other matters to do with copyrights. The WTO makes certain these guidelines are complied with to carry out fair play to all the countries involved in global trade. The Organization for Economic Cooperation and Development (OECD) works as a forum for guidelines and recommendations in subjects like taxation, anti-corruption, and environmental sustainability with the help of its best practices and coordination policies that work against international challenges [257]. Anti-Bribery Convention of the OECD is one more example of the international activity to prevent corruption which has aimed to set up the standard of canonization of bribery of foreign officials.

The United Nations (UN) is an international organization that brings together most nations to deal with matters affecting the whole world and even individual countries in areas including peace, security, human rights as well as sustainable development. Different conventions and treaties of the UN are for the global society that fosters global legal order [258]. However, there are some problems affecting international collaboration; achieving legal integration of various international legal systems, cultures, and politics is a continuous process. Another weak point is that technological developments raise emerging legal solutions like AI and digital currencies. International cooperation strategies also need to respond to these changing legal consequences. The global interactions and the legal integration present a way toward gearing to solve some of the complicated global challenges [259]. The legal work carried out by WTO, OECD UN, etc. is very helpful in framing a coherent legal structure at the international level.

Standard cyber-criminal trials serve the purpose of communicating that any unlawful action will not go unpunished [260]. Police arrests and other convictions among cybercriminals serve as deterrents for the rest to refrain from emulating the same behavior. Moreover, such legal actions highlight the need to safeguard the communities and nations, thus a need to establish sound legal framework for ensuring the security of the identified services. Most effective cybercrime prosecutions usually involve working with other international organizations [261]. It improves coordination hence making it difficult for offenders to use the territorial integrity of a country as a window to escape law. As well, the use of public–private partnerships is essential in addressing cybercrime. Synergistic efforts between and within governments and nongovernmental cybersecurity organizations and corporations enhance the alliance in combating cyber threats [262]. Thus, the information, resources, and expertise must be shared in order to effectively prepare for the emergence of the new nature of risks. Some of the emerging threats are caused by the existence of encrypted messages; solving these issues, as well as concern for privacy rights will pose the future legal systems as the ethical and regulatory challenges. As cyber threats continue to advance, adapting legal frameworks, fostering public–private partnerships, and integrating technical expertise will be crucial for building a resilient defence against the challenges in cyberspace.

The future is going to make it much worse than the current situation by unleashing Advanced Persistent Threats (APTs) which are complex and well-planned cyber attacks normally funded and conducted by organized attackers [263]. AI is another link for the discussion as it intertwines with cyber threats. Such attacks, especially the ones using machine learning algorithms with which the attack can be self-evolving, are even harder to track and curb; while attackers use AI to step up their activities. The creation of quantum computing is beneficial to cybersecurity as a promising technology; however, it also threatens cybersecurity. Quantum technologies can help to create new types of cryptographic applications but are also the main source of risks to today's cryptographic frameworks [264]. The legal responses available to meet these dynamically changing cyber threats have to be dynamic in nature. Fundamental concepts of legal regulation require elaboration, including the problems connected with deepfake technologies, surveillance society, and the legal status of the blockchain [265]. As targets of cyber threats, nations are forced to cooperate in the sharing of intelligence, legal convergence, and best practices such as extradition. More often, bilateral regional and international treaties will have to be prepared to provide relevant mechanisms for faster decision-making and reaction in combating cybercrime as it is a worldwide phenomenon. This is important to have an array of defenses that we can counteract in dealing with the ever-changing strategy of attackers. The decision to classify cybersecurity as a problem of national security further complicates the picture, as countries will focus on their interests rather than on cooperation [266]. Maintaining an effective cybersecurity level while following ethical principles and acknowledging people's rights to privacy will always be an issue. Another necessary component of future cybersecurity will be education, including worldwide, and cyber security practices. Enabling people and institutions to know what to look for and how to avoid the traps assists in facing new strategies [267]. The proposed framework indicates that education is a key component in creating defences against cyber threats. However, it is possible to build the future envisioned with the help of the Internet and the opportunities of a connected world by involving innovative processes and flexible approaches to legislation and international cooperation.

5 Cyber Security Legislation Trends

5.1 Role of United Nations (UN)

In 2021 the United Nations launched an ambitious program to establish a global cybercrime convention, an important step in international efforts to fight cybercrime. This work arises from UN General Assembly Resolution 74/247 (2019), which noted the growing threats from cybercrime, and as such, encouraged the creation of a comprehensive convention. In May 2021 UN General Assembly adopted Resolution 75/282, creating an Ad Hoc Committee to draft this global treaty. The committee's aim is to unify the legal framework in the area of cybercrime to enable better cooperation among Member States in prosecuting and investigating as well as preventing such crime. The UN cybercrime convention aims to:

- Set standard for cybercrime laws by creating offense for the access to ICT systems without permission, cyber fraud, child exploitation, and ransomware attacks.
- It encourages international cooperation towards cross border sharing of digital evidence, investigations and prosecutions.
- The technical assistance and capacity building provided to countries especially developing countries to ensure their infrastructure and legislative framework for fighting cybercrime, is strengthened.

By addressing the transnational nature of cybercrime, the crime largely fills the gaps between its various national legal systems. It would enhance global co-operation permitting countries to cooperate more effectively on a preventative and prosecutorial basis in relation to cybercrime. This initiative is critical because it addresses the transnational nature of cybercrime, where cybercriminals exploit gaps between different national legal systems.

5.2 *European Union (EU)*

In recent years, the European Union has made quite significant steps in updating its legislative basis and judicial practices to fight cybercrime. The Digital Services Act places new responsibilities on digital platforms and puts greater transparency requirements on online services, to make digital spaces safer. Medium and large companies in critical sectors across the EU are strengthened by the NIS 2 Directive in terms of cybersecurity. Both the European e-evidence regulation and directive, passed in 2023, seek to harmonize the rules for the collection and transmission of electronic evidence across EU borders. These measures will be transposed into national law by Member States by 2026. The Court of Justice of the European Union (CJEU) addressed conditions for using data obtained according to European Investigation Orders (EIOs). The court ruled that where the data has been intercepted from an EncroChat encrypted platform, the Member State of execution can share the data across borders as long as the sharing complies with the laws of that Member State.

5.3 *France*

France has implemented wide-ranging reforms especially by setting up offices dedicated to cybercrime and increasing criminal penalties. The decree (Decree No. 2023-1083; 23 November 2023) created the Anti-cybercrime Office (OFAC), which leads national efforts in combatting cybercrime, as well as investigations conducted by the judiciary and help to other authorities. The law (Act 2023-22; 24 January 2023) stipulated additional provisions to the CC and CPC to enhance the struggle against cybercrime by increasing the penalties for unauthorized access to data systems and introducing new crimes about the administration of unlawful online platforms. The Court of Cassation(21 November 2023) said that in EU law, the access to connection data necessary to instruct a provider to reveal connection data would have to be the subject of prior judicial review and that, to avoid a violation of privacy rights, such generalized data requests have to be specifically justified.

5.4 *Luxembourg*

Luxembourg amended its legal framework to better address cybercrime and the collection of electronic evidence. The Criminal Procedure Code (CPC) and the Criminal Code (CC) were amended to permit notification of the e-evidence (Law of 29

July 2023) measures via email, and the definition of IT systems has been expanded to include automatic and non-automatic data processing systems.

5.5 Hungary

New provisions for Hungary aimed at crimes committed against electronic payment instruments strengthened its legal framework. A new series of offenses related to the illegal recording and handling of data from electronic payment instruments were included in the Criminal Code as amended (Amendments to the Criminal Code; 1 January 2023):. Now, possession, production, and distribution of devices and software used to obtain such data are criminalized with penalties of up to two years imprisonment.

5.6 Malta

In the field of financial crime, Malta revised its legislation regarding electronic evidence. With the Proceeds of Crime Act amendment (Act No. VI of 2024) allowing digital evidence to be considered at confiscated assets proceedings, courts are now able to consider digital information when deciding whether it will be confiscated.

5.7 Austria

Austria is also altering its cybercrime laws to increase penalties for some crimes. The amendments also made cybercrime-relatedness (Amendment to Cybercrime Legislation; 2024) more harshly penalized.

5.8 Romania

The Romanian authorities adopted new legal measures to fight offenses against the exploitation of a child through digital means. It is an offense under this law which introduced a new paragraph under Article 374 of the Criminal Code (Law No. 217/ 2023), punishable by up to six months or three years imprisonment for adults who request minors to produce and distribute pornographic material through electronic means.

5.9 Germany

The issues of using encrypted communications in criminal investigations have been very active in Germany's courts. In a ruling confirming the conviction of defendants running a bulletproof hosting service, the Federal Court (Cyber bunker Trial) has said that services that are designed to evade law enforcement do not qualify for the legal protection afforded by the Telemedia Act or the EU e-commerce directive.

5.10 Norway

The Norwegian courts have allowed encrypted communication data to be admissible in criminal cases. The Norwegian Supreme Court (30 June 2022, EncroChat Case) said the data collected on EncroChat had been lawfully obtained under French law and could be used in criminal proceedings in Norway.

6 Discussion and Comparative Analysis

This research is based on the work of several leading scholars in cybercrime legislation and enforcement, whose excellent comparative studies highlight our theoretical and practical understanding of international cybersecurity law, for the digital economy. Shukurov and Jafarov in their study, used thematic analysis from interviews with legal professionals to highlight challenges such as legal ambiguities and digital evidence management [268]. In contrast, although their work highlights the difficulties of enforcement, my research complements it with a broader and empirical account, adding richness to our understanding of where enforcement is challenging which is especially pertinent considering international cooperation. AllahRakha's study, Global Perspectives on Cybercrime Legislation, uses doctrinal analysis to examine the cybercrime frameworks of international bodies such as the United Nations and the European Union [269]. While his work highlights the importance of harmonizing cybercrime laws, my research extends this by providing empirical evidence from law enforcement agencies, grounding the call for legal harmonization in the practical challenges of law enforcement. Yongmei and Afzal evaluated the effectiveness of Pakistan's cyber laws in a single jurisdiction; in contrast, this research is cross-jurisdictional, providing a comparative perspective that increases the relevance of results for global audiences [226]. Yongmei and Afzal's study provided important insights, but it is conducted at the scope of a nation; whereas my research examines cybercrime enforcement issues from international and global perspectives, showing that this topic is relevant for policy making not only at a country level but also worldwide which demonstrates61 there are needs to be harmonization on the policymaking achieving high successfully together.

Tikk and Kerttunen provided insight into cybersecurity governance and operational challenges on a global scale [270]. Their theoretical framework explores the full spectrum of cybersecurity policy; however, my study bridges the gap between theory and practice by examining the real-world challenges law enforcement agencies face while enforcing the law. Through these comparisons, it becomes clear that my study makes a unique contribution to the literature by providing a comprehensive and practical analysis of the fight against international cybercrime, making it a valuable resource for policymakers seeking to improve the effectiveness of global cybersecurity frameworks. Ajayi looked at the effect of mechanical progressions on cybercrime and the confinements of existing authorization systems in combating advanced computerized dangers [214]. Ajayi highlighted challenges in following and indicting cybercrime due to innovative progressions, my ponder not as it addressed these challenges but also consolidated observational proof from cross-jurisdictional case considers, giving a commonsense see of requirement deterrents over distinctive legitimate systems. Similarly, Brown identified the limitations that technological advances place on the investigation and prosecution of cybercrime [215]. Brown's research provides valuable insights into the legal obstacles and the dependence of legal tools on successful prosecution. This research work extends these findings by providing a comparative analysis across multiple jurisdictions, highlighting the importance of standardized international protocols, and proposing specific strategies for law enforcement to overcome these legal obstacles in practice.

Sumadinata addressed the global scale of cyber threats and called for increased international cooperation [271]; this work was comprehensive in its analysis of the impact of cyber threats on global security, my research builds on this by evaluating specific legislative approaches from different regions and assessing their effectiveness in real-world law enforcement situations. Singh examined the jurisdictional challenges and enforcement mechanisms involved in cybercrime, particularly under the Budapest Convention [272]. Singh's legal review provides an in-depth analysis of international treaties, but my research adds to this by highlighting implementation issues at the operational level, showing how jurisdictional challenges play out in real-world cases. Balarabe discussed the theoretical balance between digital sovereignty and international cooperation [273], our research complements this by providing data-driven insights into the practical challenges that arise in cross-border issues, strengthening the argument for a legal framework that is adaptable and flexible. Casino et al. focused on the complexities of managing digital evidence across borders, particularly due to differing national protocols [274]; our study builds on this by proposing specific legal reforms and operational strategies to mitigate these challenges, making the findings more directly applicable to law enforcement practice and policy frameworks. Through this comparative analysis, it is evident that our research makes a unique contribution to the field by combining both theoretical and empirical approaches, addressing the challenges of combating international cybercrime with a practical approach that is directly relevant to policymakers and law enforcement agencies globally.

7 Conclusion

The development of a strong and viable legal system is necessary that will be fit for combating cyber threats in today's complex digital economy. The nature of cybercrime legislation is dynamic; cyber security has become an issue that needs collective effort from government, policymakers, corporations' legal bodies, as well as citizens. Emerging threats to the digital economy are fast evolving, hence the need to design a proactive strategy that embraces stakeholders. Technology use in the personal and business setting requires the development of an approach that is dynamic to prevent the online space from being threatened further in the future. The measures shall be largely effective in enhancing the resilience of systems against cyber criminals, the observance of the individual's right to privacy, and the sanctity of the law. The world will be safer if international cooperation is encouraged, advanced technology is adopted, and relevant information is disseminated to the public. The issue of cybercrime cannot be solved solely by legal means, but also the use of technical measures, as well as the training of people who could potentially become victims of cybercriminals. The criminal justice system must be ready, aware, and perfectly synchronized at the international level to tackle the issues of cyber threats.

8 Recommendations

- All Nations collectively need to step up efforts to reduce cybercrime to facilitate the digital economy. It is possible to establish more efficient agreements and treaties with other countries that will control the sharing of information and extradition protocols, as well as the creation of cooperation of multi-national task forces to combat Trans transnational cyber threats.
- To develop legal responses around the globe, it is important to set global cybersecurity norms. Promoting the use of these standards in different jurisdictions will go a long way in ensuring that the adoption of measures for the prevention and mitigation of cyber threats is uniform.
- It is necessary to enhance the cooperation of the public and private sectors in the sphere of cyber security. Governments, cybersecurity organizations, and industries need to work together to provide the framework to share threat intelligence, good practices, and possible cooperation scenarios.
- It is crucial to educate people on cybersecurity and how to be safe from accessing the threats. More effort should be directed toward educating people, companies, and other organizations on the ability and capacity to prevent cybercrimes. Through improved training, it will ensure that the officers working as investigators are abreast with current trends in the field of cybersecurity.

International Laws and the Rise of Cyber Economies

1 Introduction

The global market has experienced the rise of cyber economies due to the rise of digital platforms, e-commerce, and online transactions that are reshaping how business is conducted across borders [9]. Digital economies or cyber economies are economic activities based on the usage of digital technologies, especially the Internet [275]. E-commerce, online financial transactions, digital goods and services, and the growing gig economy, rely on the global digital infrastructure and are part of this sector [79]. In the past decade, the digital economy has grown very rapidly. E-commerce was once a niche but now it has taken the shape of a multitrillion-dollar industry. In 2021 alone, the global e-commerce market grew to be valued at more than 4.9 trillion dollars, and this shows no signs of slowing down since internet penetration is on the rise, more people use mobile devices to access the internet, and the world is embracing digital services [276, 277]. In the last 10 years, the e-commerce sector has grown at a double-digit speed year by year [278]. A large part of this growth is driven by the growing adoption of consumers' online shopping, online payments, and the everyday existence of online marketplaces. The surge in digital transactions and online business growth due to the emergence of COVID-19 has led to an upsurge in the transition to digital business models [279].

The digital economy is strongly shaped by international law as it enables the smooth running of cross-border transactions. The issue of having a strong legal framework for regulating international digital trade, protecting consumer rights, and ensuring the security of cyberspace is one of the key challenges cyber economies faces [87]. International laws provide the required structure for protecting intellectual property, managing data privacy, and resolving legal hurdles as regards cross-border e-commerce [280]. On the other hand, they build a legal environment that helps to avoid disputes and provides a good, equal, and transparent environment for digital markets. For instance, the General Data Protection Regulation (GDPR) in the European Union or the United Nations conventions related to cybercrime, are meant to

J. Afzal, *Exploring the New Horizons of International Law Concerning Globalization of Economy*, https://doi.org/10.1007/978-981-95-1312-3_5

make sure that businesses follow global standards in data protection and online security [210]. In addition to this, there is international trade law that has dealt with the tariffs on digital goods and services to allow global trade in digital products.

In the digital world, where digital transactions are becoming more and more important to the global economy, international laws have become very necessary to govern the activities [88]. Without a global legal framework, the cyber economy could be fractured into parts; each country developing its own set of rules in the knowledge that they may have the benefit of theirs first and may then develop over time [212, 281]. International laws are the method of fragmentation prevention since they are the source of common principles and standards for digital business across borders. These laws ensure the process of consumer business, the security and trust of consumers, and the future growth of the global digital economy.

2 Key Components of Cyber Economies

2.1 E-commerce: Online Business Models, Digital Services, and Marketplaces

E-commerce, one of the key pillars of the cyber economy, has completely changed the process of business with customers [282]. With regards to online business models, a company can sell goods and services digitally [283]. These models are: B2C (Business to Consumer), B2B (Business to Business), C2C (Consumer to Consumer), and C2B (Consumer to Business) [284]. We are now in a stage of the rapid rise in digital services that have created a thriving need to provide online marketplaces to people to buy goods, access services, or start a business deal with other consumers or another business. Shoppers, both in department stores and malls, Amazon, Alibaba, and eBay have made shopping experiences easier, and more convenient, and have a wide range of products to choose from and make it easy to compare prices. Location and infrastructure no longer serve as barriers for small businesses, as these platforms have allowed them to access the bigger global markets. The same is true of the digital services offered, from e-learning platforms to streaming services to digital payment systems to cloud computing. By working together, these components enable the digital economy through trade and service opportunities without the physical stores and face-to-face interactions.

2.2 *Cryptocurrency and Blockchain: The Role of Decentralized Technologies in Shaping Cyber Economic Landscapes*

The global economy is increasingly recognizing cryptocurrency and blockchain technology as transformative to world affairs [285]. Cryptocurrency is a digital or virtual currency that works on decentralized platforms without traditional financial institutions like banks [286]. The underlying technology that enables cryptocurrencies, known as blockchain, is a secure, transparent, and immutable distributed ledger system that records all completed transactions [287, 288]. This is a technology that has seen its application moving out of financial markets to domains such as supply chain, healthcare, and digital identity verifications. The main advantage of cryptocurrency is the ability to carry out fast, low-cost transactions across borders [289]. In addition, the financial assets of the users are in their control, which makes it a favorable option for people in countries with unstable currencies. One of the characteristics of blockchain is its decentralization, which makes the involvement of intermediaries unnecessary and thereby facilitates faster transactions and eases operation [290]. This has wide implications for not only the financial sector but for industries including entertainment (digital rights) and logistics (tracking goods on the supply chain). With its potential to increase transparency, reduce fraud, and make operations more efficient, the use of blockchain for business process automation has gained fame as companies and governments have begun to embrace and adopt the technology.

2.3 *Digital Labor and Gig Economy: The Rise of Freelancers, Remote Work, and Digital Platforms*

Freelancing and temporary work have become increasingly popular in the modern world due to the emergence of the digital platform economy and the growth of the gig economy [291]. The gig economy is a form of employment where workers engage in short-term work contracts, often from their smartphones or other internet-connected devices [292]. These platforms enable employees to sell their services to the global market and have the freedom to select the number of hours they work and the kind of tasks they undertake. The shift towards remote work has continued to fuel the gig economy even more, especially with the COVID-19 pandemic outbreak and its effects. Today, it is possible to work remotely with the help of digital solutions to communicate, share information, and complete assignments irrespective of location. The utilization of remote work has been advantageous to organizations that want to cut costs that are associated with maintaining an office space while allowing employees to gain control over their working schedules. Thus, according to statistics, the gig economy involves millions of workers around the world. It has been postulated that gig economy workers are a significant segment of the population in developed countries, including the US, and Brazil, among others. The high percentage of freelancers and teleworkers proves this sector is developing fast, and the government must regulate the rights of workers in such an economy.

3 The Role of International Law in Regulating Cyber Economies

3.1 Cyber-Security and Data Protection Laws: International Legal Frameworks for Safeguarding Digital Information

Privacy and security serve as essential pillars of the digital economy. Since organizations continue to use social media and online platforms to conduct their operations, they accumulate significant amounts of personal and sensitive information, meaning that it is becoming ever more important to protect such data from criminals and other malicious parties. However, finding the right balance between privacy and global digital trade or services still appears as a major concern. Despite many initiatives, the attempt to control the cross-border transfers of personal data has been a failure in several cases [293]. Nevertheless, the European Union's General Data Protection Regulation (GDPR) is one of the most liberal and effective privacy laws till now. It is to empower users to own their data and to make organizations responsible for the processing of that data. However, one more question is quite important: Is there any single standard of data protection all over the world? Today, consumer protection standards are fragmented and at times contradictory, which puts international companies in a difficult position. Data protection is not only a legal or a technology issue; rather, it is the protection of a fundamental human right of individuals across the world. This is because in areas where the rights to privacies are not strong or effectively protected, the risks associated with data getting into the wrong hands or being lost altogether, are elevated.

California introduced the California Consumer Privacy Act (CCPA) in 2020, which grants its people significantly greater consumer rights regarding data [294]. The CCPA enables Californian residents to know what information has been collected about them from what sources and where data about them is sold. These laws like the CCPA are setting new grounds for data privacy and motivating other jurisdictions to follow suit.

As a flexible set of principles for the protection of individual privacy that enables the facilitation of cross-border data transfers among member economies in the Asia Pacific region, the APEC Privacy Framework serves as a significant element of the Asia Pacific coordination on privacy. However, such legal structures are all the more important as cyberattacks and data breaches become more frequent [295]. Taken as a whole, these international legal initiatives are working towards building a more accountable digital world where companies are being held to higher standards and people have more reasons to trust their data.

3.2 *Intellectual Property Rights in the Digital Era: How International Law Protects Online Intellectual Property (IP)*

IP has emerged as a significant factor in the global economy with companies spending millions, if not billions, in creating and protecting it [296]. Equally important is the protection of individual rights of creators and inventors as well as commercial entities. However, the flexibility of digital content diffusion is another challenge to IP rights as seen in the following ways. Above all, international law can effectively face these challenges by granting copyrights, patents, and trademarks to digital works including software, music, and films under bilateral and multilateral agreements. Co-leading this global effort is the World Intellectual Property Organization (WIPO), an agency of the United Nations [297]. WIPO assists its member states in the formulation of appropriate international legal instruments aimed at enhancing the IP systems. The WIPO Copyright Treaty is an example of creating a new international legal framework that met the demands of the digital age by granting creators more control over the use of their work and how it is disseminated. Another important legal regime is the Agreement on Trade-Related Aspects of Intellectual Property Rights (TRIPS) within the framework of the General Agreement on Tariffs and Trade (GATT) [298]. TRIPS thus set up a global standard for the protection of its IP, enabling rights owners of digital content to seek legal redress when their work is duplicated or abused. However, these frameworks are still compromised, and IP infringement continues to go rampant. It can also be noted that digital content remains easily copied and pirated, and counterfeit products remain accessible. To address these challenges, there is a need for increasingly vigorous legal regulation and enhanced interstate collaboration to respond to the changing environment in the digital space.

3.3 *International Trade Laws and E-Commerce: The Regulation of Cross-Border Digital Trade*

There are some legal risks inherent to e-commerce, mainly because most of the transactions take place in cyberspace, and each country has a different legal system. Notably, international trade laws have continued to embrace the changes of this new digital age of trade to eliminate legal complexities and hurdles that may hinder global trade. The WTO also operates in this domain, especially in the Wake of the Trade Facilitation Agreement (TFA) that entered into force in 2021 [299]. The TFA is aimed at reducing customs formalities and costs to support the supply of technology-enabled goods and services. Another WTO instrument is the General Agreement on Trade in Services (GATS), which has also extended to include services delivered through digital platforms. One of the most recent examples of digital trade regulation is the Digital Trade Chapter of the United States-Mexico-Canada Agreement [118]. It provides guidelines on cross-border transfers, data localization requirements, encryption, and privacy. These provisions make the USMCA a potential model for future international digital trade agreements. Given that digital trade is increasingly becoming prominent, international legal frameworks need to remain adaptive to issues such as digital taxation, data protection, and the regulation of digital platforms. On the domestic level, governments need to defend national interests, but at the same time, they need to engage in international efforts to maintain digital markets open and competitive.

3.4 Taxation of Digital Businesses: How International Tax Law Addresses Digital Economies and Platforms

Taxing online businesses is one of the most insistent challenges of the digital age, from Amazon, Google, Facebook, and many more. Physical location and local transaction-based traditional tax systems do not fit an internet-based business model. Also, new international tax frameworks have been about to fill this gap. This challenge has been taken on the lead by the Organization for Economic Co-operation and Development (OECD) [300]. As part of a two-pillar strategy for fair taxation of the digital economy, the European Union proposed in 2021. The first pillar is about making sure that multinational companies get taxed in the countries where their consumers live, even if the companies themselves don't have a physical presence there. The second pillar establishes a new worldwide minimum tax so that multinational corporations cannot avoid taxes by stashing profits in countries with low tax rates. In its entirety, these proposals seek to reform the international tax system and tackle tax evasion in the age of globalization. The European Union has also acted on the issue by trying to establish rules to govern the taxation of digital economies. In 2020, the EU introduced the Digital Services Tax (DST), which aims to tax revenues obtained from digital advertising, marketplaces, and data services [301]. Other members, such as the UK and France, have, however, introduced their digital taxes as the EU seeks the implementation of a common standard to apply a fair tax on digital businesses in all its member countries. The two international tax frameworks are meant to make sure that digital platforms are beneficial to national economies, and to curb tax evasion by multinational companies by shifting their profits to countries with low taxation rates. Following Table 1 shows key international data protection laws & their impact on businesses and Table 2 shows key international trade agreements related to E-Commerce respectively.

Table 1 International data protection laws (GDPR, CCPA, etc.)

Law	Region/country	Key provisions	Impact on businesses
General Data Protection Regulation (GDPR)	European Union	Requires consent for data collection, stricter penalties for non-compliance, and data protection rights for individuals	Set a global standard for data protection; forced global businesses to comply with stricter regulations
California Consumer Privacy Act (CCPA)	United States (California)	Grants consumers rights over personal data (access, deletion, opt-out)	Impacts businesses operating in California and those targeting California residents
Personal Data Protection Act (PDPA)	Singapore	Provides a data protection framework, focusing on personal data use and security	Businesses must comply with strict consent and data retention requirements
APEC Privacy Framework	Asia–Pacific Economic Cooperation	Promotes cross-border privacy protections while facilitating data flows	Facilitates global digital trade by aligning data privacy regulations among member countries

Table 2 International trade agreements related to e-commerce

Agreement	Parties Involved	Key Provisions	Impact on E-Commerce
World Trade Organization (WTO)—Trade Facilitation Agreement (TFA)	WTO Member Countries	Simplifies customs procedures, reduces barriers to digital trade	Eases cross-border e-commerce by standardizing regulations
United States-Mexico-Canada Agreement (USMCA) - Digital Trade Chapter	United States, Mexico, Canada	Ensures free data flows, prohibits data localization, and protects encryption	Sets a model for digital trade agreements globally
Comprehensive and Progressive Agreement for Trans-Pacific Partnership (CPTPP)	11 Asia–Pacific Countries	Promotes free data flows, digital product market access	Encourages e-commerce growth across member nations

4 Challenges in Regulating Cyber Economies

4.1 Jurisdictional Issues: Complications Arising from Cross-Border Digital Transactions and Differing National Laws

Jurisdiction is one of the most challenging issues of the modern world when it comes to the regulation of the digital economy. Unlike the conventional markets which are mostly anchored to a particular country or a certain region, the digital economy spans across the globe. Globalization has led many internet-based companies to conduct their business across countries hence experiencing conflicts in the laws of different countries [302]. This alone presents a myriad of questions as to which country's laws should govern a particular cross-border electronic transaction or a conflict. For example, if a consumer in one country buys a product from an online retailer in another country, it is not clear whether the law of the buyer or the seller should apply to the transaction. When legal issues are not clear or unstandardized, it results in complications, confusion, and controversies that slow down digital commerce. However, when it comes to legal matters such as IP rights, data breaches, or fraud, it becomes rather difficult to define the jurisdiction. Due to this, countries have sought to come up with international policies to standardize laws and set proper guidelines for digital trade across borders, although this is still in the process of being developed.

4.2 Privacy and Security Risks: The Balance Between International Laws and Safeguarding Personal Privacy

Organizations use social media and other online platforms to carry out their operations, they gather large amounts of personal and sensitive information that must be protected from criminals and other entities. However, achieving the right balance between privacy and data protection on one hand, and free international digital trade and services, on the other, is an ongoing issue [303]. Despite the attempts that have been made by several countries, international multi-sector initiatives to address the challenges concerning the cross-border transfer of personal data have been found to have several shortcomings. Nonetheless, the European Union General Data Protection Regulation is still considered one of the most stringent and effective privacy laws to date. Still, there is a question that remains unanswered: there is no common standard for data protection globally. Thus, enterprises operating in the international environment face challenges in the form of a dense web of conflicting rules and standards. Privacy is not just a legal or technical issue; rather, it is much more than that, it is about valuing and safeguarding the rights of people around the world to be left alone. Data privacy is a significant concern in areas where privacy laws are either limited in their scope or implemented ineffectively, which increases the risk of data misuse or loss. The problem grows as organizations continue to amass huge piles of user data for things like marketing and analytics. To address these concerns, there is a need for more international collaboration and harmonization of data protection standards across borders.

4.3 Cryptocurrency and Regulation: Legal Challenges in Regulating Decentralized Digital Assets

While speaking about cryptocurrency, we can define it as one of the most disruptive innovations in the digital economy, but it also presents many legal complexities [304]. However, cryptocurrencies like Bitcoin and Ethereum don't work anything like traditional currencies like the dollar, euro, or pound because they're not based on centralized networks. Governments cannot control, issue, or regulate these because they are not under the control of the central authority. Different countries around the world have been regulating cryptocurrencies differently. Digital currencies have welcomed some to embrace them due to the potential of serving to create financial value and increase financial inclusion. On the other hand, a few have imposed outright bans or imposed abnormally strict restrictions based on volatility, money laundering, and the potential for facilitating terrorism financing. For example, China and India have prevented or severely limited the use of cryptocurrency, whereas Switzerland and the United States have a more open approach [305, 306]. Cryptocurrencies operate in a world with no unified global legal framework. The legal ambiguity this creates leaves investors and crypto-related businesses at risk, as it's unclear what national laws will do to their operations. Moreover, the randomness of the digital assets and their association with crime at times complicates the efforts of the authorities in striking the right balance between the creation of new opportunities for the financial industry and the maintenance of the stability and security of the economy.

4.4 Censorship and Free Expression: Legal Issues Regarding Freedom of Speech in the Cyber World

Censorship and free expression in the context of cyberspace are a large legal issue that the cyber economy faces. All governments impose different rules on online content, and sometimes they conflict with the principle of free speech. Although some governments censor certain online content to maintain political stability, control narratives, or national security, others allow other people to post whatever they want. With the rise of social media platforms such as blogs, people are easily able to share and express their opinions. But at the same time, this has also brought in great concerns about the spurring of misinformation, hate speech, and other harmful content. Therefore, lots of countries have passed laws to curtail or eliminate deleterious online content. The European Union's digital services like the Digital Services Act (DSA) have certain goals [282], such as to hold tech companies accountably for the content being shared on its platform; on the other hand, the Communications Decency Act in the United States is giving the rights to the online platforms but also lets them take down the illegal content. The other way some governments impose strict censorship, and they block access to websites, to some social media platforms, or just to the entire internet service. Countries like Pakistan have the Great Firewall of Internet censorship that limits access to foreign websites and social media platforms [307]. It's attracted concerns about how rigid censorship might hinder free expression and general access to different views. The right to free expression and society's need to regulate harmful content are the central challenges in the new cyber economy. To help resolving the issue of censorship and guarantee, as well as ensuring that online platforms respect fundamental rights and prevent the spread of harmful content, this requires international agreements and frameworks.

5 Cyber Economy and Protection Laws

The GDPR, enacted by the EU in 2018, is considered one of the strongest and most sophisticated laws in the sphere of data protection. The GDPR was designed to tackle the emerging threats associated with the management of personal data as companies extended their operations to the Internet [225]. The GDPR emerged as the new standard for data protection that targets not only businesses within the EU but any international organization that processes the personal information of EU citizens [210]. Some of the essential aspects of the GDPR are the voluntary consent of users for data collection, clear and understandable information about the data processing, the right to the ensure the individual, and the protection of special categories of data. Perhaps one of the most notable effects that organizations must strengthen their data protection policies and explain them better to users. Failure to follow GDPR rules can lead to heavy fines that can go up to €20 million or 4% of the company's total worldwide turnover. The regulation has had significant impacts, especially on multinational organizations as most of them have had to change their privacy policies, update their service terms, and adopt compliance measures as required by the GDPR. Not only in Europe has the GDPR sparked the generation of other similar laws including the California Consumer Privacy Act (CCPA) which indicates a new tendency towards increased data protection.

The trade war has been ongoing between the USA and China since 2018, and the differences between the two countries have shifted from traditional commodities to digital trade, including security and piracy issues. Although the two countries levied tariffs on each other's products, digital trade was the focus when the US claimed that China was stealing intellectual property and forcing American companies to share trade secrets before they could enter the Chinese market. One of the focal instances of confrontation was the Chinese technology company Huawei, whose international activity in the field of telecommunications caused concern in the United States. Huawei was blacklisted by the American government which accused the company of posing some national security risks because of its connections with the Chinese government [308]. As a result, both countries placed restrictions on firms accused of engaging in cyber espionage, making international trade and cooperation in technology ever more difficult. This digital dimension of the trade tensions between the US and China exposed the lack of adequate rules governing digital trade due to the increasing cases of cybersecurity threats. It also highlighted the role of international conventions that protect cybersecurity and the protection of intellectual property in the rapidly growing digital world economy.

The government of Japan has been at the forefront in the regulation of the exchanges to reduce security threats and attacks on cryptocurrency accounts. Japan has established itself as the first country to approve Bitcoin and other virtual currencies as legal tender [309]. This became more apparent after the Coin check hack in 2018 where hackers successfully made away with about $530 million worth of digital assets. To this, Japanese authorities issued stricter requirements to enhance the security and stability of cryptographic exchange platforms to protect consumers. Currently, most exchanges in Japan are not mandatory to conduct a thorough KYC or AML check but are expected to register with FSA. Also, they are required to have adequate internal controls and insurance to minimize the risk posed to the users. The actions of Japan have had a substantial impact on the overall attitude toward cryptocurrencies around the world. It serves as best practice for other countries on how they should govern their digital resources. In this way, Japan has strengthened the confidence of the population and contributed to the growth and advancement of blockchain technologies in the cryptocurrency market.

The above discussion demonstrates how international laws and regulations are evolving in response to the difficulties posed by digital technologies. In addition, they also advocate for a solid legal framework to resolve issues in the fast-growing global digital economy.

6 Emerging Trends and Future Outlook

6.1 *Artificial Intelligence and Automation: Future of Digital Economies and International Law*

AI and automation technologies are gradually becoming a norm in industries, economies, and societies across the globe. Due to its capability of handling large amounts of data, AI is crucial in industries like health care, business, transport, and production. In the digital economy, artificial intelligence increases productivity, improves value addition, and personalization of services to consumers [310]. It has a significant part in the economic development of a nation, and increases as these technologies develop and advance. From a legal perspective, the use of AI across the world has its benefits and legal issues. On one hand, AI can enhance legal activities, making it possible for the processes to be more efficient. AI is already being applied in contract review, research, and case prediction, which could aid lawyers and courts in handling their work better. However, AI has been associated with many ethical and legal issues, specifically in the areas of privacy, fairness, and accountability. As AI systems are being integrated into strategic sectors like the automotive industry and the stock exchange, there is a need for international law to regulate the development and deployment of those technologies [311]. The implications of AI on the labor market can be seen as a threat as well. It is forecasted that many jobs will be displaced by automation with the help of AI, while new positions will be generated. A transition toward such a society will need new policies in workforce development, employment relations, and social protection to prevent workers from being displaced by an AI environment.

6.2 Digital Sovereignty and Global Regulation: Countries' Efforts to Establish Control Over Their Digital Spaces

Digital sovereignty is a country's capacity to control its digital infrastructure and data [312]. As the internet is playing an increasingly important role in national economies, governments are trying to assert some control over economic activities that happen on the Internet within their borders. It includes stricter data localization laws, foreign tech regulations, and control on how information flows into and out of the country based on national security purposes. A good example of digital sovereignty can be seen in the recently passed Digital Markets and Digital Services Acts in the European Union that establish rules for large platforms in the EU and attempt to regulate digital services according to the EU values of privacy and security. Likewise, places such as Russia and India have enacted legislation that compels organizations in foreign nations to keep their data locally while following local guidelines. Even though digital sovereignty empowers nations and makes them safer, it also poses the threat of the balkanization of the digital world. This is because, as more jurisdictions create their legal regulations, the regulations may differ which can limit international trade and also slow down the growth of the digital economy. The major issue in the following years is to strike a balance between national sovereignty and the connected open digital market.

Table 3 Predicted changes in digital trade agreements (Post-2025)

Agreement type	Expected changes	Key focus areas
World Trade Organization (WTO)	Expansion of digital trade provisions, new rules for AI and data flows	Cross-border data transfer, digital trade barriers
USMCA (United States-Mexico-Canada Agreement)	Strengthening digital services provisions, new rules for cybersecurity	Data protection, encryption, and cross-border privacy
EU-Japan Economic Partnership	More stringent data localization and cybersecurity rules	Data protection, cloud computing, and digital taxation
CPTPP (Comprehensive and Progressive Agreement for Trans-Pacific Partnership)	Inclusion of digital taxation and AI governance measures	Digital economy, AI regulation, and intellectual property

6.3 The Future of Digital Trade Agreements: How International Laws Will Evolve to Regulate Future Cyber Economies

Digital trade agreements aim at providing easy access to data across borders, protection of copyrights, and the setting of rules for electronic commerce [313]. They also cover newer topics like cybersecurity, digital taxation, and the protection of privacy. WTO and regional and bilateral deals, such as USMCA, and EU-Japan EPA, are examples of measures taken to liberalize digital trade. These agreements contain provisions that deal with issues related to intellectual property, cross-border data, and digital trade. However, due to the continuous advancement in technology, it is clear that the existing trade agreements will require an upgrade to reflect recent advancements in technologies such as AI, blockchain, and others. It can be assumed that further digital trade agreements will be based on questions such as data protection, digital taxation, or the regulation of new technologies like cryptocurrencies. In the future, as more countries enter into new-generation digital trade agreements, international law will be important for the formation of a fair and open global digital economy. The following Table 3 shows post-2025 predicted changes in digital trade agreements at a glance.

7 Conclusion

The challenges of governing a borderless digital society cannot be accomplished by one country alone. Specific rules need to be set by international cooperation, there should be created one set of harmonized and non-discriminatory rules to foster business success without negatively affecting consumers, the environment, and national security. When it comes to the cyber economy, cooperation is paramount—whether it is establishing a common framework for the protection of personal information or creating digital trade policies. These dynamic changes pose immense possibilities for international law to develop and expand in conjunction with innovations. With new technologies like artificial intelligence, blockchain, and other emerging technologies, there will be a need to adapt international laws. New measures need to be adopted to regulate these technologies to enhance equity and utility to all the relevant parties. This is already seen in such areas as the use of artificial intelligence, regulation of cryptocurrencies, threats of cyber terrorism, and even control of the internet in the future.

International Law and Emerging Economic Issues

1 Introduction

The development of international economies needs international law to establish the proper way for nations to work together [314]. It provides global standards that help solve conflicts and maintain good business relationships between different countries. Old legal systems find it hard to handle present-day economic situations [315]. In the middle of the twentieth century, governments established trade control measures that suited a world with basic international commerce and defined geopolitical dynamics [316]. These outdated facilities were not intended to manage current business requirements, such as digital exchange regulations, environmental development impacts, or tech company oversight roles in national economies [317]. Many countries struggle to define the legal rules for cryptocurrency assets because different nations control different parts of the business through their tax rules [318]. Fast-growing economic trends clash with slow legal appraising because this disparity leads to weak regulatory compliance and injustice [319]. International economic law developed its modern structure through events that started during World War II at the Bretton Woods Conference in 1944 [320]. States focused their efforts on revitalizing international finance and trade after experiencing protectionist policies and the economic effects of World War II during the interwar years [142]. As part of post-World War II efforts, institutions such as the IMF and World Bank developed, while the GATT and WTO set up frameworks for tariff cutbacks in trade [158]. These organizations followed established rules of international law. Each nation holds the authority to decide how to manage its economic system throughout its national borders. States must follow their accepted treaties according to the pacta sunt servanda rules [321]. The WTO's Most-Favoured Nation (MFN) and National Treatment rules help foreign products compete equally in domestic markets by requiring that member nations extend no special favors to their products [322]. The basic trade rules encounter growing problems when applied to real-life situations. Our historical belief about states controlling international trade faces challenges from the growing influence of multinational firms

J. Afzal, *Exploring the New Horizons of International Law Concerning Globalization of Economy*, https://doi.org/10.1007/978-981-95-1312-3_6

and digital platforms that work under supranational authorities. Based on states as major actors, the traditional international economic legal framework no longer fits today's diverse international trade system [323].

The main problem with current international law arises because it struggles to adapt to significant global changes and major system-based problems. The global financial crisis of 2008 showed how weak global economic controls could fail to protect the world [324]. The existing legal standards could not be enforced because leaders blocked them. People once saw the WTO as the foundation of international trade, yet its dispute resolution system currently cannot operate. The WTO system's emphasis on trade freedom does not align with modern interests to protect the environment and workers, plus preserve internet independence. International economic law combines two separate systems: old structures dependent on state approvals and treaties, plus new realities of digital trade among various power centers. The world needs new legal systems that combine adaptability to business networks with strong standards to maintain fair international trade law.

2 Globalization, Digital Economies, and the Law

Digital technology has driven a fast economic transformation across the world during the last 20 years [79]. Our traditional business system now works differently because digital markets use technology to make financial transactions easy and automatic through AI-based platforms [325]. The UNCTAD Digital Economy Report (2021) shows e-commerce sales globally increased to $26.7 trillion in 2019, while COVID-19 made consumers worldwide switch to digital platforms faster [326, 327]. Despite rapid digital economy growth, states and global authorities cannot keep up with effective responses. Digital economic growth causes severe problems for legal systems to handle. Major technology businesses Amazon, Google, Alibaba, and Meta work internationally without running permanent operations in many areas. Each separate national law finds itself unable to maintain full regulatory or tax control over digital economic activities. Digital tax rules have become one of the biggest points of dispute between nations [328]. France and India chose to tax digital services from large tech companies based on the number of service users inside their national borders. The United States announced trade reprisals to protect its companies because foreign governments target American businesses with their policies. The emerging tax issues reveal a complete lack of established legal standards. The system of international tax rules emerged in the 1920s at a time when the internet did not exist, and the concept of physical company presence continues to be used [329]. The Organisation for Economic Co-operation and Development (OECD) works to update international tax rules through its digital tax program called the Inclusive Framework on Base Erosion and Profit Shifting (BEPS), which 140+ countries have joined [330, 331]. This effort has two main pillars: the first redistribute taxes from multinational businesses, and the second creates worldwide minimum tax rates. The movement toward new tax rules advances slowly because both nations and tech face many problems in implementing changes. States participating in the framework have a shaky agreement that breaks easily, plus weak oversight of tax rules. People worry about how laws should control blockchain networks and DeFi platforms [332]. These systems transmit funds between peers directly through cryptographic transactions. The global value of digital currencies rose above $2 trillion in 2021 because of Bitcoin and Ethereum market performance [333, 334]. Different jurisdictions throughout the world do not clearly define the legal status of these platforms. El Salvador supports Bitcoin as an official payment method while China flatly prohibits cryptocurrency trades in its territory [335]. Many nations have undefined laws that neither explicitly ban nor approve certain activities.

The unclear legal rules affect both everyday investors and professional financial institutions when making transactions between different countries. Many national laws do not properly regulate how to protect consumers and stop money laundering, tax obligations, and enforceable commercial agreements. DeFi platforms generate complex legal challenges because users and disputes have no clear human authority over smart contract automation [332]. The system blocks access to legal actions when digital assets fail or when fraud occurs. The European Union started governing parts of digital commerce through laws, including the Digital Services Act (DSA) plus the Digital Markets Act (DMA), alongside the upcoming AI Act [336]. The legal systems target digital platforms to apply responsibilities for managing their content and require them to share operational details while their systems function and keep markets equitable. The AI Act serves as an early effort to establish broad AI control by classifying different levels of risk [337]. These rules have high goals yet function mainly within EU territories and need local officials to take action. Their worldwide effect becomes minimal until people around the world agree to use them as industry rules.

Both UNCTAD and the World Bank highlight that the gap between digital users is expanding [338]. Advanced economies create digital rules that most developing nations struggle to join due to their limited technological resources and insufficient governmental participation ability. During 2021, only about 50 developing nations had official laws covering e-commerce and data protection [339]. One world area now operates digital businesses under new laws, while other areas remain locked out from these rules or face unclear legal conditions. Data transfer between countries continues to pose a major problem that needs solving. The United States supports unlimited internet data movement because it sees it as necessary for business and new technology creation. Under GDPR rules, the EU protects personal data tightly but prevents data movement to regions without effective security standards. Businesses encounter multiple legal challenges because different countries operate conflicting rules, and they face penalties from both jurisdictions. India and China created separate digital sovereign rules by making companies store data within their borders and limiting outside players from accessing it. The world lacks a single legal system to manage online businesses because different nations have different rules. The nations running digital interactions lack an organization like the WTO and the IMF that can establish united guidelines. Although ITU and IGF provide coordination services, they do not possess any power to enforce regulations [340]. Digital law develops in an unplanned manner and displays contradicting elements because national interests determine its outcome instead of international agreement.

The absence of proper laws produces major problems. When there are no universal rules, businesses operate in doubt, governments miss tax opportunities, and people remain vulnerable to danger. When strong countries or areas try to control digital rules alone, it makes international conflicts worse and creates unfair access to technology. The practice of companies moving their operations to weak rules areas to escape strong rules makes worldwide oversight difficult. A plan that works at multiple legal levels is necessary to fix this problem. International efforts should combine powerful economic alliances with developing country training programs to create legally binding digital regulations. Even though soft law documents assist with regulation, they need international treaties or governing bodies to become mandatory standards.

3 International Trade Law and Protectionism in a Post-Pandemic World

The COVID-19 crisis changed how international trade law works while also affecting its basic beliefs. After World War II, nations created a multilateral system to support the World Trade Organization's rules-based system as they believed this approach would add to economic progress and world peace. The worldwide agreement on international trade standards now comes into question. The pandemic demonstrated both international supply chain weaknesses plus increased support among nations to pursue self-serving regional trade deals [341]. The development of local trading blocs is a major sign of this shift in global trade strategies. The Regional Comprehensive Economic Partnership and the Comprehensive and Progressive Agreement for Trans-Pacific Partnership now function as alternative trade agreements since WTO negotiations remain stalled. In 2020, fifteen Asia–Pacific states, including China, Japan, and South Korea, established RCEP, which became the largest economic trade bloc based on GDP [342]. The agreement helps smooth production rules and ease customs duties but does not include mandatory workplace safety or environmental protection rules. Compared to CPTPP standards, the treaty shows higher demands because Western nations want open business practices and aligned regulations [343]. Both groupings have a regional basis because nations now prefer working with smaller neighborly organizations rather than embracing the universal WTO model.

Several major problems have weakened the WTO's authority, especially because its Appellate Body stopped working in 2019 [344]. As the sole WTO member opposing new appointments, the United States has made the dispute settlement mechanism unavailable to users. The international trade system remains unsupported by the resolution of trade disputes through 2024, which promotes national self-interest and trade-response actions. The WTO lost its position as the top trade law adjudicator, while other key organizations also experienced declining trust among their members. Businesses face rising demand to secure their supply chain and bring production back home because of both international unrest and pandemic supply chain disruptions. At the beginning of the COVID-19 crisis, many countries faced urgent medical equipment procurement problems, plus shortages of pharmaceuticals and semiconductor chips. World leaders at both EU headquarters and national governments started reviewing their heavy reliance on international supply chains following these events. Under the U.S. CHIPS and Science Act, the nation receives billions of dollars to support domestic semiconductor producers, while similar plans arise in Japan and South Korea. Recent trade agreements now include clauses that let nations control important national industries. A growing number of trade agreements let governments protect specific industrial sectors from international market competition. The permitted exemptions permit states greater freedom to manage their businesses, but they diminish the essential role of free trade in trade liberalism. People criticize that letting states determine their trade policies creates opportunities for countries to use protectionist measures to their advantage. The pandemic sparked export restrictions and vaccine export policies that damaged global trade systems. Countries implemented export restrictions on medical supplies plus food items then vaccines when the crisis reached its peak. The European Union established export rules to track vaccine movements plus approved shipments, while India stopped vaccine exports to first serve its people. These actions needed WTO approval because they protected public health. In reality, their use showed that different groups had unequal opportunities to get healthcare and created important moral and legal problems with these waivers. Since its start with health supplies export controls now cover a wider range of items. Market tensions between the United States and China led to controls over essential materials like rare earth minerals and advanced technology elements [345]. The connection between international commerce and defense matters grows stronger with new trade restrictions. Using security exceptions under Article XXI of GATT becomes more common, which transforms an exception into widespread practice and puts the entire system at risk [346].

International trade law faces increasing problems because it now exists in multiple separate legal systems. The worldwide trading environment exists as a jumbled assortment of multiple international agreements and domestic trading rules. Companies, especially smaller firms, struggle more with complex legal issues and compliance requirements due to these increases. The system of global norms becomes harder to enforce because states use various legal frameworks together with bilateral power tactics instead of international dispute mechanisms. National interest concerns have grown while global cooperation has declined because of legal fragmentation [347]. During the pandemic, organizations adopted the Build Back Better slogan, which led them to increase local content production while subsidizing domestic industries and imposing strict foreign investment rules. Even though these policies may help ruling politicians, they might create endless protectionist cycles and weaken worldwide commerce performance. The plan toward unilateral actions hurts developing nations in the long run. Smaller countries need market access rules, but they have weak negotiating power against trade protectionism. Their success in market entry depends on stable trading rules that protect their access to markets. Multilateral systems get damaged more than they do, which reduces developing countries' room for growth.

4 Climate Change, Sustainable Development, and International Economic Law

The world now faces both environmental dangers and major legal problems stemming from climate change. International rules of trade, investment, and financial transactions are coming under pressure as policymakers seek effective ways to meet their climate responsibility and support sustainable practices. The climate emergency compels officials and legal experts to review whether WTO and investment rules can meet Paris Agreement targets. In 2015, the Paris Agreement became the first worldwide agreement to use the UNFCCC platform by setting 2 °C as the maximum global temperature increase limit [348, 349]. Under the new framework, countries set their climate targets, which they committed to achieving through NDC programs. Despite its importance as an environmental diplomacy milestone, the Paris Agreement needs stronger ways to enforce its rules. The informal nature of UNFCCC rules stands in direct opposition to WTO trade regulations, which consists of firm requirements designed to stop all trade discrimination and prevent market-distorting subsidies.

The WTO rules prevent countries from offering green subsidies because they create trade-distorting effects, especially for clean energy or carbon–neutral sectors. The European Union plans to tax imports through carbon border adjustments to match environmental standards with other markets. WTO members may take these actions to court because they oppose fulfilling both MFN and National Treatment rules. International trade law has not yet clearly determined if Carbon Border Adjustment Mechanism (CBAM) are legal, making future trade conflicts possible [350]. The increasing popularity of Environmental Social and Governance (ESG) standards now drives significant financial investments [351]. Developed banks and institutional funds depend on ESG standards to assess project performance and company worth. However, the integration of ESG into economic decision-making lacks a common global standard. Despite EU Sustainable Finance Disclosure Regulation (SFDR) and Task Force on Climate-related Financial Disclosures (TCFD) sustainability measures, several nations engage in financial regulation loopholes due to no universal global standards [352, 353]. International investment law through the Investor-State Dispute Settlement (ISDS) system regularly clashes with objectives that protect the planet [354]. Under this legal system, foreign investors can take court actions against host nations that change their laws to reduce expected financial gains. Nationwide environmental laws exist to benefit citizens. The Vattenfall company became known internationally through this case. Vattenfall sued Germany for stricter environmental rules under their international investment treaty in this example [355]. Investors under ISDS provisions have taken action to fight against decisions like discontinuing fossil fuel financial support and rejecting mining permits due to environmental reasons.

International environmental agreements should count as stronger evidence than trade and investment rules in legal interpretations. Today, Multilateral Environmental Agreements (MEAs) and economic treaties work separately, which creates disputes between them [356]. Adding MEAs to trade and investment agreements will let both systems work better together. Countries experiencing development should get assistance while pursuing their climate targets without losing progress. The amount of financial support, as well as technology and training programs, must be expanded on a larger scale. A green transition needs to serve everyone fairly on Earth and stop allowing powerful investors to harm weak communities across the world. Environmental justice needs to guide all economic law updates to create a fair system [357]. We must acknowledge past industrial nations' duty while letting impacted people take part in court activities and follow modern science and human rights rules for legal systems. The creation of an equitable and eco-friendly worldwide economy needs active changes to our legal framework beyond market self-regulation.

5 Development Finance, Debt Crises, and the Role of International Institutions

The global economic system heavily relies on funding for development projects. It supplies money to create infrastructure and develop both education and industry, plus healthcare systems in developing nations. After World War II, the IMF and World Bank began operating to help developing nations through financial resources and expert guidance [358]. The current model of conditional lending practiced by these institutions, along with their underlying power inequalities, receives increasing scrutiny due to their effectiveness in creating sustainable development. People frequently discuss whether the IMF and World Bank help or harm developing nations. Borrowing countries receive loans only when they follow specific economic reforms that the IMF and World Bank require in their financial packages. The necessary reforms usually include budget cuts, public asset sales, and deregulation, plus lowering government support programs. The planned economic stability programs often fail to produce the expected results because they weaken public spending and social services while making the rich and poor communities more unequal. The ongoing effects of Structural Adjustment Programs (SAPs) from the 1980s to the 1990s continue to shape economic planning discussions about national self-rule in Africa's sub-Saharan region and Latin America [359]. The biggest obstacle in development finance comes from unequal rights that countries have in dealing with public debt problems. Countries that default on foreign debt payments face an unorganized and uncoordinated loan restructuring process. An acceptable system to coordinate creditors from public and private institutions does not exist at the international level. Each creditor group handles negotiations separately, and treatments remain unequal because large groups delay debt restructuring, which causes ongoing economic turmoil. The broken-up debt settlement structure lets a powerful few major creditors and bondholders decide terms that benefit them over others. Debt distress grows more urgent in today's world because many African and Asian countries now face financial trouble. As reported by World Bank research, most developing nations face high debt risks or are already in debt distress. The impact of COVID-19 requires governments to use more loans to strengthen healthcare and recover their economies. Debt payments in many nations use too many public funds that should instead support basic government services.

Chinese lenders have increased their loans, and emerging institutions such as the BRICS Bank now influence global debt management [204, 360]. China now leads other nations as the biggest lender to developing countries through its Belt and Road Initiative [206]. Chinese loans typically do not follow the IMF and World Bank standard conditions, but these loans concern many people about how clear financial records are handled, they question whether the recipient countries can pay back their debts [361]. Some nations struggle to include Chinese debt terms during restructuring procedures because China refuses to join international debt relief programs in Zambia and Sri Lanka [362]. The BRICS Bank and Asian Infrastructure Investment Bank (AIIB) join other new financial institutions to change the way development finance works [363, 364]. These institutions help emerging economies find funding with better conditions while strengthening their control over financial rules. The institutions also have not created reliable ways to protect borrowers or monitor their actions. Experts say that international financial law's rules on debt between nations make borrowing nations dependent. The established rules for debt contracts primarily benefit lenders in countries with strong legal systems. Without global protection against financial market risks, debtor nations keep experiencing financial crises over and over. A single holdout creditor from NML Capital forced Argentina's national recovery plan to stall by gaining court approval from the United States in their case [365].

The economic imbalance makes it hard for nations to develop their economies according to their priorities. Heavily indebted nations must limit their investments in basic needs due to the debt restrictions imposed on them. The requirement to pay hard currency debt limits how governments spend money while forcing them to sell products abroad, even when these export models might harm their people or the planet. The global community now agrees that nations require an official system to manage unmanageable debt. This system would work as a special court for states to handle debt problems through organized and effective structures. A debt workout system should treat all creditors fairly while protecting agreements from creditor groups that delay decisions, and it must include standards to evaluate debt sustainability using social and environmental criteria. Several nations under the United Nations umbrella want a debt framework, but prominent creditors refuse to help. With no established rules in place, temporary programs such as the G20's Debt Service Suspension Initiative and the Common Framework for Debt Treatments help reduce debt pressure temporarily [366]. These arrangements depend on the country's willingness and include only public debt, yet do not tackle fundamental financial problems. There is also a risk that short-term relief will simply delay the reckoning, rather than offer a path to sustainable recovery.

6 Case Studies and Regional Responses

Under today's global technology and economic changes, regions and countries now design separate legal systems to defend their economic plans while strengthening their national independence. This section analyzes four distinct situations showing how different regions handle their economic problems, including the EU's push for digital independence and Africa's push for AfCFTA regional trade [367, 368].

6.1 The European Union: Digital Regulation and Economic Sovereignty

The European Union leads digital economy regulation worldwide as it pursues digital sovereignty. EU rules strive to decrease dependence on foreign digital infrastructure so the EU can control its data assets. The European Union uses these major laws, including GDPR, DSA, and DMA, to show its digital sovereignty [369]. The laws want to make business fairer while also defending customers and making Big Tech companies take responsibility for their content and behavior. GDPR started in 2018 to regulate data protection needs and made global technology companies update their systems to prevent heavy fines. The DSA and DMA require large online platforms known as gatekeepers to follow rules against using market power and to present clear explanations of their algorithms [370]. These internal rules impact digital governance discussions all around the world through their global reach. The EU establishes strict regulations to protect its economic independence. The region wants to establish global market standards instead of directly following digital rules created outside its borders, particularly by America and China. The new regulations caused problems between the United States and the European Union while creating worries about splitting global rules.

6.2 Africa's AfCFTA: Legal Construction of Regional Economic Power

While the EU has an established framework that links its member states, the African Continental Free Trade Area (AfCFTA) aims to connect African markets through its youthful legal plan. The African Continental Free Trade Area (AfCFTA) opened in 2021 to become the biggest free trade region in the world based on its member nations, which total 55 African Union members [371]. Its main purpose is to remove tariff barriers from 90% of products while making it easier for capital and people to flow across borders and driving industrial growth through enhanced integration [372]. The AfCFTA framework builds its legal basis through documents that regulate trade in products, services, disputes, and intellectual property rights. The agreement ensures value creation happens within Africa through its rules of origin policy. The legal basis supports African nations to develop their economies by making goods with higher value while trading goods between African countries. Yet challenges persist; the lack of proper infrastructure and trade limits, along with weak administrative systems, blocks complete usage. The transfer to one legal system throughout the region needs solid political leadership to make it work. Despite current challenges, AfCFTA has the potential to benefit the region over an extended period. The agreement outlines a development-oriented trade system that puts inclusive growth and country self-rule before market deregulation standards.

6.3 US–China Trade War: Tariffs, WTO, and Sanctions as Legal Weapons

The US-China trade war of 2018 introduced modern weapons like economic penalties instead of diplomatic approaches for geopolitical objectives [373]. The United States started tariffs on $360 billions of incoming Chinese products in 2018, using Section 301 of the Trade Act of 1974 to fight trade abuse and illegal intellectual property theft. China activated tariffs on American imports after the US tariffs started [374]. Both China and the United States took legal cases to the WTO, but their progress was limited due to a WTO Appellate Body crisis made worse by the U.S. blocking of judge selections. The United States placed export controls and sanctions through the International Emergency Economic Powers Act (IEEPA) to block US technology sales to Chinese organizations ZTE and Huawei [375]. This dispute demonstrates the growing trend of states using legal tools as weapons in international economic politics instead of relying on traditional cooperation. WTO rules displayed their weaknesses since they failed to control major sources of US-China conflict, which include state capitalism support, along with technology and subsidy imbalances.

6.4 South–South Cooperation: Redefining Legal Norms from the Margins

South-South Cooperation (SSC) serves as a different model for international economic relations to evolve [376]. South-South partnerships differ from North–South donations since they place equal value on shared benefits without requiring countries to submit to outside authority. The rise of South-South cooperation shows in programs such as the Bali Strategic Plan and BRI alongside the IBSA Dialogue Forum [377]. South-South cooperation now provides special finance terms and distributes technology with specific development parameters. Contracts include specific terms that let parties handle changes smoothly and support nations in keeping control of their development decisions. The New Development Bank represents a new approach that differs from the conditionality requirements of the IMF and World Bank loans. Critics do not accept this model as it comes with several problems. South-South legal cooperation between developing nations now challenges standardized international trade rules coming from Western nations as they work to establish their universal standards.

7 Virtual Assets Law Regulatory Framework

A few years ago, virtual assets hardly existed, but today they are a common part of society and have changed our views on money, ownership, and technology. Back in 2009, Bitcoin started as a way to create a decentralized digital currency, but it has expanded to include many other types of crypto and digital assets [378]. At the moment, digital currencies guided by blockchain influence are transforming various industries, pushing millions of people worldwide to invest in digital currencies. The speed at which growth is happening is astonishing; technology has allowed virtual assets to offer services to people who could not get them from standard banks. They are also using new techniques for raising funds, including Initial Coin Offerings (ICOs) and token sales [379]. NFTs have now started to shake up the art, music, and entertainment fields. Generally, the way businesses operate financially and with technology is changing a lot nowadays. Many virtual assets rely on blockchain technology, which allows transparent and unchangeable ledgers to exist without needing a central authority. Decentralization ensures that transactions are processed quickly, come at lower costs, and are open to people from all countries. With the help of smart contracts, complex financial products and apps are built more easily. The new systems can assist in streamlining tasks, lowering costs, and giving confidence to users in ways older systems generally struggle with. Still, as technology changes so much and quickly, laws and regulations are often not as updated as they need to be. The rules in traditional law focus on conventional money and big, centralized financial organizations, not decentralized, digital, and worldwide virtual assets. This creates significant regulatory challenges; there are several pressing concerns for regulators and governments in deciding whether a certain virtual assets falls into the category of a currency, security, or something different. Which groups should be responsible for supervising cross-border transactions made on decentralized networks? How can regulators prevent people from being taken advantage of without stopping all innovation? Since there are no clear and standardized rules, regulations are not uniform around the world. In some places, there are friendly rules in place to encourage virtual assets use and advancement. There are also jurisdictions where governments have chosen to be strict or even ban cryptocurrencies because of concerns about money, consumer risks, and shady activities. Because laws vary from one country to another, global businesses encounter many problems with compliance and may try to take advantage of inconsistencies between countries.

7.1 Overview of Virtual Assets

Virtual assets are a fresh idea covering many forms of digital value. Fundamentally, virtual assets are only digital and can be moved, saved, or traded online. Unlike traditional ways of exchanging money, they are based on technologies like blockchain, which do not depend on just one central authority. This separation means that ownership, control, and the way we transfer value are understood differently now. Virtual assets are important because they represent digital value [380]. While virtual assets are not tangible, their worth is real, and they can be traded for other assets or services online [380]. Anyone can access them instantly if they have an internet connection, which makes them accessible to everybody around the world. The use of blockchain technology in virtual assets is helpful for users, but it is proving a challenge for regulators to control them well. Each virtual assets has its special trait and is used in multiple ways. Crypto assets, such as Bitcoin and Ethereum, exist only in the digital world and can be used for transfers between people without banks. Their transactions are secured and recorded by the blockchain, allowing for a clear and public copy of the ledger. Stablecoins, unlike most cryptocurrencies, are worth a fixed amount backed by US dollars or gold. With their price tied to a stable assets, stablecoins are suitable for everyday use and act as a link between old finance and cryptocurrencies. Unlike other cryptocurrencies, utility tokens are used as an entry to services or products that run on blockchain technologies. A typical example of a utility token allows its owners to pay for data storage or be part of a smart contract-run community.

They are similar to stocks and bonds, as security tokens show ownership, profit pieces, or voting rights in a company. They are governed by laws meant to keep markets safe for investors and honest. They try to use the advantages of blockchain and keep the legal rules for existing securities. Recently, NFTs have received a lot of attention from the public. Unlike cryptocurrencies, every NFT is different and proves ownership of something specific, like artwork or music. With NFTs, artists and collectors can now easily create and own their digital property, although there are tough issues around how their value is determined and who truly owns them. There are many different virtual assets, which makes it more difficult to set regulations. As the functions of tokens vary, each type calls for a specific set of regulations. For example, putting strict regulations on utility tokens could reduce innovation, while not closely watching security tokens could leave investors facing risks they should not encounter [381]. In addition, some virtual assets are not covered by the existing rules, making it difficult to use them. Since technology in virtual assets keeps advancing, new tokens and platforms are always emerging, often compromising the categories and bringing about unexpected qualities unnoticed by current laws. Being able to change with the times is crucial for regulators since the environment for virtual assets evolves so fast.

7.2 Key Challenges in Regulating Virtual Assets

Virtual assets are especially hard to regulate because they evolve and have special traits very quickly. Properly classifying these assets is one of the hardest things. In the traditional financial system, assets are grouped as currencies, commodities, and securities, each with its own rules. As a result, virtual assets are recognized differently by different groups of experts. It is sometimes thought of as a commodity by some, yet others consider Bitcoin a currency. Some regulators treat ICO tokens as securities and subject them to stricter guidelines according to the law [382]. A lack of agreement as to what virtual assets are complicates matters for regulators, companies, and investors. If the definition of these assets is not agreed upon, enforcing laws can become very challenging [383]. The issue of jurisdiction further complicates the matter; with virtual assets, people across the globe can trade easily on decentralized networks, without the use of intermediaries. Without physical borders for these virtual assets, it is difficult for regulators to know who is responsible for compliance. As providers can be anonymous and located globally, it's hard for regulators to determine who should apply the rules. Due to virtual assets being traded across borders, investigating and prosecuting crimes can be difficult for regulators. When there are no equal rules worldwide, criminals may look for weaker countries in which to commit violations, called regulatory arbitrage. Protecting consumers and investors is very important; because virtual assets markets are so volatile, many retail investors are hesitant to invest in them. Many scams, frauds, and security breaches in the virtual assets world can cause serious financial problems. Platforms fail to keep investors safe because the regulations are not strict or clearly defined enough. Therefore, stronger rules are important to ensure people are truly protected. When regulation is followed well, companies have to share all relevant information, outline any risks, carefully monitor what they are doing, and help as soon as issues are identified.

It is harder to protect consumers because of money laundering and terrorist financing. Most virtual assets transactions are private, so it is easy for criminals to dodge identification checks. Regulators require all virtual assets service providers to introduce AML standards, which include verifying their customers' identity [384]. Yet, since the industry is advancing so swiftly, it's hard to make sure the rules are respected. It is not easy to find a balance between rules and protecting virtual assets users' privacy. In addition, decentralized platforms are expanding rapidly, which makes it difficult for authorities to monitor their operations. Market unfairness and complaints about the credibility of virtual assets decrease people's trust in the market. Whenever regulations are not strong and technology is too advanced, it is difficult for authorities to observe and control the market. Some exchanges get exploited due to the lack of staff to supervise all transactions; for example, a fake exchange or price manipulation harms the market and affects trust. Because laws are not the same in every country, it is difficult to ensure fairness across the globe. The growing pace of changes in these fields leads to even greater complexity. Because rules are made before new risks are discovered, regulators may create those that are too safe or too unsafe for investors. To overcome these issues, regulators should grow their knowledge, collaborate with other regulators and the industry, and use new technology to monitor developments in virtual assets.

7.3 Common Global Regulatory Approaches

Regulators are developing new plans to secure virtual assets and promote progress in the industry. With the help of classification, regulators can develop regulations suitable for each type of virtual assets. Doing this ensures that everyone, whether in the market or the regulator, is applying the same set of rules, which helps all parties feel safe. Regularly, regulators worldwide require Virtual Assets Service Providers (VASPs) to submit and obtain a license, such as exchanges, wallets, and custodians [385]. This measure is important for avoiding money laundering and similar crimes and for maintaining conformity with all required regulations. The system of licensing makes VASPs answerable for their actions, thus safeguarding users. It is equally important for banks and other financial institutions to focus on AML and CTF compliance. Authorities encourage VASPs to observe suspicious acts and confirm the identities of their customers because these systems can be misused for financial crimes. If anyone suspects something illegal is happening with finances, they should inform the appropriate officials. They adhere to rules and principles agreed upon by different countries, as shown by the initiative of the Financial Action Task Force (FATF), which enforced the 'Travel Rule' for sending and receiving information during transfers. Various authorities expect risk and change in the value of virtual assets to be clearly explained to ensure informed choices by users. Several authorities have limited who can buy high-risk products, while others have refused to permit some products altogether. They are intended to safeguard new investors against big losses and to promote clear information.

Regulators are increasingly paying attention to the taxation of virtual assets. Agencies responsible for taxes are deciding that virtual assets are generally considered property or assets that are taxed under capital gains tax. With proper guidelines, users can stay on the right track regarding their taxes, contributing more tax income to the government. If virtual assets are considered securities, such as some tokens sold through ICOs and security tokens, securities laws are put into effect. It requires virtual assets issuers and traders to follow established processes for registration, telling investors about the risks, and safeguarding them. To promote both innovation and regulation, many places have established things like regulatory sandboxes. Sandboxes let virtual asset businesses try new products and services under supervision, as the regulatory requirements are low in the first phase. Case Studies of Regulatory Frameworks in Different Jurisdictions are given in Table 1. This way of thinking supports experimentation, helps regulators stay informed about new technologies, and ensures the right regulations are put in place without stopping innovation too early.

The United States has a lot of different rules and agencies that regulate virtual assets, including the Securities and Exchange Commission, the Commodity Futures Trading Commission, and the Financial Crimes Enforcement Network, each of which handles different parts of this space. Companies often find it confusing when different agencies rule over the same aspects and give different instructions about cryptocurrency. Because the regulations are sometimes confusing, some have called for simpler regulations at the federal level. In addition, the European Union plans to make its cryptocurrency rules similar in every country by creating the Markets in Crypto-Assets (MiCA) framework [386]. With MiCA, the EU wants to have only one set of rules for cryptocurrencies that every member state must follow, to help make things simpler for those working with digital assets. Its focus on protecting people buying crypto and creating safe markets is an important move to help bring virtual assets into the EU's financial system with strong rules in place. Singapore shows how you can find the middle ground between following rules and coming up with new ideas. The country's Payment Services Act requires virtual assets service providers to get a license and sets strict rules to prevent money laundering and terrorism-related crimes. Simultaneously, Singapore helps fintech get better by giving businesses chances to test out new ideas in regulated areas, so they can try things out before being fully supervised. Japan took a leading role in regulating cryptocurrencies, considering them legal and urging virtual exchange platforms to sign up with authorities. Having well-defined rules at launch made investors believe in these markets, particularly since much effort is put toward protecting consumers and fighting against money laundering. In opposition to this, China prohibits both the buying and selling of cryptocurrencies and the mining of them. The government says it introduced these rules

Table 1 Case studies of regulatory frameworks in different jurisdictions

Jurisdiction	Regulatory approach	Key features & challenges
United States	Fragmented multi-agency system	Multiple regulators (SEC, CFTC, FinCEN) with overlapping roles; regulatory uncertainty; complex compliance for businesses
European Union	Harmonization through Markets in Crypto-Assets (MiCA)	Single regulatory framework across member states; clarity for issuers and service providers; consumer protection focus
Singapore	Balanced licensing and innovation support	Clear licensing under Payment Services Act; strong AML/CTF rules; proactive innovation facilitation through sandboxes
Japan	Early adopter with strict consumer protection	Cryptocurrency recognized as legal property; mandatory exchange registration; robust AML and investor safeguards
China	Restrictive stance with CBDC development	Ban on crypto trading and mining; emphasis on financial stability and environmental concerns; active CBDC pilot projects

to strengthen the financial system and to care for the environment. At the same time, China is experimenting with using its own Central Bank Digital Currency (CBDC), which may demonstrate that it prefers to have more control over digital money than with decentralized cryptocurrencies. What these case studies reveal is that countries adopt a wide range of regulatory ideas, such as the US's detailed approach led by agencies, the EU's centralized method, Singapore's putting innovation high on its list, Japan's structured way of jumping in early, and China going slowly while relying on the government. Every country's approach provides useful insights into how governments can respond to fast changes in the virtual assets space.

8 Emerging Issues

The regulation of virtual assets is currently changing fast, showing how various and sometimes contradictory trends are shaping the future of finance. For example, DeFi platforms are considered one of the biggest tests for current financial regulations. DeFi lacks central authorities, so it is unclear who should be responsible and where problems should be handled. So, there is now a governance gap where typical ways of enforcement, which depend on noticeable parties, often cannot work effectively. Figuring out how to regulate systems based on codes and communities rather than companies is a challenge for regulators, leading to major questions about whose responsibility it is to safeguard consumers and avoid large disruptions. While DeFi can provide access to finance for more people and spark new ideas, not being regulated leads to greater chances of fraud, market manipulation, and system faults, so fresh regulations are needed to guide it and its open approach. CBDCs are set to change the way virtual assets operate and how the monetary system works. State-issued digital currencies from central banks could help replace private crypto coins and stablecoins as the preferred digital payment method. Modeling the benefits of CBDCs, we observe that they may help payments run more smoothly, offer more access to banking services, and improve the transmission of decisions from the central bank. Still, adding these cryptocurrencies to the market leads to more complications with regulations. It could lead to less use of commercial banks, alter the balance of power in digital finance, and raise issues concerning privacy and surveillance.

Regulators must ensure that transparency does not come at the cost of users' privacy. They should make sure that their monitoring activities do not reveal the identities of anonymous virtual assets users. Above all, being upfront with users might discourage those who care about privacy and lead them away from using the platform for its intended purpose. Poor supervision, on the other hand, could allow crime to thrive. As a result, authorities should avoid making regulations that could lessen the appeal of privacy for those who use virtual assets. Besides, firms must request that new standards keep up with the pace of technology. When rules are not updated, they can leave gaps for exploitation and discourage the development of new virtual assets services. If regulators do not have any flexibility, there is a danger they will either suppress new technologies or not notice new dangers. To solve this challenge, we need to apply principles in regulation, talk frequently with those in the industry, and rely on the best compliance technology to ensure the rules don't get outdated.

9 Conclusion and Future Outlook

For the past 20 years, the global economy has transformed quickly and intensely because of digital advancements, climate concerns, global politics, and growing income disparities. The present global economic rules continue to follow old methods of regulation, even though they should be updated. This chapter shows how current global economic advances exceed the fixed organization and separate features of international law. Several legal systems globally are behind in managing new tax policies for digital assets and crypto transfers while facing debt and environmental policy dilemmas. International law systems were developed when states followed predictable patterns, and technology/economy moved more slowly. New digital finance systems involving programmed trading and international data sharing push against established legal rules about the place of authority, national rights, and risks to investors. International law needs to adjust to new technologies; the proof remains unclear on this topic. International institutions show rough progress toward change since the EU digital governance and AfCFTA continent-wide initiatives stand apart from most other international organizations. This lag has serious implications; business risk increases while consumer protections weaken when legal rules remain unclear, allowing powerful states and companies to avoid proper accountability. The result is that people lose faith in universal rules, and the gap between wealthy nations and developing nations grows wider. When multiple entities create rules about newer topics such as AI technology and trade sanctions, they usually make problems worse than finding solutions. The need for multilateral governance change is important at this moment. The WTO, IMF, and World Bank need to transform their decision-making process along with their basic functions to include more nations and better serve everyone equally. Developing nations must have the authority to define the rules that affect them, particularly in digital trade, debt handling, and environmental finance. Today, inclusive governance needs to become a basic organizational requirement to build support and maintain peace. A future economic law system should serve justice while protecting nature and adapting to threats. The global system must develop practical rules for handling data and AI applications, as well as add climate protection terms to trade deals and establish methods to solve government debt problems. Our society must understand the problems market systems create so we can add more social and environmental security to our economic agreements. The true need is not just to update laws but to build a new legal system. The fast-changing global conditions force us to adjust international law or see it fade away in the face of international emergencies. A future-ready legal framework that involves everyone helps us deal with unknown risks today to make progress together.

Decentralized Currencies and Digital Economy: Stability and Implications of Digital Currency

1 Introduction

The relationship between law and digital currencies is an innovative field that is constantly developing and involves the legal analysis of technological and legal advancements [387]. This is true because traditional legal systems have well-defined characteristics of money and how it is to be regulated. However, most of these definitions do not fit into digital currencies, hence making it difficult for the lawmakers to classify and regulate them under the existing laws since they have some characteristics of both money and securities. For instance, Bitcoin and other cryptocurrencies exist in a legal limbo—concerning their nature, it is not entirely clear whether it is property or money. For taxation in the United States, cryptocurrencies are considered to be property, while in other countries, they may be recognized as currency and may even be classified as a commodity [388, 389]. This absence of a legal definition often causes a lot of confusion among businesses, users, and regulators. There are no laws governing the use of digital currencies and this makes it possible for them to be used in illicit business-like money laundering or fraud [390]. Addressing these concerns involves the application of the law to the matter, a matter which should be done with consideration of the pros and cons of digital currencies.

Digital currencies are different from the usual physical money, such as the US Dollar, Euro, and others, because they are virtual and are not backed by any particular country. This means that they are not printed or issued by central banks like traditional money. However, they work on peer-to-peer networks through the use of blockchain technology. They operate based on cryptographic algorithms and peer-to-peer networks for their creation and use, which sets them apart from traditional currencies [391]. When we break down the types of digital currencies, we can classify them into two main categories.

1. Central Bank Digital Currencies (CBDCs): These are digital currencies that are issued and managed by a country's central bank as a digital form of the physical currency [392]. However, CBDCs are centralized, thus they are under the control

J. Afzal, *Exploring the New Horizons of International Law Concerning Globalization of Economy*, https://doi.org/10.1007/978-981-95-1312-3_7

of the government or the central bank of the country implementing them. They are a direct demand on the central bank and are often viewed as how governments can retain influence over the monetary system as they introduce digital technologies into the economy. For instance, China is working on its central bank digital currency, the Digital Yuan, and the European Central Bank is contemplating the idea of a digital euro [393, 394].

2. Cryptocurrencies: Cryptocurrencies are digital currencies that are not controlled by any central authority and are based on blockchain technology, such as Bitcoin and Ethereum [287]. Due to the instability and absence of legal frameworks that govern the use of cryptocurrencies, the subject is a center of legal controversies regarding its categorization and utilization.

Blockchain is the underlying technology that supports most of the digital currencies and thus knowledge of it is helpful in the understanding of the functionality of the digital currencies [378]. In its simplest form, a blockchain is a database that contains records of transactions and is spread across many computers so that the information contained in the records cannot be altered. Every list of transactions is enclosed in a "block" and these blocks are connected in a linear sequence, hence the term "chain" in the name blockchain. One of the significant characteristics of blockchain is that it is decentralized, and no one owns the database, as it is the case of centralized databases [395]. This makes it more secure as any change of information in one block will require changing all the subsequent blocks, which is almost impossible. These characteristics make the technology reliable and secure as compared to the traditional financial systems since it is decentralized as well, and its records are not changeable. For instance, through the application of blockchain, it is possible to transact directly with another party without the involvement of a third party like a bank. This creates the potential for faster, cheaper, and more efficient ways of conducting transactions, especially in cross-border transactions, which can be time-consuming and expensive. In addition, smart contracts, which are self-executing contracts with the actual terms of the contract written in code, enabled by blockchain technology, can transform many sectors apart from the financial sector.

> *"The future of money is digital, but its legal foundations must be carefully crafted to ensure security, fairness, and stability"*

2 Legal Classification of Digital Currency

One of the most discussed topics related to digital currencies is the appropriate legal classification of such currencies [396, 397]. This classification has serious consequences for how they are governed and managed within the larger economy. What status should be given to digital currencies: money, assets, or commodities? The answer to this question is not simple, and it depends on the jurisdiction of the country.

As Money: It is also for this reason that some have discoursed that stablecoins, in particular, are money in the sense that they act as a medium of exchange. Nonetheless, due to their instability, cryptocurrencies such as Bitcoin cannot be considered as stable money, which is why many people classify them differently.

As Assets: In most jurisdictions, digital currencies are considered an asset or property for taxation. This implies that every person or company is required to declare their income or losses in the course of engaging in or using cryptocurrencies. For instance, the Internal Revenue Service (IRS) in the United States has classified cryptocurrencies as property, which are taxed at capital gains tax. This legal classification has important consequences for the taxation and regulation of digital currencies.

As Commodities: Some countries, such as the United States, have recognized some digital currencies, such as Bitcoin, as commodities in the manner of the U.S. Commodity Futures Trading Commission. This brings them closer to the definition of assets such as gold, which are sold in commodity markets. In this regard, cryptocurrencies are regulated in some way, especially when it comes to derivatives.

At the moment, there is no legal definition of digital currencies worldwide due to the lack of a standard legal regulation of such currencies [398]. In the United States, digital currencies are regulated by both securities and commodities laws as well as tax laws, while in other countries, such as Japan, they are considered as money or even legal tender in some cases. The absence of a specific global policy is problematic and difficult for businesses, users, and regulators.

3 Legal and Regulatory Landscape of Digital Currencies

3.1 Current Legal Frameworks

The use of digital currencies is on the rise, and this has put pressure on governments and financial regulators to establish laws to govern them [309]. These are important steps to protect the financial integrity of consumers and to curb other vices such as money laundering. Nonetheless, it is crucial to note that digital currencies are borderless, and they are not tied to conventional financial systems, which makes the regulation of such currencies exceptionally difficult.

United States Regulatory Landscape: The U.S. employs a multi-agency approach to digital currency regulation:

1. On its part, the SEC has categorized some cryptocurrencies such as Bitcoin and Ethereum as commodities while others may fall under securities depending on their features.
2. Cryptocurrencies are regulated in the United States by the Commodity Futures Trading Commission or CFTC for short in trading of derivatives.
3. Currently, FinCEN regulates AML (Anti Money Laundering) and CFT (Countering the financing of terrorism) policies for crypto transactions.

European Union's Unified Approach: The EU has recently passed the Markets in Crypto-Assets Regulation (MiCA), which:

1. Develop a coordinated regulatory environment in the member states
2. Implements licensing requirements for crypto assets providers
3. Establishes consumer protection measures
4. Addresses potential risks to financial stability

People's Republic of China: In China, the policy has been more of a restrictive one; Chinese authorities have restricted the financial industry from providing related services for cryptocurrency transactions and have suppressed cryptocurrency mining. It has been experimenting with CBDCs through the Digital Yuan in an attempt to retain control over the digital economy [399]. Nevertheless, there are several challenges that lawmakers experience whenever they are addressing the issue of digital currencies. First, the lack of centralization of many digital currencies also means that governments cannot control the creation and use of such currencies. While traditional financial systems have the advantage of having central authorities that can oversee the banks and transactions, digital currencies work on peer-to-peer networks and are not bound by any country or organization. This poses a problem in enforcement and thus brings about legal ambiguities. Second, the nature of digital currencies is that they are highly volatile, which makes the regulation of such currencies even more challenging. Cryptocurrencies are highly volatile, and their volatility affects other aspects of the financial market. For example, Bitcoin was at $5,000 in 2018 and rose to $65,000 in 2021, but then fell again [400]. This causes instability and risks to investors and regulators due to the uncertainty of digital currencies.

3.2 The Role of Central Banks

Two key questions arise about the regulation of digital currencies: whether central banks should regulate digital currencies and if so, how. The central banks have always been the central authorities responsible for a country's monetary policy especially on matters concerning the national currency [401]. As with other forms of digital money, people have asked whether central banks should retain such power in the digital world. Opponents argue that central banks should develop new electronic money called CBDCs to develop the financial industry and retain control over the money [402]. In this way, with the CBDCs, central banks will be in a position to control the digital currencies' transactions to avoid fraud and financial instabilities. Thus, CBDCs may be legal and regulatory assets that decentralized cryptocurrencies are not endowed with. For example, CBDCs can be designed with some regulatory features like KYC and AML, which will enable tracking of the same [403]. This would allow governments to have full control over their respective monetary systems and, at the same time, benefit from the digital currencies in that they would be cheaper and faster methods of transacting. Nevertheless, CBDCs have legal issues. CBDCs would require changes to legal tender laws to be classified as legal tender as well as the development of policies by the central banks to make them safe, non-inflationary, and acceptable. There is also the question of how CBDCs would coexist with existing private cryptocurrencies. Would governments be able to control or limit the use of non-state-issued digital currencies.

3.3 Cross-Border Regulation

Another problem that is inherent in digital currencies is that they are global [79]. As for traditional money, it is issued and controlled within the country, while digital currencies can be used all over the world. First of all, there is an issue of jurisdiction; if a person from one country engages in cryptocurrency business with a person from another country, then which law should be used? The decentralized system of digital currencies means that the transactions that take place are out of the jurisdiction of any particular country's laws. This is a problem of enforcement as legal procedures may become cumbersome if the participants are in different jurisdictions with different laws. Also, there are problems associated with the fact that most of the platforms that deal with virtual currency transactions are cross-border, therefore, the regulation of the platforms is difficult. For instance, a particular exchange established under the laws of a specific country may allow users from across the globe, and thus, it may be almost impossible for any given country to control the exchange. This is made worse by the fact that there are no generally acceptable rules to regulate the use of digital currency. While some are trying to have more comprehensive regulatory structures like that of the European Union, some have developed a dispersed one. This leads to a lack of harmony in the regulation of similar activities—a factor that goes against the grain for both business entities and users. For instance, as the EU is developing MiCA to establish a legal framework for cryptocurrencies [404], countries like Pakistan and South Korea have followed the opposite strategy and put bans or limitations on some activities connected with cryptocurrencies. Another challenge is that there is no coordination in the regulation of the Internet [405]. This can make countries with stringent regulatory measures put their clamp down on cryptocurrency activities to shift to nations that have relatively relaxed rules and regulations on this form of venture, hence providing room for the perpetration of unlawful deeds. Also, there are issues of tax evasion, especially for the international market, since it becomes easier for people to engage in illicit activities since the transactions cannot be easily traced.

4 Stability and Security of Digital Currencies

One of the most significant challenges digital currencies face is their stability or lack thereof. Cryptocurrencies such as Bitcoin and Ethereum have been volatile in the market, with daily volatility being more than 10% or even more [406]. This high volatility can be attributed to several factors such as market sentiment, speculation, regulatory actions and news, and microeconomic factors. The main reason behind this is that cryptocurrency is a volatile market. Digital currencies are normally volatile and speculative, which means that their prices are influenced by the trader's sentiments and expectations and not by the basic economic principles of supply and demand [407]. This characteristic hinders its capability to be used to forecast the price change and most investors consider cryptocurrencies as highly risky investments, thus increasing the volatility. Other factors that impact the stability of cryptocurrencies include security threats and risks in the market. Frauds, scams, and thefts are quite rampant in the cryptocurrency industry, and major exchanges and wallets have not been spared. Large-scale thefts are capable of causing investors' confidence to drop and this results in a steep drop in the prices of the shares. For instance, the Mt. Gox hack in 2014, when $450 million worth of Bitcoin was stolen, hurt the cryptocurrency's reputation and market [408].

These fluctuations can have a wider impact on financial stability. In conventional financial systems, central banks and governments can intervene to correct the situation in the markets in situations of disequilibrium. However, there are no authorities that can prevent fluctuations from occurring in the case of cryptocurrencies. The lack of such a mechanism implies that large-scale crashes can have severe impacts on investors and the general economy, especially given that cryptocurrencies are increasingly being adopted into mainstream financial systems. The unpredictability of cryptocurrencies also makes them difficult to use as a reliable store of value, thus not being suitable as a means of exchange for goods and services.

4.1 Security Concerns and Legal Implications

Since most digital currencies are unregulated and operate independently, security is one of the biggest challenges for consumers and the authorities [304]. Cryptocurrencies are also vulnerable to hacking, fraud, and theft, which have an adverse impact on user trust as well as reveal weaknesses in the digital money system. Regarding the legal standpoint, some measures of protection exist, although these differ from country to country. Laws regulating consumer protection regarding digital currency transactions are still quite limited, and many of the exchanges that exist do not offer the same level of protection and recourse as conventional financial institutions. In the case of a hack or loss, many people have no legal redress, especially if the exchange is not regulated.

The legal issues associated with such security threats are best addressed by new legal frameworks that are specific to digital currencies. The nature of digital currencies cannot be addressed by traditional legal structures such as banking and securities laws. For instance, although cybercrime laws may offer some legal redress, they are usually inadequate where the offenders are unknown or are located in other countries. Moreover, since the use of cryptocurrencies is pseudonymous, it becomes very hard to identify the culprits behind the crime.

The regulators and lawmakers will have to put in place proper laws that protect consumers from fraud and theft through the use of digital currencies [409]. These may include demanding that exchanges keep insurance or adopt higher security measures like the use of multi-sig wallets to minimize hacking instances. Furthermore, collaboration between international organizations will also be important in addressing cross-border cybercrime and making sure that the culprits are apprehended no matter the country they are from.

4.2 Liability and Accountability

When a digital currency transaction goes wrong, such as in the case of a lost transaction, fraud, or hacked account, a fundamental question arises: Who is legally responsible for the loss? The answer is not always clear, and this legal uncertainty adds to the complication of cryptocurrency use. Unlike conventional financial systems, where banks or any other third-party service providers are liable for losses or fraud, cryptocurrencies are usually completed directly between two parties. This poses a problem of who is to blame in case of any mishap. In case of a loss of funds as a result of hacking or a particular transaction, is it the exchange, the wallet service, or the user that is at fault? In some circumstances, this issue is aggravated by smart contracts or decentralized finance (DeFi) protocols [410]. Here, the transactions and agreements are embedded in the blockchain and are self-executed.

While there are traditional legal principles governing contracts and torts, they may not be very helpful in the case of digital currency [398]. For example, in the case of a contract, rules of offer and acceptance as well as performance come into play, but due to the decentralized, anonymous nature of digital currency, it is difficult to enforce. In the case of a loss of money through fraud or hacking, the current tort law may provide some redress, but proving negligence or fraud in a decentralized environment is challenging. Unfortunately, legal systems are not as advanced as technological ones when it comes to digital currency regulation. Regarding liability enforcement and protection of victims of cryptocurrency incidents, there are several issues such as class action lawsuits, arbitration clauses, and jurisdictional issues. The issue of who bears the loss in case of loss of digital currencies is still not well defined in the current laws. Nevertheless, it can be stated that more detailed rules will be required to safeguard the consumers and define responsibilities in the context of this emerging market segment.

5 Digital Currency and Financial Systems

The introduction of cryptocurrency has brought about several problems in the traditional banking and financial industries. Traditionally, the role of financial intermediaries was played by the banks that were involved in financial intermediation, provision of loans, financial payments, and regulation of money circulation in the economy. However, this role has been threatened by digital currencies in the following ways.

First, digital currencies can act as an effective substitute for the banking system, but at the same time, it is not a part of it [411]. Cryptocurrencies like Bitcoin and Ethereum allow the transfer of funds from one person to another without the involvement of a financial institution. Some of the advantages of this form of transaction are the lower cost of the transaction and the time taken to complete the transaction. Moreover, digital currencies are more inclusive in the sense that they can give a chance to use various financial services to people who have no bank accounts or limited bank accounts, especially in developing countries. However, such a change has led to the emergence of questions regarding the centralized control that was previously offered by banks. Apart from being intermediaries in payment systems, traditional banks have the role of maintaining the stability and integrity of the financial system. Without these institutions, the risk of fraud, cybercrime, and financial instability increases. With the increased use of digital currencies, regulators and financial institutions have to consider the advantages of decentralization against the detriment of the global financial system. It is still a matter of discussion whether digital currencies should be incorporated into the existing financial system or not. On the one hand, the adoption of digital currencies in traditional banking systems could bring some other advantages, for instance, the efficiency of transaction settlement. Critics of the idea to keep cryptocurrencies separate also have their opinions and points to support it stating that decentralization is one of the key strengths of digital currencies [412]. In being outside the realm of the conventional banking system, digital currencies offer an option that is not restricted by the rules and money supply changes. This could increase the amount of funds available to consumers and could reduce the costs for consumers as well. However, this is a risk that without integration, the digital currencies will further fragment and contribute to the formation of an unstable financial system.

With the increase in adoption and acceptance of digital currencies in the financial markets, financial regulators have the responsibility of dealing with the risks that come with the currencies. Cryptocurrencies and digital currencies are volatile by their nature, and their popularity has brought the issue of financial insecurity into focus. Lack of regulation of digital currencies can result in market bubbles, fraud, and other economic shocks [413]. The function of the financial regulators is therefore to ensure that the financial system is stable while at the same time being innovative. Currently, financial regulators are required to regulate risks associated with digital currencies and safeguard consumers against fraud and misuse of the digital currencies for activities like money laundering and financing of terrorism. AML and CFT measures are crucial when it comes to digital currencies because the latter are pseudonymous by their nature [414]. Authorities also have to prevent digital currencies from destabilizing the existing financial systems by creating excessive fluctuations or eroding confidence in domestic currencies.

On the one hand, the regulators must be careful in regulating the new digital currencies while on the other hand promoting innovation. Other benefits can be associated with the use of digital currencies because it is fast, cheap and inclusive. These laws are very rigorous and may even hamper this innovation and the achievement of the full potential of digital currencies. In this respect, financial regulators have the task of maintaining, on the one hand, the stability of the financial system and on the other the promotion of innovation in the Cryptocurrency market. One possible solution to this problem can be the development of coherent and transparent rules for the regulation of digital currencies and their advantages and disadvantages. These should include matters concerning consumer protection, market transparency, taxation, and anti-money laundering but at the same time, should not hinder the emergence of new technologies and business models in the cryptocurrency space. For example, the European Union's Markets in Crypto-Assets Regulation (MiCA) is an attempt to establish a single set of rules governing digital currencies in the member countries. MiCA's objectives are to enhance the efficiency of the market and protect consumers, without allowing digital currencies to become a threat to the financial system. This way, MiCA can guide cryptocurrency providers and users to avoid market manipulation and fraudulent activities.

6 Privacy and Data Protection in Digital Currency Transactions

One of the most debated aspects of digital currencies is their impact on privacy. Although digital currencies provide a measure of anonymity in transactions, they pose many legal issues concerning privacy and user protection [415]. Cryptocurrencies like Bitcoin are linked with anonymity; while the details of the transactions are recorded on the blockchain, they are not linked to the identity of the owners. This has made digital currencies attractive to those people who want to be out of reach of the government or any financial institutions. However, there are questions regarding the extent of anonymity that is provided by digital currencies. In many cases, it is possible to track transactions back to the individuals, especially when the transactions are conducted through exchanges that demand the identification of their clients as per the AML policies. This means that, to some extent, digital currencies are not secure when it comes to the privacy of the users. This is because if the transactions are connected to a person's identity, his or her financial details may be exposed to the government, hackers, or any other party of their choice.

The issue of privacy in the use of digital currency involves the legal aspect, especially concerning the protection of data and civil rights [225]. Privacy is widely regarded as an individual right in many countries, and consumers may have a right to their data. Hence, the degree to which digital currencies infringe on this right remains questionable as to whether users of these products can achieve the benefits of the cryptocurrencies without compromising on privacy. As more people embrace the use of digital currencies, it will be challenging to determine the extent to which individuals' right to privacy should be protected as opposed to the extent to which it should be regulated to reduce fraudulent activities such as money laundering. Some of the digital currencies that are not very considerate of the privacy of their users may be at risk of being banned since they may violate the data protection laws or the privacy rights of the users.

6.1 Data Protection Laws

Cryptocurrencies and their users are under pressure from data protection laws and more, especially in regions like the European Union, which is governed by the GDPR law [210]. GDPR established rules on how organizations should manage personal data and demanded that companies collect, store, and process this information about the rights of the users. In terms of digital currency platforms, this implies that they are bound by the law to protect and respect the privacy of their users. For instance, platforms that provide a marketplace for the buying and selling of cryptocurrencies may be required to meet the requirements of the GDPR if they gather information on EU individuals. According to GDPR, the following are some of the requirements that apply to digital currency platforms:

1. Ensure that the users give their consent to be subjected to the collection of their personal information.
2. Protect data, and put measures to avoid cases of data theft or hacking of the data by unauthorized persons.
3. Enable the user to request and obtain his or her data, rectify it, or erase it from the database.
4. Inform the users of the data breach within a certain period if their data is leaked.

Furthermore, GDPR mandates that any online platforms that are established in the EU must have a Data Protection Officer who will be in charge of data processing and compliance with the law. However, digital currencies and blockchain technologies are not fully compliant with traditional data protection laws. Blockchain technology is fixed and open; for this reason, transactions are irreversible and can be viewed by anyone. This is a contradiction with the GDPR's "right to be forgotten", or the right to obtain the deletion of personal data relating to the data subject. Since once a transaction has been written into the blockchain, it cannot be erased, there are concerns about how GDPR can be implemented on the blockchain.

6.2 Regulatory Actions on Privacy

Due to the increasing concern for privacy and data protection, there are several steps that the regulators might take to ensure that the digital currency platform complies with user privacy and data protection. It can be expected that regulatory authorities will continue to address the privacy risks in a way that does not hinder the development of the industry. Another possible policy measure is the adoption of legislation that is aimed at protecting the privacy of users of digital currencies. For instance, in the United States, the regulators may expand CFPB jurisdiction to cover digital currencies and ensure that privacy laws are in line with the current financial laws. In Europe, there may be additional changes to MiCA to include more detailed rules regarding the privacy and data protection of cryptocurrencies.

The regulators may also demand the application of the KYC/AML measures without violating the privacy rights of the users. Although KYC and AML regulations are crucial for combating money laundering and financing terrorism, these regulations are an invasion of privacy as they involve personal data collection [416]. In the future, regulators may try to find a way to use anonymization techniques or zero-knowledge proofs that let authorities check identities without disclosing the data. Such measures could help to achieve a balance between compliance with the law and the protection of the users' rights. In addition, international collaboration may prove to be essential in the future as regards the regulation of digital currencies and the protection of users' rights. Because digital currencies are not bound by geographical locations, privacy laws need to be standardized in different countries to avoid exploitation of the law. For instance, the data protection laws in one country may be different from those of another country thus leaving some individuals with little protection for their data. The FATF is an organization that will assist regulators around the world to work together to have a common strategy towards issues of privacy of digital currencies [417]. Another possible way of regulation can be the inspection of the exchanges associated with digital currencies to check whether they respect the privacy of their users or not. Regulators could require exchanges to undergo regular security audits, transparency reports, and risk assessments to identify vulnerabilities and ensure that user data is protected.

7 The Impact of Digital Currency on the Global Economy

Another good thing about the advent of digital currencies is that they can increase financial literacy in developing nations. Many millions of people are still excluded or under-banked and cannot use such simple financial services as savings, credit or insurance. In rural or other underdeveloped regions, there is little or no infrastructure for conventional banking, and thus, many people cannot be integrated into the global economy [411]. Digital currencies may be viewed as a solution to this problem since people can engage in economic activities without necessarily going through the banking systems. The lack of restrictions and availability of cryptocurrencies and digital wallets to anyone with an internet connection and a mobile phone has made it possible for anyone in developing countries to have a bank account. For instance, an individual living in a rural village can make payments for utilities, accept payments for goods or services, or even conduct international business without physically going to a branch. Moreover, stablecoins—cryptocurrencies backed by more stable assets such as the US dollar—can be viewed as solutions for countries with unstable currencies. These digital assets can offer more reliable sources of funds in countries with high inflation rates or devalued currencies, which will help citizens protect their value better than their national currency. However, several legal concerns come with the use of digital currency in the developing world. The main issue is that many such nations lack adequate legal provisions that may guide the process. Lack of technical know-how and resources makes it difficult for governments to monitor the use of digital currencies, thus leading to fraudulent activities, market control, and financial crimes. Other risks include the ability of capital controls to be bypassed and an increase in money laundering, especially in parts with little or no regulation. They also pose legal issues of taxation, consumer protection, and sovereignty of money. Increased usage of cryptocurrencies may hamper the government's capacity to track transactions for taxation purposes and may deny them the much-needed revenue for public service delivery and developmental projects. Most countries still lack proper legal frameworks to regulate digital currencies, and most authorities are not prepared to enforce the current laws or to protect users in this new financial frontier.

In the current world economy, digital currencies have had a tremendous influence on the global markets. These currencies are gradually becoming popular and are being used in global trade to a greater extent. The conventional cross-border payment systems involve third parties such as banks, which makes the process slow and expensive, especially for small business entities and individuals. On the other hand, digital currencies promote direct buyer–seller transactions that are more efficient and cheaper in the international market. For instance, organizations across the globe can use Bitcoin or Ripple (XRP) to clear transactions immediately [418], unlike traditional bank transfers that take time and are costly, especially in cross-border money transfers. This could significantly reduce trade costs, especially for small businesses in developing countries that are locked out of the global market due to high transaction costs and cumbersome banking procedures. In addition, digital currencies provide new payment systems that operate beyond the monetary borders of a country. This is especially useful in areas where there is a limited banking system and opens new opportunities for countries with limited access to foreign currency for trading and financing. However, some legal issues arise when it comes to controlling the international movement of cryptocurrencies. As the currencies functioning on the distributed systems, digital currencies are beyond the particular national regulation. This is because it is very challenging to regulate and oversee inherently international entities. For example, let's imagine a real business case where a company from one country buys products from a seller in another country: this process can be done without involving the financial systems and legislation of both countries, through the use of cryptocurrencies. This lack of oversight raises concerns about the potential for money laundering, terrorist financing, or other illicit activities, as digital currencies can be used to obscure the identities of the parties involved. Cross-border regulations also pose problems in the aspect of taxation. If a person or a company engages in digital currency transactions in many countries, it becomes difficult to decide which country has the power to tax such a transaction [212]. The regulation of digital currencies varies from country to country and how they are taxed; therefore, when the users or the businesses transfer money from one country to another they may be cheating the system. However, it should be noted that fluctuations in currency can also be a menace to international business. Even though digital currencies are fast and cheap to transact with, their volatility of value negates their use as a medium of exchange. For instance, if the value of Bitcoin reduces drastically before the payment is made and received by the recipient, the recipient will be paid in less value than expected thus incurring losses and reducing confidence in digital currencies as a stable mode of payment.

Legal harmonization is one of the critical issues that need to be addressed to regulate digital currency transactions across the world. Since digital currencies are cross-border in nature, the countries will have to harmonize their laws to ensure that they can meet the challenges that arise from decentralized finance. The absence of international cooperation in the creation of digital currencies can lead to the emergence of legal loopholes that can be filled by wrongdoers, which will in turn hinder the widespread adoption of digital currencies.

8 Legal Challenges and Future Directions

Although financial regulators have tried to develop guidelines that deal with the use of digital currencies, several legal issues are still unanswered [79, 218].

1. Classification and Definition: The first of the key areas of doubt is the legal classification of digital currencies. What are they? Currencies, commodities, or assets? For taxation purposes, certain countries have categorized cryptocurrencies such as Bitcoin as property while others consider them as commodities or even as a currency. Such an absence of clarity creates uncertainty on how digital currencies should be regulated regarding taxation, consumer protection, and regulation.
2. Jurisdiction and Enforcement: The second area of vagueness is the issue of jurisdiction. One of the advantages of digital currencies is that they operate in a global environment, thus the transactions can take place across the borders. This poses a problem in trying to ascertain which country's laws should be applied where there is fraud, theft, or contractual disputes. For example, when a person in one country engages in a fraudulent transaction using a cryptocurrency, who is legally right to enforce the law, the authorities of the country of the user, or the country where the platform is located?
3. Legal risks: There is no legal protection for consumers who engage in the use of digital currencies. It is noteworthy that in case of fraud, theft, or loss of funds, the users may have limited legal redress at the moment. Current consumer protection laws were developed for the conventional banking and financial sectors and may not be easily translatable into digital currencies. This leaves the consumers exposed to risks that may negatively affect them and slow the growth of the use of digital currencies.

8.1 Potential Legal Reforms

As highlighted above, the current legal framework may be insufficient to address the risks posed by digital currencies effectively, and there might be a need to pass new laws and reform existing ones. Despite the fact that some of the issues may be covered by existing legislation, it is necessary to consider that digital currencies have their peculiarities.

1. New Legislation: New laws could be passed to define and regulate digital currencies more effectively. This may include laws that pertain to the areas of taxation, consumer protection, fraud, and security requirements for the trading platforms of cryptocurrencies. Better definitions of the laws would assist the governments in enforcing the laws and the market to run efficiently since the business people and the consumers would know their roles and responsibilities.
2. Amending the Existing Laws: In another approach, what could be done is to modify the existing laws on financial regulations to suit the requirements of digital currencies. For instance, it is possible to add cryptocurrencies that meet specific requirements of securities laws and to extend AML and KYC rules to digital currency trading platforms. These amendments could assist in regulating digital currencies as part of the existing financial system while at the same time allowing lawmakers to address new issues when they emerge.

In either case, legal reforms should be versatile enough to allow for new technological developments and changing business practices in the future. The legal framework for regulating digital currencies could become irrelevant in a very short period of time due to the development of the technology used in digital currencies; therefore, future-proofing is crucial in any approach.

8.2 Future of Digital Currency Regulation

Looking ahead, the future legal landscape for digital currencies is likely to evolve significantly. With the growing acceptance and use of digital currencies in the global market, there will be pressure to have a standard and complete set of rules on the use of digital currencies across the globe. This could entail the formulation of global laws that would set standard guidelines on the use of digital currencies, especially in the global market.

1. A Single System: Another significant feature of the future development of digital currency regulation will be the formation of a single system. Since the use of digital currencies does not have geographical boundaries, cooperation will be important in establishing coherent rules on the use of these currencies. International organizations such as the Financial Action Task Force (FATF) that has put in place standards on anti-money laundering could assist in the fight by providing direction on how the war should be conducted. This would eliminate the problem

of having multiple regulators each with their policies and procedures where doing business and consuming digital currency should be streamlined while at the same time preventing the use of the same for unlawful purposes.

2. Traditional Cryptocurrencies: As the world gradually opens up to cryptocurrencies, Central Bank Digital Currencies (CBDCs) issued by the government could be another form of cryptocurrency. CBDCs would be under the regulation of the government, and hence would be regulated by the government but they would be based on the technology of digital currencies and hence they would be fast and more accessible. The adoption of CBDCs may lead to increased legal certainty in the use of digital currencies in the economy by setting specific standards for the use of digital currencies.
3. Regulation of Digital Currencies: The regulation of digital currencies will therefore be adaptive and responsive to the existing digital environment. This is a very important aspect since the rate of advancement in technology is very high and so is the risk that comes with it hence the need for regulation to adapt to the changes that come with the advancement in technology. It is now possible for lawmakers to pass dynamic regulations that can easily be changed to address new emerging issues, unlike the case with rigid regulation.

8.3 Improving International Cooperation

Therefore, enhancing international cooperation will be crucial for developing a single legal regime for digital currencies. To counter cross-border incidences like taxation, fraud, and market manipulation, countries will have to cooperate more. International cooperation in setting rules for regulating digital currencies might also contribute to the simplification of the legal framework and decrease the number of cases of regulatory competition where companies operate in countries with less strict requirements. For instance, the governments of various nations could come up with a common policy on taxation for digital currencies to ensure that users of digital currencies are charged across the globe for their income earned in digital currencies. Likewise, the data protection and anti-money laundering laws could be aligned so that the use of digital currency can be done safely and with efficiency and compliance with the standards of users' identification and transaction reporting.

9 Conclusion

This chapter has looked at the legal perspective on digital currencies and the opportunities and issues that come with them. Cryptocurrencies like Bitcoin, Ethereum, and Central Bank Digital Currencies (CBDCs) have various benefits, ranging from enhanced access to financial services and the possibility of disrupting international trade. However, their decentralized nature, volatility, and lack of clear regulation present significant legal uncertainties. Different major legal issues of digital currencies were discussed, including the problem of the definition of their legal status, whether it is money, commodities, or assets. We also talked about the question of the jurisdiction that governs cross-border transactions and the problem of consumer protection in cases where there are no adequate laws and regulations. In the same regard, the question of privacy has been an area of concern with the use of digital currencies being associated with anonymity and at the same time requiring some form of regulation to avoid unlawful activities. The use of digital currencies also raises important issues in the global economy, such as: How do they fit into cross-border payments? How are they a threat to traditional financial systems? However, the use of digital currencies facilitates the speed and reduction of costs, but they are still prone to volatility and security issues that pose challenges to regulators to safeguard consumers and financial stability.

Law plays a crucial role in determining the evolution of the digital currencies of the future. With the growth of the adoption of digital currencies and cryptocurrencies, it becomes paramount that the legal systems of the world come up with ways of dealing with these new technologies. The legal systems must ensure that the efficiency, the increase in the number of consumers, and easier cross-border operations do not come at the cost of consumer protection, financial stability, and the fight against unlawful activities such as money laundering and fraud. The regulation of digital currencies should be conducted to ensure that the new financial instruments do not destabilize and compromise the security of the global financial system. This entails the provision of extensive measures that include; sound consumer protection measures, stringent AML/KYC measures, and enhanced cybersecurity measures. Moreover, the regulation of digital currencies has to be international since these currencies are global products and their regulation should be consistent around the world. Therefore, legal systems will have a critical role in defining this change to promote the development of digital currencies and protect consumers, businesses, and financial markets. Lawmakers should therefore continue to encourage the use of digital currency as potentially revolutionary tools in the management of the world economy while at the same time establishing sound, secure, and transparent frameworks that can support the full potential of digital currencies.

Globalization of Economy and Regulatory Laws of Digital Currency

1 Introduction

Economic globalization is now a major factor in creating a transnational power structure that mostly functions outside of the conventional interstate framework, i.e., transferring national public governance responsibilities to international commercial organizations [419, 420]. This structure is far more deeply ingrained in certain elements of national states than is generally recognized; the judicial, legislative, and executive processes that allow international capital to be accommodated within national jurisdictions are governed by the state and demonstrate this internal dimension. Therefore, economic globalization represents a significant restructuring of governance at both the national and transnational levels and should not be interpreted solely in terms of cross-border trade and investment flows [421, 422]. This enlarged area of power is influenced by a number of different institutional frameworks, including the global human rights regime and the international network of nongovernmental organizations (NGOs), in addition to the rise of a new private institutional order connected to the global economy. Therefore, it is crucial to examine its current features rather than assuming that they are consistent with earlier incarnations. The state's economic role and obligations have changed in the current era of globalization; many state officials today contend that, especially in highly developed economies, national budgets are no longer able to support the social welfare obligations that were constitutionally required in earlier decades [423–425]. A decline in the scope and exclusivity of international law may result from the emergence of a largely privatized international institutional order, in which strategic actors are a variety of private firms rather than the national governments of major states. This changing institutional structure has its normative authority, which is different from and perhaps contradicts the conventional master normativity of the modern era. For those who study international law, this change poses a crucial query: do these new circumstances lessen the normative authority of international law?

J. Afzal, *Exploring the New Horizons of International Law Concerning Globalization of Economy*, https://doi.org/10.1007/978-981-95-1312-3_8

This new conformity, which has its roots in private power but manifests itself in public, helps denationalize institutions, laws, and resources that have historically supported the goals of national states. This new institutional order is distinguished by its ability to de-nationalize formerly national policy areas and privatize previously public ones [426]. Both the denationalization and privatization processes are the product of changes that have taken place inside the national state, or more specifically, within certain of its essential elements [427, 428]. States increasingly act as institutional hosts for the mechanisms enabling economic globalization, even the most powerful governments have experienced significant internal changes [429]. This poses a basic question: given their crucial role in enacting and controlling international economic processes, to what degree can certain institutional elements of national states still be regarded as "national"? In contrast to previous stages of economic growth, the modern state is essential in managing the relationship between foreign players, such as multinational firms, international markets, and supranational organizations, and national legislation. The current stage of globalization is unique in several ways because of this changing dynamic.

2 De-nationalized of Economy

States have been forced to actively promote globalization by an increasing worldwide consensus, which is frequently fuelled by political pressure and economic imperatives [430, 431]. As a result, national governments now have responsibilities and are ultimately responsible for protecting the "rights" of global capital [432]. Thus, the defense of capital rights is ingrained in a certain kind of state structure that is influenced by both an international legal framework intended to foster economic globalization and Western legal traditions about contract law and property rights. Although the state continues to play a significant role in determining the legal framework of economic activity, its power is becoming more and more incorporated into and occasionally subservient to a larger global power structure [433]. The link between the state and the global economy is frequently described using terms like deregulation, financial and trade liberalization, and privatization [434, 435]. The independence of a nation's central bank, which enables it to enact policies in line with global economic demands, is one of the essential prerequisites for that nation's integration into international financial markets. Central banks have historically operated as domestic organizations that address domestic economic issues [436]. But in the last few decades, they have played a crucial role in putting monetary policies into place that encourage the growth of international financial markets and the larger global economy. Although this independence has reduced political power and corruption at home, it has also made central banks important players in the globalization process. These changes bring up important issues regarding how international law is developing; the scope and exclusivity of international legal frameworks may be revised. A shift towards governance structures that go beyond conventional state-centric legal standards is suggested by the growing reliance on informal, sector-specific regulatory networks [437, 438]. This will further integrate national economies into a global system that is not fully governed by international law [439, 440]. Theorizing this change necessitates acknowledging the de-nationalization process; this change entails a planned restructuring of some institutional sectors rather than a total overhaul of governmental institutions. New norms within the state can be established by a small number of state agencies, legislative efforts, and executive choices, especially when they engage with influential transnational corporate entities. These specialized changes are changing important facets of government, frequently functioning outside the conventional purview of international law, even though the majority of the state's bureaucratic apparatus is still in place because of institutional inertia. The demands of the global financial system have also prompted central bankers, who have long participated in international coordination, to start a new phase of cooperation. In addition to producing policy alignments that are put into effect at the national level, these interactions also help to create an international regulatory framework that functions outside the bounds of conventional international law. The creation of a strategic operational field where some state operations are somewhat separated from the larger institutional framework that has historically been centered on national priorities is a noteworthy result of these changing dynamics. Cross-border interactions between governmental organizations and commercial sectors, designed to meet the needs and circumstances influenced by economic globalization, are what define this field [441]. The de-nationalization of institutions and services that were once regarded as purely national is one of the endogenous processes that contribute to globalization inside the national sphere [426, 427]. Crossing national boundaries and interacting with private entities on a targeted basis, this transnational field is extremely crucial. Unlike typical diplomatic agreements or international treaties, it does not involve the state in its totality. Rather, it is influenced by the actions and policies of particular state subcomponents that have direct contact with businesses and international markets, including legislative initiatives or central bank objectives. As a result, laws and regulations gradually converge across countries to provide the structural prerequisites for globalization [442]. It is a hybrid environment that is based in an increasingly institutionalized cross-border network of private companies and somewhat grounded in the current interstate structure. This is a significant departure from the historically cohesive character of state responsibilities in favor of an unbundling of state tasks, in which some facets of governance function apart from the conventional relationship between sovereignty and territory.

This change has been significantly influenced by outside factors functioning outside of the conventional interstate system rather than being solely an internal evolution within states. This new normative order has been established and enforced by a wide range of private actors, from small organizations to significant international players. The global capital market's growing normative power in influencing national economic policies is at the heart of this change [443]. The logic of capital markets has gained significant influence in ongoing negotiations between nation-states and global economic actors, frequently dictating key aspects of national policymaking. While the extent of this influence varies across states, acknowledging that some retain more sovereignty than others, it remains a defining feature of contemporary economic governance. This shift is exemplified by several key elements, such as the prioritization of central bank autonomy, strict anti-inflation policies, exchange rate stability, and the broader set of economic conditions commonly associated with IMF conditionality. This change might be seen as the privatization of the power to set norms, a process in which private and international financial interests increasingly control tasks that were formerly the purview of state government. States' normative authority and the effectiveness of international law are directly impacted by this privatization, which may make it harder for them to protect the interests of the general public.

3 Globalization of Trade Market

International trade generally promotes economic development by guaranteeing the most effective use of resources and optimizing economic expansion [444]. Therefore, how does the law influence both internal and international economic frameworks and facilitate trade? The nations that have developed into capitalist regimes that yet place restrictions on absolute private property rights and capital flows are home to the most developed economies in the world. The Organization for Economic Co-operation and Development (OECD) member nations devote between one-third and half of their GDP to social spending plans [445]. Property rights and the rights of employees, renters, and people to access clean water and air are balanced in these economies. Even though laissez-faire economics may seem appealing in theory, every wealthy country has adopted a mixed economy not as a compromise that reduces efficiency, but rather to improve it by fixing the structural flaws in uncontrolled markets. Although markets are strong forces for resource allocation and growth, their failures are systematic and intrinsic rather than isolated occurrences. Due to its inherent dynamism and narrow-mindedness, markets frequently price crucial components of economic growth inaccurately or catastrophically.

Extreme volatility is a common occurrence in financial markets; internal market processes do not automatically rectify their inefficiencies [446, 447]. As evidenced by recent Wall Street scandals and the stock market bubble, powerful financial actors use their influence to misdirect capital allocation, which can occasionally result in economic inefficiencies worth trillions of dollars. Economic systems do not arise exclusively from the intellectual insights of economists and legal specialists, as the past 150 years of history have shown [448–450]. Instead, political conflicts inside nation-states, influenced by the interactions of citizens, political parties, and economic interest groups, are what give rise to the various types of managed capitalism seen in different countries. Democracy is a basic tool for setting the rules that govern markets, even though it may not always produce the best policies due to its inherent complications [451]. Regulations are necessary for any market to operate, and they establish the parameters of economic activity, regardless of whether they are created by authoritarian or democratic administrations. Ironically, these well-established lessons are frequently overlooked when the conversation turns to cross-border trade and transnational money movements.

The global economy is even more prone to volatility than domestically managed economies because it functions outside the purview of national regulatory bodies. The idea that a market system, which is inefficient in its most laissez-faire form within countries, suddenly becomes optimal when applied to international trade is not supported by any evidence [452]. The role of law is more complicated and frequently unclear in the context of international trade; fair trade standards between countries with different economic models can be established by legal systems to encourage equity [34, 453]. While some states may place more emphasis on public investment and social welfare, others may prioritize economic liberalization. These variations should be considered by a well-designed trade policy so that trade can continue equitable terms. To shape a global trade system, it is imperative to differentiate between these various legal tasks. The law-and-economics school's proponents frequently support the widespread belief that the main goal of the law is to foster an environment that supports the growth of the free market. Although it is acknowledged that a worldwide coordinated approach to economic governance is necessary, creating and implementing such a framework is made more difficult by the lack of a centralized global authority.

Following World War II, the World Bank and the International Monetary Fund (IMF) were instrumental in reviving international trade and financial flows [454]. There is a stark difference between the Bretton Woods organizations' current activities and the vision of their founders [455]. The system's designers realized in 1944 that deflation was likely to result from unchecked international financial flows and that competitive currency depreciation posed serious risks [456]. To enable member countries to seek full employment at home, the IMF was created to stabilize national currencies without pressuring economies into contraction. Global policymakers today, however, have a quite different viewpoint; instead of maximizing economic development, the Bretton Woods institutions, especially the IMF, have developed into tools for imposing a single economic model, frequently putting the interests of banking and business elites first. A laissez-faire system, which is unstable, unreliable, and harmful to human welfare, has been essentially reinstated as a result of private capital's rising independence from national governments' regulatory authority as global markets have grown. A lot of acceptable state interventions—such as those for social investment, stabilization, and economic development—are thought to conflict with WTO regulations or accords like the North American Free Trade Agreement (NAFTA) [457]. By avoiding national courts and legislatures and instead using special NAFTA tribunals, companies from member countries can contest democratically adopted environmental measures as trade restrictions under NAFTA's Chapter 11 process. The OECD suggested a similar program called the Multilateral Agreement on Investment, but it was eventually shelved because of strong opposition.

The loss of national sovereignty in favor of global market forces despite growing inequality might be justified if neoliberal policies continuously produced prosperity. However, more volatility and widening gaps within and between countries have resulted from the move away from mixed economies and towards uncontrolled markets. It is important to understand that striking the right balance between human development and commercial expansion is a political decision rather than an inevitable economic one. According to traditional free-market theory, markets naturally allocate resources in the best possible way, and any government interference—whether through taxation, regulation, or public investment—distorts this allocation and impairs economic performance [458, 459]. However, well-thought-out interventions can improve efficiency and justice if markets regularly misprice inputs and outputs or cause instability. Simple market theories do not apply to real-world economies; while some high-growth civilizations are extremely unequal, others are very egalitarian. In the same vein, many economic models have both prosperous and suffering countries.

Recent stock market scandals have shown that deregulation frequently opens the door for insider opportunism, which so-called "self-regulating" market mechanisms neglect to prevent until serious harm has been done [460]. Consequently, income disparity becomes even more; inequality increases as societal restraints on the market erode. Therefore, we need to rethink a mixed economy—one that promotes sustainable growth while guaranteeing equitable human development—for both efficiency and equality. When markets are allowed to operate independently, they are unable to produce the accountability and orderly balance required for a healthy and just economy. For example, the fall of the Soviet Union paved the way for the emergence of "gangster capitalism" in Russia, proving that unregulated markets can lead to instability rather than order. Historically, societies that have successfully increased democratic involvement have also controlled market excesses, making democracy a lived reality for everyone rather than just a theoretical concept.

4 Globalization of Investment and Its Implications

The International Monetary Fund (IMF) used neoliberal stabilization policies in collaboration with commercial banks and recently elected administrations who were more focused on the market [461, 462]. Instead of encouraging economic management and combating financial instability, the Bretton Woods institutions ended up enforcing market liberalization and austerity [463]. Reducing public spending, depreciating currencies, deregulating businesses, privatizing state assets, opening national capital markets, and fostering an atmosphere that is conducive to foreign investment are some of the strategies that have been recommended. By bringing pricing into line with economic fundamentals, these policies seek to improve market efficiency. In theory, foreign investment and economic growth should be stimulated by the flow of capital into nations that offer high returns. These stabilization measures, however, have produced a range of outcomes in practice. They have been successful in guaranteeing debt repayment and creating markets, but they haven't always helped vulnerable communities or underdeveloped nations. As seen by the Asian financial crisis of the late 1990s, they have frequently resulted in speculative financial inflows rather than long-term, profitable investment [464, 465]. By purposefully "getting prices wrong" to direct low-cost capital into domestic businesses, some of the most prosperous developing economies have prospered. Prioritizing domestic savings and strategic investment, these countries restricted or only permitted foreign money under rigorous guidelines. Significant sacrifices were made elsewhere as a result of structural changes, but the expected financial gains were frequently insufficient. According to neoliberal economic theory, marketization should encourage convergence as wealthy investors seek out profitable growth prospects in developing countries [466, 467]. Theoretically, these investments would benefit everyone by boosting economic growth and producing large profits. However, the reality of the last few decades has been divergence rather than convergence. Per capita earnings in the Global South have decreased in comparison to those in the Global North, except a few Asian nations, all of which implemented policies that went against laissez-faire economics.

Both the growth of North–South trade and the expected inflow of direct foreign investment and portfolio capital into emerging countries have mainly failed to materialize. Instead of relying on foreign investment, the majority of countries still produce money domestically through industrial profits and local savings. Foreign investment frequently varies erratically, which makes national economies even more unstable [468]. Global economic potential is limited by a system that is overly inflation-averse and geared toward the interests of bondholders, foreign exchange speculators, and private investors. Regardless of temporary sacrifices, attaining real human development is impossible while global economic growth only coincides with population growth and income distribution is still unequal. The cumulative effect of IMF-led structural adjustments frequently causes global economic decline rather than development, even when certain nations need fiscal restraint.

The basic problem of managing a global economy will not be solved, even if the Bretton Woods institutions adopt a wider variety of development models. Following World War II, national governments successfully created mixed economies that balanced market forces with social stability. However, in a globalized economic climate, it is becoming more and more difficult to maintain this equilibrium. Society runs the risk of collapsing if market forces are allowed to control every element of life, including labor laws and environmental regulations. People still expect their governments to offer political rights, healthcare, education, and economic security even though they are part of a global economy. People blame national politicians, not multinational firms or global financial institutions, when economic conditions worsen [469]. Ironically, the more state sovereignty is undermined by unbridled globalization, the more people seek protection from their governments. The majority of regions lack institutions that can provide democratic economic monitoring, in contrast to the European Union, which has established transnational governance structures. Widespread political opposition has resulted from this weakening of sovereignty as well as the growing influence of international corporations that lack accountability.

Governments that insist on regulatory control run the danger of being branded as protectionist in a world where markets are becoming more liberalized. Global capital, which frequently looks for jurisdictions with cheap labor, lax regulations, and low tax burdens, may find it difficult to recruit nations with strong social policies and efficient taxation [470]. Recent regulatory actions, however, from anti-money laundering to environmental protections, show that national governments still have a lot of influence. Globalization has the potential to worsen inequality, fuel political turmoil, and impede human progress if it is not controlled [471]. Strengthening national and international institutions that can guide markets toward more expansive social and economic objectives is necessary to address these problems. To guarantee that market economies serve a wider range of human interests, the biggest task, however, is to replicate such institutions globally. Unless it fits with their corporate or geopolitical agendas, nation-states are frequently hesitant to give up actual sovereignty to organizations that oversee global governance. For attaining successful global governance necessitates striking a careful balance between upholding national sovereignty and encouraging international collaboration in the interests of social justice, sustainable environmental practices, and fair economic growth.

5 Regulatory Laws of Digital Currency

The necessity of regulation in modern financial markets applies to the world of digital currencies as well. The inherent volatility of cryptocurrencies and systemic risks from wholesale operations involving digital currencies raise serious financial stability issues [472]. The crypto sphere has been no stranger to the devastating collapse of multi-billion-dollar exchanges, indicative of why stronger regulatory targeting is needed, along with the traumatic volatility of said markets. As so much fraud, scams, and technical vulnerabilities persist in digital currency markets, initiatives for increased consumer protection are necessary [473]. Most digital currencies are pseudonymous, making them appealing to anyone who wants to launder money or otherwise engage in illicit financial activity [474]. The inherently decentralized character of digital currencies presents challenges in terms of tax collection and regulatory compliance, necessitating new forms of international cooperation.

One of the main legal ambiguities regarding cryptocurrencies is the question of basic classification, as in, should cryptocurrencies be viewed as securities, commodities, or currencies. This uncertainty has led to jurisdictions developing differing approaches to regulation and resulted in a fragmented global regulatory landscape. Challenges remain in cross-border regulatory coordination and enforcement from decentralized networks [475]. The rapid pace of technology development presents another difficulty concerning regulation, since regulators are required to ensure adaptability while simultaneously preserving stability in the market. But there were also great opportunities, with greater financial inclusion from broader digital currency adoption, payment system efficiencies, and regulatory technology (RegTech) innovation [476]. By its nature, the collision of technology and finance in digital currencies is raising novel regulatory challenges that even the best-established financial rules are ill-designed to solve. The decentralized qualifiers and the non-local access to many digital currencies have prompted the need for new virtual economies to be developed [477]. Regulators will have to protect consumers and the financial system while encouraging innovation and technological progress. This balancing act has translated into a variety of regulatory approaches that are being implemented, which demonstrate extreme differences in national priorities and risk appetites.

6 Digital Currency Regulations

The regulatory landscape for digital currencies has become torn into an intricate tapestry of international frameworks and national approaches, mirroring the vast range of commercial speeds at which national domestic jurisdictions are responding to the new products of the digital economy. The Financial Action Task Force (FATF) has become a major global standard setter for digital currency over the past couple of years [189]. In 2019, the Financial Action Task Force (FATF) promulgated its groundbreaking guidance on virtual assets and virtual assets service providers (VASPs) [478], creating the right so-called Travel Rule that requires the transmission of certain identifying information for cross-border transactions. This guidance, which more than 200 jurisdictions have adopted, requires VASPs to obtain and transmit information about the originators and beneficiaries of digital currency transactions over $1,000 [479, 480]. The implementation of these standards has greatly increased the transparency of digital currency transactions and has bolstered international collaboration to combat financial crime. The BIS, through its research and policy recommendations, has made a significant contribution towards regulatory discourse. The Bank for International Settlements (BIS) Committee on Payments and Market Infrastructure (CPMI) has also outlined principles guiding the design and implementation of CBDCs, arguing that financial stability must be preserved, and has come up with guiding principles on the design and implementation of CBDCs [481–484]. The IMF report in September 2021 noted that a coordinated approach to digital currencies would mitigate risks of regulatory fragmentation. The IMF has devoted special attention to the entities behind stablecoins and the potential consequences stablecoins pose for monetary policy and financial stability, pushing for coherent regulatory frameworks that cover both systematic risks and consumer protection.

The U.S. has a patchwork of regulations surrounding digital currencies, with various regulatory agencies weighing in on the issue. The SEC has made sweeping moves to regulate digital assets that are deemed to be securities, as in its recent landmark case against Ripple Labs. Importantly, the CFTC regulates derivatives on digital currencies and has identified both Bitcoin and Ethereum as commodities. The Financial Crimes Enforcement Network (FinCEN) supervises compliance with anti-money laundering regulations for digital currency businesses, and the Office of the Comptroller of the Currency (OCC) has issued guidance on banks' participation in digital currency activities [485, 486]. One of the most comprehensive regulatory sets in the world—the EU's Markets in Crypto-Assets (MiCA) framework [487]. Enacted in 2023, MiCA lays out a single regulatory framework for digital assets in the EU, covering market transparency, consumer protection, and financial stability.

The framework also PINPOINTS specific requirements for each of the various types of digital assets, both owned digitally and in "stablecoin" form, and provides a licensing regime for crypto-assets service providers. The enforcement of MiCA is an essential milestone in the direction of regulatory harmonization in the EU, which is a piece of information in itself for others to comply with. China has taken a hard regulatory line, essentially banning most types of cryptocurrency trading and mining. During this time, the People's Bank of China (PBoC) has been developing its own central bank digital currency (CBDC), the Digital Yuan, with a tight grip on the digital currency ecosystem [393, 488]. This tactic is part of a broader strategy by China to control its financial system and achieve technological independence. The country's regulatory stance has a far-reaching implication for the global digital currency market, especially mining as well as trading volume. Russia has taken a mixed approach, embracing the adoption of cryptocurrency early, only to impose stricter crackdowns on it. In 2021, the country issued a Digital Financial Assets Law that establishes a framework for the regulation of digital currency, including strict limits on how cryptocurrency may be used to make payments [204, 489, 490].

7 Digital Currency and the War Against Money Laundering

Forex AML Challenges Combination of digital currencies and anti-money laundering rules poses one of the most significant challenges of contemporary financial regulation [491]. Financial Action Task Force (FATF) is an intergovernmental body founded to assist in forming an integrated global response to combat money laundering and terrorist financing, which has been instrumental in the creation of international requirements for cryptocurrencies related to anti-money laundering (AML). The organization's guidance related to virtual assets, released in 2019, was a watershed moment in the domain of digital currency regulation, as it provided the first truly comprehensive point of reference for AML compliance in the digital assets space. That guidance, adopted by over 200 jurisdictions, was also the first to introduce the term Virtual Assets Service Provider (VASP) and set out several obligations that would be imposed on such entities under the FATF Recommendations. However, even the paraphrase that contained "Travel Rule" was a big step in the right direction in the field of AML regulation for digital currency. Cryptocurrency exchanges have become key nodes in the wider ecosystem of tradable digital currencies, subjected to higher and higher levels of anti-money laundering (AML) duties [492]. Crypto exchanges know your customer (KYC) requirements have gone beyond that of traditional financial institutions, adding layers of verification and monitoring [493]. These more rigorous criteria are in place due to the specific risks involved with digital currency operations, such as the possibility of immediate cross-country transfers and the implementation of confidentiality improvement technologies. Transaction monitoring systems are getting more complex, using artificial intelligence and machine learning to spot patterns of illicit activity. Because many digital currencies are pseudonymous and blockchain-based transactions can be complicated, implementing these systems has been especially difficult. In recent years, technological solutions such as blockchain analytics tools have allowed for more effective monitoring and analysis of digital currency transactions.

By and large, there have been some landmark cases in the enforcement of AML regulations, which have resulted in many evolving regulatory approaches and practices that have emerged from the industry. The Binance case, which came to a head in 2023 when Binance settled with U.S. authorities for $4.3 billion, is one of the largest enforcement actions to date [494, 495]. This case exposed the significance of effective AML policies and the repercussions of non-compliance. It's interesting to note that, as part of the settlement, its terms mandated specific improvements to KYC, transaction monitoring, and reporting procedures. The 2022 collapse of the crypto exchange FTX exposed major gaps in anti-money laundering (AML) supervision and compliance [496–498]. The investigation revealed significant commingling of customer funds and insufficient AML controls, resulting in recommendations for more regulatory oversight and tighter compliance measures. This case has had a specific impact on regulatory approaches and practices for digital currency exchange and custody arrangements.

8 Summary

Applying securities laws to digital currencies is one of the most complicated and fastest-moving frontiers of financial regulation. Since the advent of Initial Coin Offerings as a mode of fundraising, their regulation has seen significant shifts. That's because ICOs cannot skirt existing securities laws, and the SEC's approach has been specifically geared towards promoting that ICOs comply with existing securities laws, which are concerned with registration and disclosure obligations. As a result, new frameworks for token offerings have emerged, such as Security Token Offerings (STOs), which are designed to align clearly and meet security regulations. The European Union's approach to ICO regulation, reflected in the MiCA (Markets in Crypto-Assets) framework, serves as an alternative regulatory model MiCA lays down particular rules concerning token offers, having rules on disclosure obligations and marketing prohibition. This framework takes a more nuanced view of digital assets and their differing nature, while still ensuring investor protection. To this day, there are challenges for regulators and market participants over the classification of digital assets as securities, commodities, or currencies. Under the CFTC's interpretation of the Commodity Exchange Act, Bitcoin and Ethereum are classified as commodities, resulting in a possibility of overlapping regulatory frameworks for digital assets. The resulting dichotomy has precipitated jurisdictional overlap and coordination difficulties among regulatory agencies. New forms of digital assets, like governance tokens and non-fungible tokens (NFTs), have complicated classification issues even more. These assets commonly have features of both securities and commodities, requiring shades of regulatory responses. The growing complexity of digital assets structures has led to a need for guidance from the SEC (among other bodies) and the SEC's approach to classification of digital assets has evolved, but there are challenges in fitting these structures within traditional securities law concepts. Cross-border coordination amongst regulators is fast becoming a necessity, as the issue of digital assets securities is already being felt internationally. IOSCO has been at the forefront of developing international standards that address regulatory challenges posed by digital assets. To that end, the International Organization of Securities Commissions (IOSCO) has been at the leading edge of developing international standards that address the regulatory issues raised by digital assets. Its 2020 Report on Digital Assets Trading Platforms (link) set out key high-level principles for regulating digital assets markets and investors. International cooperation on digital assets regulation has become easier with the development of regulatory sandboxes and innovation hubs. These initiatives give regulators the ability to try out novel regulatory methods and preserve investor safety.

We must acknowledge that markets need both freedom and regulation to promote human progress. Rethinking global economic governance is also necessary; it would be beneficial to return to policies that place a higher priority on employment, economic growth, and financial stability. It is also necessary to combat the destabilizing impacts of speculative currency trading, maybe by enacting laws like a Tobin tax on financial transactions. The shortcomings of state socialism have already been demonstrated, as millions of people were deprived of their freedom and prosperity due to overbearing state control. Examining how legal frameworks influence economic results is equally crucial, whether their purpose is to safeguard the interests of those in positions of power or to maximize human potential. Millions of individuals are directly impacted by the discussion of global economic governance, making it more than just an academic issue. The law might serve as a tool to safeguard private wealth, or it can encourage a balanced approach to development.

Nomenclature of the Digital Economy and Contemporary Theory of Digitalization

1 Introduction

The term "New Economy" refers to an economy influenced by technology, digital development, global effects, and innovation [499, 500]. Unlike the past, when the economy relied upon industrial items, the New Economy houses digital assets and focuses on information, knowledge, and services [501]. These changes require us to look at our rules and laws for managing economic matters and to decide on changes to guide our actions and what is legally required of us. Moving forward, the New Economy is being driven by the shift to intellectual property, information, and technology infrastructure [502]. These days, many businesses benefit a lot from intangible things like data analytics, artificial intelligence, software updates, and digital platforms. Google, Facebook, Amazon, and Apple lead in many fields, not just through goods but also by using their data and what they offer online. Property rights in traditional law revolve around clear ownership of physical possessions, but these kinds of assets are unique and can lead to big challenges for regulators [503]. How it is decided who controls, owns, and has rights to resources that are intangible and can be instantly copied and sent elsewhere is the first important legal matter. In addition, the New Economy brings new market forms and work models that greatly alter the way traditional economies operate [504]. An example is that long-term, secure jobs are now being replaced by more flexible, shorter-term jobs found on platforms, freelance marketplaces, and online workplaces. A change of this kind makes it seem that our current employment laws, labor rights, and social protection systems may not be enough. Since they are made for stable job relationships, these legal frameworks have a hard time guaranteeing fairness and protection in the moving digital economy [505]. So, the law must now address these shifting relationships to guarantee the rights of workers are upheld, economic fairness is maintained, yet the economy does not become too rigid. Importantly, it changes how players in the economy compete and markets are regulated. Nearly all digital platforms are like monopolies, thanks to network effects, which make the platforms even stronger

J. Afzal, *Exploring the New Horizons of International Law Concerning Globalization of Economy*, https://doi.org/10.1007/978-981-95-1312-3_9

when more users use them [506]. Because of this power, people have doubts about the fairness, competitiveness, and creativity in the industry. Traditional antitrust laws were intended to control prices and obvious market control, but today they are not enough to address data control, biased algorithms, and big tech, making it hard for others to enter the market. Worldwide, regulators find it hard to explain bad market practices because common aspects such as pricing do not fully capture the damage done to both consumers and small businesses [507]. Consequently, competition laws must be reconsidered to deal better with digital situations.

On top of that, the New Economy is being globalized, making it even harder to regulate. What happens with digital goods and services is not limited to one nation, which can cause problems with deciding rules, taxes, and laws. For instance, international digital services tend to avoid standard taxes, which means governments miss out on money and big tech companies get special benefits [508]. For this reason, we require a strong argument to help fair international rules for taxes, accountability, and transparency, so that economic disruptions and differences among nations are avoided. Concerns about privacy and data protection are now major issues introduced by the New Economy [509]. Physical companies now depend on huge amounts of personal data, taking in information from many customers. We must ask if gathering personal data is legal and fair, and whether existing privacy laws do enough to guard people's rights against the activities of businesses or governments. One way to overcome these issues is shown by the GDPR, which provides guidance, especially about how to store and use data, and requires that organizations get proper consent, be transparent, and be accountable [87, 282].

1.1 Cryptoeconomy

From a legal point of view, the crypto economy is an evolving area that links new financial methods with technology [387]. Primarily, the cryptoeconomy consists of conducting economic actions using blockchain technology, cryptocurrencies, and decentralized finance (DeFi) [510]. Because these activities lack central control and are often private, they are especially complex to manage from a regulatory standpoint. Older legal systems have trouble keeping up with the decentralized patterns seen in the cryptoeconomy [511]; a major challenge faced in the crypto economy is how to define cryptocurrencies legally [304, 512]. Many places in the world categorize digital currencies differently—they may regard them as commodities, securities, or currencies, or introduce them as their class. As a result of this legal uncertainty, any business or investor working with cryptocurrencies would have compliance challenges. It is also a major legal issue to implement anti-money laundering (AML) and counter-terrorist financing (CTF) rules [513]. The fact that they are nearly untraceable and allow for cross-border transactions makes cryptocurrencies more likely to be linked with illegal activities. Internationally, regulation has found it difficult to prevent financial crimes while still encouraging new ideas in the industry. As an example, the Financial Action Task Force (FATF) has proposed rules for virtual assets service providers (VASPs), making them follow AML, including the 'travel rule' that requires both sender and receiver information to be in each crypto transaction [514, 515]. Even though this approach improves transparency, many argue it weakens the central points of cryptocurrencies: privacy and decentralization. On top of that, it becomes more complex when cryptocurrencies are used in transactions and are then taxed [388]. Taxation of crypto gains is not the same in every jurisdiction [516]. Because rules are not similar across countries, there is a chance for some to avoid taxes by changing where they do business, which complicates the system. In addition, the international and decentralized characteristics of the crypto economy oppose existing laws and enforcement [304]. Since there are no central bodies in blockchain networks and since they are global, illegal activities and disputes commonly involve countries without clear legal boundaries. Because of uncertainties about which country to follow in such disputes, investors may not feel protected, and dealing with lawsuits become difficult.

1.2 Gig Economy

Because of the rise of gig work on digital platforms, how we work has been undergoing a quick transformation [517, 518]. Even though this change makes work easier and more lucrative for people, it also leads to problems with existing employment rules. Critical analysis uncovers a broad range of legal issues about labor, taxes, and liability, suggesting that current laws must be reassessed logically. The gig economy is mainly about the unclear way people are classified as workers [519]. Uber, Airbnb, and Upwork, like other tech platforms, prefer to treat workers as independent contractors instead of employees. Such a distinction has legal significance as being an employee generally gives you certain rights to minimum wage, healthcare, pension, sick pay, and a safer workplace. Because of the uncertainty over their employment status, gig workers are not always able to benefit from the basic rights and protections of the workforce [520]. Platforms say that they consider gig workers to be independent contractors mainly because the workers enjoy flexibility and independence in what they do [521]. Still, according to studies, many platforms control several aspects of work, such as pay, customer handling, conditions, and schedules. All around the world, judges are now carefully analyzing this arrangement. Especially, legal decisions like those from the UK Supreme Court versus Uber have made it clear that gig workers not only have a lot of control over their work but also deserve employee benefits as a result [522, 523]. From the point of view of taxes, the gig economy makes it hard to fit into the structures created for standard employment [524]. People who work as gig workers often use several apps and operate across many regions, which complicates income and taxation. Platforms often say they don't employ workers, so they are not responsible for collecting taxes or providing tax information. Legitimate workforce individuals deal with most administrative tasks, leaving them with little help or knowledge, which sometimes leads to failing to pay taxes or unknown errors. Managing financial responsibility and dispute handling is important for Financial Intelligence Units (FIUs) [525]. Under traditional employment, the employer is responsible if accidents or misbehavior happen during work. At the same time, these platforms are usually given their responsibilities and often deny any liabilities to gig workers. If an accident happens involving an Uber driver, who is responsible and who gets what compensation becomes a question. Companies legally disconnect themselves from these situations, something that employees, often low on funds, cannot do without serious consequences. In short, legal structures used today do not make it clear who is responsible which hurts the interests of vulnerable gig workers.

1.3 Virtual Economy

The virtual economy refers to the exchange of goods, currencies, and services that only happen inside digital platforms and virtual environments [526, 527]. Transactions in virtual economies mostly focus on assets that don't exist physically, so they bring up unique issues that need targeted thinking and careful attention. Mainly, the virtual economy consists of virtual land, characters in digital games, game items, and exclusive cryptocurrencies from those platforms or digital games. New online worlds such as Second Life, Fortnite, Roblox, and different online multiplayer games have made it hard to tell apart the economy of the real world and the virtual economies found there. People involved in crypto use virtual currencies to get and sell digital assets, which sometimes can be transformed into actual money [380]. Even so, due to being digital and decentralized, these transactions are not regulated, so it's unclear what certain laws mean for matters like legal rights, taxes, and defending consumers. A main legal problem is figuring out who owns different digital assets. There is real money to be made with virtual items like rare collectibles or land. On occasion, people have bought these items for thousands or even millions. Yet, according to the law, it is not always clear who owns virtual assets. Services usually tell users they own little or nothing, allowing the service to shut down access or erase digital assets if it wants to. Because of this, users who spend real money are often unable to take legal action if things go wrong, calling for better rules and consumer protections. As a consequence, governments lose considerable income, and the situation can cause unfairness among market actors. Sometimes, a person who makes big profits by selling virtual goods can escape taxation because the laws on the Internet are not always clear. When virtual economies become bigger and connected to traditional ones, well-structured laws are needed to avoid over-taxation while not stopping people from taking part. It is easy for manipulation, money laundering, and illegal trading to take place within the virtual economy of online games and virtual worlds. Those involved in crime find it easy to cover their illegal tracks with virtual currencies. At the same time, present regulations are not sufficient to identify, stop, and address such economic crimes online. I would suggest making rules simpler, starting safety checks, and organizing global partnerships to address and control illegal economic actions online. There are also instances where it is unclear which laws apply, which adds further difficulty to regulation. As virtual economies are present worldwide, it is very hard to decide which country's laws should be applied. Because of this, it is not easy to enforce rules, settle disputes, or protect consumers. If a user lives in one nation and makes transactions on a platform from another nation, it can cause legal, user rights, and regulatory concerns.

2 Phenomenon of Digitalization

Digital technology and platforms are heavily used in the fast-moving digital economy. It is not as simple to define the digital economy as it seems at first glance. Three approaches are commonly combined: the bottom-up approach, the trend-based top-down approach, and the tiered or flexible method. Each method brings certain strengths, weaknesses, and reasoning, and exploring these can help us see why this classification matters and how it shapes our view of digital phenomena.

A bottom-up approach puts importance on being practical and clear. At the outset, individual industries or companies are studied to find out if their work or products are suitable for the digital economy. When a company essentially operates through digital tools such as software developers, online retailers, or online platforms, it belongs to the digital economy. It is straightforward because the proof and numbers support the decision about entity is digital or not much easier. This method may have difficulties because it looks back at history instead of planning for the future. Since it relies heavily on current activities, it may overlook fast-evolving trends and businesses whose operations significantly change due to innovation. A classic bookstore could become a big online retailer after making changes quickly. Although this bookstore could ultimately be included in the digital economy when considered from the grassroots, its progress may not initially be recognized, reducing how quickly it fits this category. There is also uncertainty about exactly what level of digital use is needed, so judgments might differ widely between scholars.

In contrast, a top-down or trend-based approach looks at large digital transformation trends and explains how these translate into the economy. To use this method, analysts initially pinpoint important digital trends like artificial intelligence, greater cloud computing, or a rise in e-commerce. The approach, at this step, reviews the spread of important digital trends across the economy, examining what impact they have on existing businesses, new business models, and society. The fact that workers are prepared ahead of time is one important factor in this technique. This approach lets stakeholders anticipate significant shifts and respond faster to them. By noticing early on that AI and automation will have a big effect on manufacturing, services, and agriculture, policymakers and businesses can organize and plan better for training, investing, and setting up rules in advance. On the other hand, using trends could be questioned because the forecasts it relies on may not always correspond well to real-life changes. Due to its anticipation of trends, the factor may exaggerate or minimize a trend's actual significance for practice or the economy. As an example, although blockchain was expected to reshape both finance and contract management in a short period of time, it has reached economic adoption and achieved its impact at a much slower and limited pace than people expected. Consequently, this approach might mistake what exactly is included in the digital economy. Therefore, the flexible or tiered approach was introduced to bridge the two different ways of learning. The method tries to find a middle ground between the definite structure of the bottom-up approach and the flexible creativity of the trend-based approach. It does this by grouping digital economy activities into core and non-core segments. The "core" includes companies that mainly rely on digital advantages such as digital platforms, online marketplaces, and software services. Meanwhile, the "non-core" contains traditional sectors that also use digital technologies, for example, retail shops now use the Internet to sell, and factories use smart technology.

The reason for this strategy is that it can change with new information. Because each industry is digitalized differently and over time, a strict classification system is likely to become out of date or less useful. Something that works as a digital service today might be essential for the business tomorrow. Recognizing this flexibility allows classification to respond to both new technology and the economy. In addition, the tiered system helps policymakers make better decisions by giving them a more detailed overview. For instance, government policies for digital infrastructure and data are not the same as those for digitally transformed fields such as agriculture and logistics. Because of this, the necessary changes in the market can be handled with more efficiency. At the same time, this suppleness does not make the system free from challenges. Discernment between what is a core digital sector and what is not can be challenging and often controversial. It is becoming harder to define the difference between traditional and digital industries. As an illustration, the automobile industry, once mainly traditional, now makes heavy use of digital technologies, including software for autonomous cars, GPS maps, and immediate data analytics. Putting this type of sector in the core vs. non-core list can sometimes be difficult, leading to misunderstandings and possible inconsistencies when carrying out specific regulations.

3 Contemporary Theory of Digitalization

In this section, the author presented the concept of the Contemporary Theory of Digitalization (CToD). The purpose of the Contemporary Theory of Digitalization is to provide a logical framework for digitalization within the organization, and for organization to organization across the globe. There are three levels of CToD Level 1, Level 2, and Level 3. Following is a brief description of these three levels.

3.1 Level 1 of Contemporary Theory of Digitalization

Level 1 of the Contemporary Theory of Digitalization deals with the Digital Border of an organization/state, the Digital Regulations, and the Digital Governance of an organization/state. The first level of CToD is also known as the 3D level of Contemporary Theory of Digitalization. The focus of this level is on the basic digital infrastructure of an organization/within the organization.

Digital Border: An organization/state needs to define its digital border and area of operation.

Digital Regulations: An organization first needs to define/design its Digital Regulations. These regulations are basic rules and laws and by-laws of an organization or institute.

Digital Governance: An organization or institution needs to define its Digital Governance mechanism. Digital Governance is also known as the e-governance mechanism.

3.2 Level 2 of Contemporary Theory of Digitalization

Level 2 of the Contemporary Theory of Digitalization deals with the operational rules within the organization. The second level of CToD is also known as the 5D level of Contemporary Theory of Digitalization. It consists of Digital Goods and Services, Digital Infrastructure, Digital Obligations, Digital Privacy and Security, and Digital Rights.

Digital Goods and Services: An organization or institute needs to clearly state its Digital Goods and Services as per the regulations designed in Level 1. An organization must follow the major treaties i.e. General Agreement on Trade in Services (GATS) and General Agreement on Tariffs and Trade (GATT).

Digital Infrastructure: An institute or organization needs to design digital infrastructure in light of regulations and governance mechanisms defined in level 1.

Digital Obligations: After the basic regulations defined in Level 1, in this section, an organization must define Digital Obligations at the organizational level and personal level.

Digital Privacy and Security: An organization or institute needs to clearly define and state its Digital Privacy and Security regulations. Organizations must follow the leading international privacy and security treaties including the OECD Privacy Guidelines, the EU's GDPR, and national laws like China's PIPL.

Digital Rights: There must be properly defined digital rights within the organization/state.

3.3 *Level 3 of Contemporary Theory of Digitalization*

Level 3 of the Contemporary Theory of Digitalization focuses on digital connectivity between organizations. It may be institute to institute or even state to state. The second level of CToD is also referred to as the 7D level of the Contemporary Theory of Digitalization. It consists of Digital Assets, Digital Connectivity, Digital Defense, Digital Diplomacy, Digital Exchange, Digital Relations, and Digital Sovereignty.

Digital Relations: Organization to organization/State-to-State digital relations encompass how states interact and collaborate through digital technologies, shaping international relations, diplomacy, and governance.

Digital Connectivity: Digital Connectivity allows to connect and access information through digital networks outside the organization/state, including the Internet, mobile networks, and other digital infrastructure.

Digital Sovereignty: Digital Sovereignty ensures that organizations or states have the right to control of their digital assets, data, and technologies. It encompasses control over physical infrastructure, software, standards, and the data generated and used. Mother organization has the right to take proper measures to ensure its Digital Sovereignty in this digital era.

Digital Assets: Digital assets are anything created and stored digitally that has or provides value. Protecting digital assets involves implementing various measures to safeguard them from unauthorized access, use, disclosure, disruption, modification, or destruction. The organization must ensure the protection of its Digital Assets while making digital relations with other organizations.

Digital Defense: Digital defense encompasses a broad range of practices, policies, and technologies aimed at safeguarding data, privacy, and operational integrity in the digital world. While interacting with other organizations or states digitally, an organization or state has the right to digital defense.

Digital Diplomacy: Digital Diplomacy means the use of digital technologies, particularly the Internet and social media, to achieve diplomatic goals and engage with foreign audiences. Organizations ensure the proper mechanism of Digital Diplomacy in this digital world.

Digital Exchange: Digital exchange is an online platform that facilitates the trading of digital assets. While interacting with other organizations or states digitally, there must be a Digital exchange platform.

4 Taxonomy of Digital Economy, Digital Law and Contemporary Theory of Digitization

4.1 Digital Infrastructure

The digital economy, digital communications, and digital services depend on digital infrastructure [528]. Among its physical parts are data centers, optical cables, satellite networks, mobile towers and undersea internet cables and non-physical pieces include cloud computing, cybersecurity systems, and systems that manage digital identities [529, 530]. To achieve digital transformation's benefits, countries need strong digital infrastructure. Digital infrastructure is now being treated as a legal and regulatory issue related to public and national security, rather than just a set of technical matters [531]. Just like roads, electricity, and water systems have rules to keep them open and dependable for everyone, digital infrastructure should too. The point is simple: in today's digital era, being connected digitally and online is necessary for everyone who wants to be part of society and the economy [79]. So, it is up to governments and organizations to guarantee that digital infrastructure can be accessed, is affordable, and stands up to challenges. Providing equal access to digital infrastructure is one of the biggest legal issues in this field [532]. In several developing areas and in rural parts of developed nations, there aren't enough or any digital tools, causing a lasting divide between those who do and those who do not have access. Because of the high costs involved, building infrastructure in low-income or remote areas can be insufficiently profitable for private companies without specific guidance and public support. For this to happen, the government usually makes certain things necessary such as helping set up free services, providing infrastructure funding, or involving the private sector, to bridge the divide. Taxation is needed for social stability and to make the economy grow over time [533]. When people are digitally excluded, they often cannot participate in the economy. Data sovereignty and managing important digital infrastructure are significant concerns [534]. Since most of the worldwide data infrastructure is run by private multinational companies, people often ask who is in charge of essential communications and data. Therefore, certain countries are adopting laws that say information generated within their borders must be stored and used within their systems. Even though these rules help protect countries and ensure security, they also create worries about splitting the internet worldwide and making things more costly for businesses. Regulating digital infrastructure now emphasizes considering the importance of environmental sustainability [535, 536]. The digital technology sector relies on data centers that use a lot of both energy and water. Since climate change is a big concern, authorities need to assess how digitalization helps society relative to how it affects the environment. More people are asking for green rules that require energy-efficient technology, carbon disclosure, and the adoption of renewables in building and powering digital systems. Finally, the topic of who owns and controls crucial digital infrastructure is becoming more involved with political relationships. Building and maintaining 5G networks is now treated as a key priority for countries [537]. The argument over Huawei and 5G in Europe and the U.S. shows clearly that digital infrastructure is now a main concern in global politics. It is necessary to strike a balance between innovation, foreign investment, and the country's resistance to threats and vulnerabilities.

4.2 Digital Regulations

Legal measures are created through digital regulations, intended to control how people use the Internet and other digital areas. Because digital technologies are present in nearly all areas of modern life, including online sales, social platforms, banking, and artificial intelligence, clear and unified rules are indispensable to deal with risks and achieve fairness and openness. Whereas standard regulations are fixed, digital rules must be flexible because technological changes can occur quickly in the digital landscape [538]. Data protection and privacy are major points that digital regulations focus on. Because digital companies store a huge amount of our information, there is a high risk that it could be misused or hacked [539]. Due to new regulations, users now enjoy more control over their personal information, as seen with the "right to be forgotten" in the GDPR. USA California and Brazil have similar sets of laws in data legislation—the California Consumer Privacy Act (CCPA) and the Lei Geral de Proteção de Dados (LGPD), respectively [540, 541]. The regulations set high standards for companies, so they must inform users and get their consent while failing to comply could result in penalties. It is important to ensure consumers are willing to stay involved in online tasks. Digital regulation emphasizes managing the issues of moderating content and misinformation. Facebook, Twitter, and YouTube have strong effects on public views and the workings of democracy. The lack of appropriate rules allows hate speech, untrue information, radical propaganda, and cyberbullying to be widely spread. The Online Safety Act that Australia adopted primarily aims at cyberbullying and online harassment by making it necessary for platforms to rapidly take down harmful content after a notification [542]. Singapore has an act, called POFMA, which places responsibilities on platforms and content creators to address fake news [543]. In addition, rules for digital platforms face obstacles related to the way algorithms are developed and used. Decisions that matter to society, such as who to hire, who gets access to credit, and who is prosecuted, are now largely decided by algorithms. Laws in this area ensure that algorithms are clear and fair to prevent any chance of bias or unfairness [544]. The sector of financial technology and cryptocurrencies is part of digital regulations, but it is constantly developing and is marked by regulatory confusion [304, 545]. New opportunities are created by cryptocurrencies and DeFi platforms, but there are serious risks in terms of stability, safety for consumers, and illicit actions such as money laundering. In this way, Switzerland and Singapore created special regulations that encourage innovation and recognize potential risks [546]. On account of these unique rules, they are now leaders in worldwide blockchain and digital finance. An important issue that is emerging is helping everyone be part of the digital world. More and more, regulations are seeing that inclusive digital policies can help prevent further dividing those who have fewer opportunities. Making sure accessibility is maintained by putting new laws in place, like the U.S. Americans with Disabilities Act (ADA) [547], which now applies explicitly to digital spaces, ensures individuals with disabilities have equal access to digital services. This unique dimension of digital regulations highlights their broader societal role in promoting equity and social justice.

4.3 Digital Goods

Usually, digital goods vary from physical products because they are stored electronically rather than as things we can touch. Examples are software, e-books, digital music, movies, online courses, video games, and virtual currencies. Because digital goods never run out and can be shared quickly, they bring various economic, legal, and regulatory issues not found with other products [548]. Since digital goods are intangible, they raise legal issues related to how property rights are usually understood [549]. Originally, laws for property focused on things that could be seen and controlled without much question. Using software or listening to digital music, consumers typically only acquire a limited right to use the items. For example, when buying a movie or e-book online, users commonly can't sell, lend, or share it like they can a physical movie or book. It becomes an issue for logical thinking when we consider consumer rights since people are charged the same price even though they hold fewer rights compared to the real thing. Regulators struggle to handle the taxation of digital goods. Traditionally, tax rules focus on location, who owns the property, and where it is used. Since digital goods can reach people immediately and anywhere online, it is difficult to decide which country's taxes should be applied. It is very difficult for countries to find a fair way to tax digital products due to how easily businesses can shift their activities to more tax-friendly areas. First of all, digital products have consumer protection issues that are not the same as those in traditional markets. Before you buy, it can be tough to know what you're getting is truly genuine or not. As a result, some digital goods may not match what the promotion promised. Because of this, regulators require tight disclosures and refund plans from app stores, demanding they make the system's features and usage rules clear. Online app stores now provide clear product explanations, what device it works on, and consumer reviews, so users are protected and can trust the service. The simple process of making extra copies and stealing digital goods is another issue. Effortlessly copying, sharing, and accessing digital goods online makes IP enforcement very difficult.

4.4 Digital Services

When we talk about digital services, we mean services that are delivered using technology online [550]. On the list are cloud computing, streaming apps, online banking, digital marketing, e-learning, telemedicine, social networking, and app-based transportation, including Uber. In contrast to digital products, digital services need subscriptions or repeat usage, leading to frequent contact between buyers and the company. Digital services are different from other services because they create unique legal and regulatory issues [551]. There are many challenges surrounding the shape of the contract between the people using the service and the provider. Most digital services ask users to agree to a set of terms that few usually read. Most of these contracts favor service providers, with parts that shield them from risks, impose limits on user rights, or permit them to make alterations without consulting users. Therefore, people involved in writing laws may question: should consumer protection rules be increased for digital service contracts when the service matters a lot such as communication, banking, or education. Privacy and data protection are important parts of regulating digital services. Personal data collection, processing, and monetization a standard revenue practices for many services. For instance, services such as social media and search engines are not charged for, but companies use user data to place targeted ads. Another major regulatory concern is consumer protection and service quality. Digital services, particularly those in health (telemedicine), education (e-learning), or finance (fintech), carry real-world consequences when they fail or malfunction. Is an inaccurate health diagnosis as a result of an online consultation considered a legal concern? If a platform fails at the moment of a market crash? In contrast to classic services, digital service providers usually try to distance themselves from blame by adding detailed disclaimers to their terms of use. Therefore, specific standards of accountability are necessary, including minimum performance guarantees, ways to address disputes, and solutions in cases of service failure, especially for services that work with or instead of important public infrastructure. Antitrust actions and digital legislation such as the EU's DSA and DMA are meant to push platforms to be more transparent, easier to integrate, and answerable to rules [552, 553].

4.5 Digital Assets

Digital assets are assets that exist online and can be measured for their worth [554]. Among them are cryptocurrencies such as Bitcoin and Ethereum, non-fungible tokens, digital securities, domain names, libraries of online content, virtual real estate, software licenses, and data. With so much taking place online now, digital assets are important for managing both personal and business prosperity. Yet, the development of artificial intelligence is triggering several legal, regulatory, and ethical issues that existing laws find hard to manage. The main question about digital assets is this: what exactly is ownership in digital formats? Under traditional law, having ownership means being able to control something physical. Even so, digital assets can be duplicated, sent elsewhere, or accessed online without the owner realizing it. It leads to important challenges in protecting rights, preventing unauthorized use, and understanding what property looks like in the digital world. Besides, decentralized systems called blockchains typically hold digital assets which makes it harder for legal rules to be applied. Since no central agency oversees the space, disputes can be hard to resolve. This type of network makes it difficult to enforce contracts, settle disputes, and assert rights. Many people think cryptocurrencies help democratize finance, but some believe they are also linked to money laundering, tax evasion, and fraud. A fast-emerging type of digital assets—also called non-fungible tokens (NFTs)—brings about new legal challenges [555, 556]. NFTs are unique pieces of digital artwork, music, or collectibles and are commonly promoted as showing who owns a digital asset. Please note that holding an NFT as a legal owner still might not allow you to use the content it shows in any way you want. Because of this difference, buyers might feel confused and consider pursuing legal action over intellectual property. It shows that there is a requirement for clear laws that specify what happens to rights while owning a digital assets and guarantees that those laws are communicated upfront.

4.6 Digital Bonds

Digital bonds are a modern evolution of traditional bonds, issued, managed, and traded entirely through digital platforms, often using blockchain or Distributed Ledger Technologies (DLT) [557–559]. Like typical bonds, they indicate that someone lends money to an entity, but they are issued, tracked, and traded differently. Digital bonds make markets faster, more efficient, and easier to follow, but they also lead to important legal and regulatory questions that may conflict with the present rules [560]. At first, digital bonds do appear to have many attractive qualities. Because digital bonds are automated and no longer depend on clearing houses and custodians, both costs and the time required for settlement can be lowered [561]. For example, blockchain technology can allow a two- to three-day bond transaction to happen in just a few minutes. The speed and convenience of these bonds make them appealing to both government and big corporate issuers looking for fast ways to access capital. Nevertheless, the new trend introduces new complexities in terms of the law. The majority of security laws were prepared imagining paper or central system records, rather than what is used nowadays. Using blockchain means that registrars, custodians, and settlement agents are no longer required to do the same traditional tasks [562, 563]. The blockchain serves as the source of truth in digital bonds, recording who holds what, when transactions happen, and when the assets become payable. The acceptance of digital ledgers as proper evidence of ownership is a key legal question. Some jurisdictions have not yet fully included blockchain evidence as part of their legal systems. It creates important challenges for absorbing the risks and handling disputes for investors. Should the parties in a digital bond transaction disagree on the terms or when it should be carried out which court is in charge and which standards will they use? Rules need to be updated to consider decentralized records as legal evidence and to outline ways for resolving problems that arise with digital transactions. Ensuring oversight and investor safety is also very important.

Regulators are at risk of not seeing what goes on in digital bonds, making it harder to detect pitfalls, unless security measures are put in place. However, governments and major financial institutions are now beginning to make use of digital bonds. In 2021, the European Investment Bank conducted the world's first blockchain-backed bond, using the Ethereum platform [564, 565]. Major business institutions such as the World Bank have begun to check digital bond markets by running pilot projects. These moves show that digital bonds are not theoretical—they are real, and growing fast. But without legal clarity, they remain risky territory for mainstream investors and vulnerable to abuse.

4.7 Digital Inflation

Digital inflation means inflation caused by digital economies, digital assets, and technology-based financial systems [566, 567]. While traditional inflation happens due to having too much money, cost increases, or greater demand for real products, digital inflation results from excess virtual tokens, price speculation, and stronghold pricing by some digital businesses. Since digital inflation doesn't follow traditional trading rules, we need to reconsider traditional economic models and use them in this new environment. After all, digital goods offer infinite copies while their production cost is almost nothing [568]. Artificial shortages, market abuse, and a few strong digital companies are the issues behind rising prices, rather than simply limited production. NFTs such as digital art and collectibles, have seen their prices rise fast by hype, the feeling of exclusivity, and investors angling for a profit [569]. If many digital assets are made or their popularity falls, the market value can plummet—much like in a deflationary crash. On the other hand, when buying activity spikes, the prices can rise sharply like in inflation. The challenge becomes even bigger with cryptocurrencies and decentralized finance (DeFi) [570]. Even though Bitcoin is built to decrease in supply over time, the crypto industry includes a variety of tokens that people can easily produce which often happens without regulation. The fast spread of countless altcoins and meme tokens can drive asset inflation, as digital "value" increases faster than the real economy's growth. This not only distorts digital assets markets but can also spill over into traditional financial systems, especially when mainstream investors are involved. Digital inflation also results from the power that major e-commerce sites hold [571]. In a traditional economy, the presence of competition always helps maintain fair prices. To regulators, digital inflation is a sign that the rules of competition law, protecting customers, and financial oversight should be strengthened. Authorities should be aware that in digital industries, monopolies often hide their influence in pricing and are stealthily built into online systems and recommender tools. Also, regulators should have the ability to detect speculative bubbles and inflation in digital assets markets that are typically hard to follow and lie beyond the ordinary banking sector. On top of that, it might require more effort for monetary policy to work when digital inflation emerges. Central banks fought inflation by affecting interest rates and controlling the money supply in the past.

However, when digital currencies or tokenized markets take over more economic activity, the traditional tools of the banking system may no longer work. As a result, governments are now taking steps to add digital currencies (CBDCs) to their tools, so they can both keep up with the times and ensure the country's economy remains stable.

4.8 Digital Border

Digital borders mark the boundaries where data, content, and online services change as they move through different countries. Unlike traditional borders, digital borders depend on regulations, laws, and tools such as firewalls, data region rules, filtering of content, and censorship tools [572]. Countries are trying to control the digital field more, leading digital borders to play a bigger role as they highlight the legal, political, and ethical challenges between global connectivity and national management. It was typically believed that the internet would be a place where information could move freely across all countries, cultures, and continents. As networks and devices have become more common and problems over matters such as privacy and control have advanced, authorities have set up "digital borders" to bring back control over cyberspace. They exist to organize what data enters or leaves the country, provide guidelines over what residents are allowed to access, and identify the organizations operating within its digital boundaries. Data localization laws are one of the clearest ways to show digital borders [573, 574]. All data collected by or within the nation must be managed on servers that are housed within the country's borders. India, Russia, and China have put in place laws that require all personal data to be stored inside their borders. Controlling the information people see on the internet is another way digital borders operate. Laws and technology allow governments to prevent users from accessing certain websites, platforms, or sources of information. The Chinese government's "Great Firewall" is the most noteworthy case, censoring international social media, news sites, and search engines, and closely controlling those in the country. Iran, North Korea, and presently, Russia are also creating systems to censor the internet. Although these actions are mainly supported for reasons of safety, protecting culture, or stability, they cause major concerns regarding people's rights to speak and have access to information. According to the law, digital borders create new issues when it comes to jurisdiction and sovereignty. Digital borders influence the economy; a number of nations put these barriers in place to help their businesses compete with foreign technology companies, much as they have done with traditional tariffs. Although digital protection can lead to fresh local solutions, it can also lower competition, discourage new developments, and decrease what consumers have access to. As a result, if international platforms are forbidden in favor of homegrown companies, only one brand might dominate, with less innovation in the digital space. As a result, entering the global market becomes complicated for companies, since they need to follow a mismatch of laws and technical rules in different countries.

Essentially, digital borders increase the chance that the internet might become fragmented into separate internets ruled independently by each country. A certain level of regulation guarantees safety, but making the internet too restricted or nationalist may go against what makes the internet free.

4.9 *Digital Sovereignty*

Digital sovereignty refers to a nation's ability to control and regulate its own digital infrastructure, data, and cyberspace activities without undue dependence on foreign technologies or platforms [575, 576]. As data moves freely across borders today and many important digital structures are run by international companies, digital sovereignty serves as an important part of national sovereignty. It highlights how states are motivated to protect what matters to them, safeguard people's rights, and control the digital area. The idea became well-known due to increasing worries about surveillance, online attacks, and foreign tech businesses. When Edward Snowden disclosed the global surveillance done by U.S. intelligence, it revealed how vulnerable national data is on the open internet. Just like Facebook, the global importance of companies like Google, Meta, and Amazon has increased concerns about digital power and the impact it might have on national policies, cultural independence, and the economy. One form of digital sovereignty can be seen through requirements for local data storage of personal or sensitive data. But having digital sovereignty has also sparked some debate. Critics worry that this will cause the internet to split into separate "splinternets," meaning that each country will have its own digital rules [577, 578]. This might stop new global ideas from coming about, cause conflicts in international business, and prevent people from expressing themselves openly. It is difficult to align a nation's interests with the need for international teamwork. Digital sovereignty truly supports nations by empowering them to defend citizens' data, boost the local digital economy, and develop democratic standards in the digital world, even while engaging with the rest of the world.

4.10 *Digital Defense*

Digital Defense means make sure to use suitable methods for online security against hacking, spying, deliberate disruptions, and false information [539, 579]. With a larger reliance on technology for communication, finance, government, health care, and protection, societies are more at risk from cyber issues. Therefore, digital defense should be regarded as central to the country's security, independence, and safety, and not only as a matter of technology or the military. Traditional military dangers are clear: stay within national borders and use similar force, but cyber attacks are invisible, go across borders, and can be quite different in approach. Even a single hacker or a small gang using malware is able to disrupt power grids, reveal sensitive documents, or immobilize major organizations. Because of this, digital defence is hard: it needs to be proactive, able to adapt, and must be well-connected with both civilian and business networks that are often hit first in cyber battles. Cybersecurity policy serves as a basic component of digital defense by creating measures to protect key infrastructures such as power grids, water supplies, healthcare centres, and networks for sending calls, messages, and data. Many governments now consider these sectors essential to society and implement new laws to make sure security standards, threat monitoring, and response plans are in place. In the same way, the European Union's NIS Directive and CISA in the United States are essential in protecting against cyber events [580, 581]. It is extremely important yet challenging to handle legal matters and reactions in digital defense. Assigning a cyberattack to a specific actor, such as a foreign government, is both difficult and could be considered sensitive. Even so, it is challenging to act against infractions when there is no clear attribution under international rules. As a result, countries often choose to use cyber tools to push back against others but without causing a full-scale conflict. For this reason, more states are looking to develop and follow worldwide agreements on state actions in cyberspace, similar to those in military conflicts. Another part of digital defense is fighting information warfare, which helps to prevent deception campaigns that use the internet to make people doubt major institutions and divide society [582, 583]. It is important for governments, tech companies, and members of civil society to join forces to find, disprove, and block false information, while doing so while respecting democratic and freedom of speech values.

4.11 Digital Person

Digital person is the idea that a virtual identity or persona exists from the information we share and store online [584, 585]. This does not just include information on social media—it concerns every bit of digital activity someone leaves behind: their biometric information, the sites they browse, AI-made avatars, virtual assistants, and digital clones created from their voices and actions. Because of the line between real and digital identity is getting blurrier, we must find ways to legally protect people as digital entities. Because the world is so connected now, almost everyone creates an immense amount of data, even if it is unintentional. Not only our open actions, but also things like tracking where we are, recognizing our faces, recording what we buy online, our preferences, and habits. This combination then creates a special digital identity that people and organizations can use to guess, project, and influence our behavior. From a legal point of view, this set of data is considered an extension of ourselves, yet most laws view it as something businesses own, instead of individuals. Such cases provoke questions related to a person's identity and rights. Would it be fair to grant a digital person legal recognition if its data came from you? After death, who gets the rights to your digital personality being copied by AI or your voice being emulated, if you've agreed to it? More people are now talking about digital identity that exists after someone dies, as well as deepfakes, to illustrate how such representations can be controlled without the subject's consent. If the law does not protect them, people might lose possession of their private digital information. Some legal experts support the creation of digital personhood to protect what individuals do in the digital environment [586–588]. This means seeing digital identity as part of a person's human dignity and protecting it in law as we do physical identity. Thanks to this recognition, handling consent, privacy, and intellectual property could change.

4.12 Digital Rights

In the world of technology, digital rights mean ensuring everyone has the same basic rights as in the offline world and that they are respected and safe online [589, 590]. Such rights include freedom of speech, the right to privacy, access to information, data protection, the ability to ask for personal data to be deleted and also include completely new rights introduced by internet use, like the right to access the internet or to be identified online. A main principle of digital rights is that using the internet should not take away your rights [591]. People deserve legal protection for their speech and sharing of information, whether they are online or meeting in person. Based on this, countries are now working together to align human rights laws with cyber issues. Because of massive data collection and surveillance capitalism, it is increasingly difficult for people to enjoy their right to privacy online. There is a common practice of companies and governments acquiring a lot of people's data while hiding the procedure from most individuals. Technology examines people's actions to mold their opinions, guide their decisions, and anticipate their feelings [592, 593]. Another cornerstone is the right to freedom of expression online. While the internet has democratized speech, it has also given rise to challenges like hate speech, misinformation, and platform censorship. Balancing this right against societal harms is complex. Should platforms be held responsible for what users post? Should governments dictate what can and cannot be said online? The answer lies in building legal frameworks that uphold free expression while ensuring transparency, due process, and accountability in content moderation. Gaining access to the internet is now seen as a digital priority.

4.13 Digital Obligations

Digital obligations involve the roles and tasks that individuals, corporations, governments, and digital platforms must complete in the digital world [594, 595]. Just as digital rights are expanded to support users on the Internet, digital society also requires those making use of digital technologies to follow certain legal, moral, and technical rules. These rules are necessary so that everyone feels safe, accountable, and trusted in the digital world. While digital rights ensure individuals what they can do, digital obligations state what they are required to do to maintain the integrity of the internet. Users, companies, platforms, and states each have responsibilities that are important in themselves and also connected to larger issues.

4.14 Global and Ethical Obligations

In an interconnected world, digital obligations extend across borders. States need to work together on cybersecurity, cross-border data sharing, and AI rules. Tech companies, especially those that operate worldwide, should respect human rights, even in places with weak laws.

4.15 Digital Banks

Digital banks rely on digital services and do not have physical sites like conventional banks [596, 597]. You can find savings and checking accounts, loan services, money transfers, and investment tools all available via the bank's website or an app. Banks are leading a transformation of global finances by making banking more accessible, efficient, and creative. Yet, their use also generates issues that require careful resolution to keep the financial system fair, stable, and trustworthy for all. Convenience and lower fees are the main reasons people like digital banks. Because they do not have to support physical banks, digital banks often charge less, pay higher interest, and make banking easy for customers. Mobile banking lets customers take care of creating new accounts, securing loans, and handling their funds all through their mobiles. Having this convenience is most important in places where the usual banking services are not well-established. It makes sense because it brings underserved populations into the official economy and allows them to make use of necessary financial services. Legal rules and regulations for digital banks are constantly changing. While regular banks operate under tight rules, digital banks sometimes use easier ways to obtain licenses, for example, fintech sandboxes or only having a few purposes listed in their charter. As a result, innovations take place, but authorities sometimes struggle to cover them. Many digital banks use information from their users to provide custom services and make decisions using software [598, 599]. Although it gives people greater convenience, it can leave their personal information at risk of being used or misused. These frameworks need to support widespread encryption, safe storage and use of data, and easy accountability for any data breaches. If user data is not safeguarded, it can damage the trust that bank customers have in their financial institutions. Moreover, digital banks have caused more competition and worries about how the financial system could be threatened. Although fintechs weaken monopolies in regular banking, when they are uncontrolled, they can become risky for the larger financial market. When digital banks enter speculative investments or use invasive data analysis without careful control, they might make financial crisis worse. As a result, regulators and central banks ought to enable digital banks to operate with larger financial systems and connect easily to national payment networks and interest rate changes.

4.16 Digital Wallet

Digital wallets are virtual systems that are used to keep your personal and payment details safe for shopping or transactions [600, 601]. Users no longer need physical money or cards to make payments; they can do so instantly with their phones, tablets, or computers, both on the Internet and at stores. Some examples are Apple Pay, Google Wallet, PayPal, AliPay, and the mobile apps offered by banks. Although digital wallets offer many advantages and make more people financially included, they bring about legal, financial, and ethical problems that need to be addressed by wise and progressive laws. Digital wallets are mainly attractive because they are practical and fast. Payment apps simplify the buying process, make it possible to do things without money or cards, and are compatible with various digital services available today. In many developing parts of the world where traditional banking services are unavailable, digital wallets give millions the first opportunity to join the mainstream financial system. Because these tools are available to more people, they help youth, gig workers, and those in rural communities become financially included. Still, there are some legal and regulatory issues surrounding digital wallets. In several jurisdictions, they are considered to occupy a space somewhere between banking and technology. Banks must adhere to AML, KYC, and consumer protection laws and are required to hold full financial licenses [602, 603], but many e-wallets skirt these rules due to their light or minimal regulation. Being unsupervised may lead providers to fraud, share private information, or fail to deliver goods and services. Rules for digital wallets ought to resemble those used for traditional financial institutions to protect users while still allowing new ideas to flourish. There is also a major concern about privacy when it comes to what we do with data. Any transaction made through a digital wallet is recorded and used to gather valuable user information. At the same time, access to this data can often help provide better services for people, but it also provides the possibility for destructive profiling, giving away users' information, or even being monitored by the government. Many people agree to give away their data by just clicking on "I accept" in the terms of service. Since digital wallets contain private banking details, they are seen as the main targets for hackers. Many people deal with phishing scams, leaked data, and their accounts being taken over. Providers should set up effective encryption, add multi-factor authentication, and install fraud detection systems. On the other hand, people who use the internet need to stay literate and practice safety online. Both the government and providers of digital wallets should work together to inform the public about fraud and provide options for victims to report it.

4.17 Digital Trading Exchange

On a digital exchange, people trade digital assets, including cryptocurrencies, tokens, digital securities, and goods or services [604, 605]. An exchange might be centralized (CEX) and be managed by a company that holds your money, as with Binance or Coinbase, or it may be decentralized (DEX), like Uniswap and PancakeSwap, which rely on blockchain technology and enable direct trading between people. Because e-commerce is becoming a major part of the digital economy, these platforms are prompting concerns about the law, and regulations, securing users, and ensuring financial stability. Basically, digital exchanges help offer liquidity and price discovery to emerging digital markets. They give users the option to trade digital currencies for cash, swap different cryptocurrencies, and buy or sell tokenized things like NFTs and digital securities. In principle, they give everyone the ability to invest in opportunities that were once accessible only to a select few. Digital exchanges, however, create significant legal and regulatory problems. Firstly, there are unclear regulations to deal with. Different countries are unsure about how digital exchanges are controlled since they could be considered securities, commodities, or money service firms. Because of this unclear situation, some exchanges have been able to expand swiftly in countries with little government supervision. Before developing a legal strategy, what types of things are being traded must be determined. A token promising ownership or future returns from a company should be considered a security and come under securities law. But if it is used to trade, it is potentially classified as a currency or a commodity. If consumers are not classified correctly, there may be problems with enforcement, harm to individuals, and bigger risks for the system. Most digital exchanges do not face the same strict rules about being transparent, undergoing audits, or providing capital as regular stock markets. Due to malicious hacking, poor management, or fraud, users may lose their holdings, as FTX experienced last year. To ensure such disasters do not happen, strict rules are needed about safe storage, audits, holding back reserves, and separating user funds. Similar to banks preventing gambling with deposits, digital exchanges must have limits on using user funds. Market manipulation is also a common problem, as is insider trading. Without proper supervision, some exchanges may allow dishonest practices like wash trading, pump-and-dump schemes, or front-running. For regulation to work well, it should consists of real-time monitoring, regular reporting, and strong policies against conflicts. Also, cross-border exchanges in the digital world add additional challenges to enforcement. A person in one nation may trade through an exchange located abroad, which operates by a distinct set of rules. For this reason, countries should collaborate and make regulations through bodies such as the Financial Action Task Force (FATF), which has produced guidelines on Anti-Money Laundering (AML) and Know Your Customer (KYC) recommendations for VASPs [384, 479, 606].

5 Summary

The purpose of the Contemporary Theory of Digitalization is to provide a logical framework for digitalization within the organization, and for organization to organization across the globe. The first level of this framework focuses on the basic requirements of digitalization within the organization including Digital Regulations, Digital Governance, and Digital Borders. The 2nd level is based on the rules and regulations made in the first level. The second level includes Digital Goods and Services, Digital Infrastructure, Digital Obligations, Digital Privacy and Security, and Digital Rights. The third level focuses on outside-organization or state digital linkage. this level includes Digital Assets, Digital Connectivity, Digital Defense, Digital Diplomacy, Digital Exchange, Digital Relations, and Digital Sovereignty. For further clarification, in this chapter, the author explains key terms related to the Contemporary Theory of Digitalization in the context of the Digital Economy and International Law.

Potential of International Law and Digital Economy

1 Evolution of the Digital Economy and Its Global Impact

1.1 Rise of the Digital Economy

The transition to the digital economy is conspicuous as a transformational shift changing international trade and business in contemporary times. The economy, in the past, depended on industries such as agriculture, manufacturing, and services, all of which followed consistent procedures on how to produce, distribute, and consume goods and services [607]. Conventionally, labor markets and commerce in these sectors were split and localized within the borders of the countries. Yet, the digital age began in the second half of the twentieth century, driven by the introduction of the internet, which dramatically transformed the operations of businesses and how customers interacted with the market [608]. A key turning point in the digital economy was the blistering growth of the internet in the 1990s that opened unprecedented global connectivity to both people and businesses [609]. The advent of the internet played a pivotal role in igniting the e-commerce revolution as Amazon and eBay became prominent players that revolutionized retail and empowered sellers to reach the world through the internet. At the same time, organizations such as Google, Amazon, Facebook, and Apple became world economic powerhouses from being small players. These companies created new business models based on digital infrastructures, platforms, and data, which profoundly influenced today's digital economy.

1.2 Global Economic Transformation

The digitalization of technologies has revolutionarily transformed the economic makeup of society, empowering businesses to create and implement new approaches

J. Afzal, *Exploring the New Horizons of International Law Concerning Globalization of Economy*, https://doi.org/10.1007/978-981-95-1312-3_10

in terms of operation and customer interaction. Digital practices have completely transformed industries such as trade, finance, communication, and logistics, leading to processes that are faster, cheaper, and more streamlined [610]. Digital commerce has accelerated international transactions, and online payment systems such as PayPal, Venmo, and WeChat have facilitated worldwide financial transactions significantly [611, 612]. With digital tools such as email, social media, and video conferencing, how organizations interact with customers and communicate across national boundaries has undergone a fundamental shift. Moreover, alternative business models have been introduced through the opening doors brought by the digital economy, especially the Gig Economy [613, 614]. Exiting vintage full-time positions, this trend introduces flexible, project-based employment that augments possibilities for organizations and individuals. Companies such as Uber, Airbnb, and Freelancer.com have promoted self-employment, thus changing the relationship between employers and employees radically [615]. Furthermore, the arrival of Fintech has led to a never-before-seen revolution in banking, payments, and the insurance industry. This progress creates a more inclusive global financial system, especially for people who do not have access to traditional banking. In other words, the digital economy has increased the potential of economic activity in organizing and performing. The value of data is another major economic consequence of the digital economy. Data has become one of the most valuable possessions in the modern economy. Tech giants such as Google and Facebook produce massive data from their users, which they use to drive advertising earnings. Analyzing big data has also created new chances for businesses to track consumer behavior, provide enhancements, and offer a personalized experience. Consequently, those companies that dominate data and use it are among the strongest players in the global economy.

1.3 Digital Economy's Effect on Traditional Economic Sectors

Digital transformation is changing industries like manufacturing, retail, and banking. In manufacturing, technology improvement in the form of 3D printing, robotics, and AI is slowly eroding traditional assembly lines, which are giving way to more flexible and personalized production [616]. While this leads to an increase in efficiency, it also leaves job losses and adds problems to labor laws that are rooted in old industrial practices. Its rapid growth has swamped brick-and-mortar stores, causing companies to transform or close shop. Retailers now must cope with competing not only from nearby shops but also from giant global players like Amazon, thereby leading to discussions on data privacy, rights of clientele, and tax laws. Also, retailers face the issue of complying with different e-commerce regimes in various countries, which vary significantly. Transformations in operations and customer engagement strategies among financial institutions are being brought about by technological changes such as online banking, mobile wallets, and cryptocurrencies. The innovation of fintech providers has brought in mobile banking and P2P lending, which makes it imperative for traditional banks to respond to volatile regulatory environments [617]. Meanwhile, regulators must guarantee both security and simplicity to promote the industry. High rate of technological change often leaves conventional industries struggling with more legal difficulties, particularly in consumer protection, safety standards, and taxation on digital assets and cryptocurrencies.

2 Current International Legal Frameworks Governing the Digital Economy

Along with the development of technology, international legal frameworks have advanced to regulate digital transactions, protect individual information, guarantee copyright protection, and handle online security threats. Such structures ensure the smooth running of the market and enable the continual development of digital innovations [618]. Although individual nations and regions have made their own rules, there is still a lack of a united federal system.

2.1 International Trade Law and Digital Economy

Digital economy advancements have changed trade regulations as new clauses have been implemented to regulate online deals, data transfer, and products in the digital world. The World Trade Organization (WTO) supervises global trade in digital commerce, among others [130]. The Trade Facilitation Agreement (TFA), which came into effect from the year 2021, aims to enhance trade efficiency through streamlined customs rules and facilitate world trade, especially cross-border data sharing and digital ID exchanges. The GATS, which is supplemented by the WTO, specifies regulatory standards for digital services industries such as cloud computing, online learning platforms, and the selling of financial products. However, balancing the interests of national industries with progressive trade policies, data protection, and the issues surrounding privacy preservation is a major problem. Despite attempts to control the transfer of data and govern data localization, the current framework of the WTO is not sufficient for complex issues in digital trade. Such trade pacts as the USMCA, RCEP, or EU Digital Single Market have a great impact on the governance of digital commerce in their respective regions. For instance, USMCA provides rules to enable cross-border flow of information, which deters data localization policies, which have helped in fostering digital sector development in North America. Similarly, covering 15 countries in the Asia–Pacific, the Regional Comprehensive Economic Partnership (RCEP) focuses on digital trade and data flows but allows countries to govern their domestic regulations [619]. By harmonizing digital rules within Europe, the EU Digital Single Market aims to facilitate effective trans-border trade through e-commerce, digital services, and data for all members.

2.2 Data Protection and Privacy Laws

As the bedrock of digital commerce, comprehensive measures to guard against data abuse and intrusion into privacy are necessary now for supervising the digital milieu. In this regard, there is a noteworthy role played by the General Data Protection Regulation (GDPR), which has been enforced since 2018 in the European Union. The GDPR empowers individuals to take control of their personal data because they have the right to access, amend, or delete their personal records from organizations. Organizations are forced to ensure that there is data security, and severe penalties apply to those who do not. The implications of the GDPR have gone further than Europe, with countries like Brazil and Japan adopting similar data protection laws. Its wide-reaching impacts have made the GDPR a global model aimed at advancing digital privacy as the number of cross-border data transfers keeps increasing. Another regulation that has become important is the California Consumer Privacy Act (CCPA) [620]; it came into force in 2020 as well, especially in the U.S. Authorities behind the CCPA may not be as thorough as that of the GDPR, but California residents have both the right to know what data the companies are gathering, access their information and ask for it to be removed. The effects of the CCPA are beyond the borders of California, and businesses across the world are amending their privacy practices to meet the provisions of the CCPA. Both GDPR and CCPA emphasize the need to protect data in today's global economy, and an increasing number of countries are sitting on similar privacy legislation. However, cross-border data flows are a formidable challenge, especially if the considerations are conflicting across different countries.

2.3 Intellectual Property Rights in the Digital Era

Intellectual Property (IP) plays a crucial role in the digital economy, especially given the increasing importance of digital products and services, including software, e-books, music, movies, and online content, among others. The WTO's Trade-Related Aspects of Intellectual Property Rights (TRIPS) agreement regulates how IP is protected internationally, including patents, copyrights, and trademarks [133]. TRIPs charted out minimum benchmarks to protect the IP in WTO member countries, to create an incentive to innovate by creators and businesses. However, in the era of digital IP enforcement, there are peculiar challenges in terms of digital piracy and online distribution of content. Because of the ease of duplicating and disseminating digital property (music, films, software – any kind of content that can be digitalized), enforcing ownership of IP has become too hard, and the problem has intensified across borders. There is currently heated debate about the right balance to strike between IP protection and the free movement of information and creativity, and this in the context of ever more user-generated content (YouTube, Instagram, for instance). IP protection under TRIPS is essential, but most contend that it must be adjusted to reflect online reality, i.e., the rise of open-source software and difficulty in regulating AI-generated content.

2.4 Cybersecurity Regulations

With the world becoming more interconnected through digital technologies, there is a huge concern about the security of networks, systems, and data. Cybersecurity is vital for ensuring the integrity and trust of the digital economy because breaches of the system call into question public confidence and disrupt global markets [621]. International law serves a crucial role in governing cybersecurity practices using the Budapest Convention, the first international treaty concerned with cybercrime and digital system protection. The Convention sets a framework of actions that should be taken to combat cybercrime and increase international cooperation on cybercrime investigation and prosecution. It has more than 60 signatories, which is the legal rationale behind cross-border cooperation in cybersecurity. Nonetheless, cybersecurity regulations are still inconsistent, with some countries putting national security before international cooperation. Global cooperation against cyber defense is imperative, but a lack of a universal legal framework for cybersecurity precludes there being uniform standards in application in various countries. This emphasizes the need for greater integrated frameworks at the international level to combat the increasing cyber threats in the digital economy.

3 Challenges in Regulating the Digital Economy

3.1 Jurisdictional Issues in the Digital Age

One of the great difficulties in the governance of the digital economy is jurisdiction—the power of a country to enforce its laws across boundaries. The primary foundation of any traditional legal system is the assumption that laws operate only in a territory [622]. However, the nature of the digital economy (in which transactions, data flows, and services across national boundaries) has made this concept ever more difficult to apply [275]. For example, a company such as Facebook or Google functions worldwide, collecting and using data from users worldwide. The moment a legal controversy emerges, for example, one related to a breach of privacy or data protection laws, the question is: Which laws apply, which country's laws apply, and which court decides? The matter of enforcing national laws across borders is particularly complex in that the laws regulating privacy, data usage, and consumer protection vary from country to country. For example, the GDPR of the EU has strong stipulations on the collection of data limits, and it has made the privacy rights of individuals a core right. Although they operate from outside the EU, such platforms like Facebook are required to respect these regulations when dealing with data from EU citizens. We can speak about the contradiction between companies' aspiration to function on a global scale and the necessity of having legal guarantees at the local level. Besides, issues of sovereignty are brought before as digital companies are functioning across international borders. Tech giants such as Amazon enjoy relatively fewer constraints because of the multiplicity of laws that govern their undertakings in various jurisdictions. This scenario leaves a legal gap, hence making it challenging for countries to regulate tech firms within their jurisdiction. By avoiding more stringent rules in some jurisdictions, tech firms from countries with less strict rules can carve out regulatory loopholes that leave the disadvantaged groups and sovereign states vulnerable to risks.

3.2 Regulatory Gaps and Fragmentation

The rapid development of the digital economy has outpaced the capability of the international legal bodies to adapt, leading to gaps between the regulations. There are countries that have progressive laws of the digital economy, but others are lagging, therefore, there is ambiguity and disparities in the standards of consumers and businesses that do business globally. For instance, some states have inadequate privacy regulations, while others practice strict measures, which leave the guidelines for cross-border business activity unclear [623]. Businesses that have a global presence often find it difficult because of these different laws, and they need to tailor their activities to fit the local laws. Such a violation of regulations presents major challenges to consumers. There is a need for clarity for consumers to have their data rights when interacting with digital platforms. For instance, consider the case where one nation's consumer is given better protections against online scams/security gaps than another consumer, simply by virtue of their relevant legislation. Lack of a comprehensive framework encourages more opportunities for exploitation, misinformation, and mistrust among consumers and, therefore, hinders the growth of the digital economy [624]. It is possible to create a coherent system of global regulations, which would strengthen consumer protection and make the expectations from businesses that operate in more countries clear. The major challenge lies in developing an agreement that would accommodate the various perspectives and requirements of different countries and regions in the world.

3.3 The Issue of Legal Enforcement and Dispute Resolution

The complexity of legal diversity and various jurisdictions' dispute resolution procedures causes difficulties in imposing legal decisions in the digital economy. With regard to international trade, standardized bodies such as the WTO are usually in a position to determine disputes. However, trading in the digital world presents new barriers; one of the key mechanisms is Investor-State Dispute Settlement (ISDS), which allows corporations to denounce government policies causing financial damage to their claims [354]. Opponents say that these mechanisms can undermine public policy objectives because businesses can say that preventive regulations limit their profit-earning potential. In certain cases, a private arbitration is also applied when resolving digital disputes, but this practice is often ridiculed because of the secrecy and tendency to support big corporations. This lack of transparency and honesty produces a digital marketplace that does not favour consumers or smaller businesses, which have nothing to rely on regarding resolution of disputes. In addition, international arbitration tends to be expensive and slow, and it is beyond the reach of many, especially in the less developed states. Another of such hurdles is enforcing legal decisions beyond borders. A verdict that comes from a court in one nation may not necessarily hold in another, and especially if the judgment is against the country's local laws. Each and every nation is not ready to grant recognition and execution of foreign judgments [625]. These sporadic tenacities of law undermine confidence and reduce the ability of international law to effectively regulate the digital economy. Unless there is a system of rules that is consistent and fair for disputes, digital world is still not balanced and hard to obtain justice in borders.

3.4 Ethical and Moral Dilemmas

As the digital economy develops, it brings more layers of ethical challenges, especially in such spheres as privacy, freedom of expression, and lack of control over the power of giants in tech. Rapidly developing technology companies now collect tremendous amounts of personal data, usually without the user comprehending the scope of the surveillance. This has resulted in increased public voices for increased data protection measures. At the same time, such social media sites such as Facebook and Twitter that determine what the user views or doesn't view have raised major issues about free speech and digital censorship. The proliferation of the role of artificial intelligence in formulating critical choices such as hiring or providing loans further complicates the issue of ethics. There is some level of anxiety regarding biased algorithms, particularly when such systems determine life-changing consequences. To uphold public confidence and equity, AI should be written, implemented, and used in an open, fair, and responsible manner. Simultaneously, companies are using big data to anticipate consumer behaviour and guide their actions in ways that may be imperceptible to many, and their consumers are unaware of how their information is put to use and any form of control they could have over such matters. This lack of transparency, therefore, provokes major questions about digital rights and user autonomy [626]. If that is not enough, the increasing influence of tech giants such as Google, Amazon, and Apple are a major threat not to the market but also to democratic governance. These corporations cut deep across other sectors than commerce as they shape policy, change consumer habits and re-design labour standards. The central ethical question is whether they are being held to account, or are they being given free rein to exercise their power in ways which pervert competition, abuse workers, and disadvantage consumers? This is necessary to develop a just, transparent and inclusive future in the digital realm.

4 The Role of International Institutions in Digital Economy Governance

4.1 The UN and Digital Economy

The UN is also a strong regulator of the digital economy, especially through UNCTAD (United Nations Conference on Trade and Development) [127]. UNCTAD's efforts on the digital economy involve technology transfer, building of capacity, and setting regulations for global data flows [627]. Various agencies of the UN have acknowledged that for economic development, there is a need for digital technologies, particularly for developing countries to make use of the fruits of digitalization. UNCTAD has presented frameworks on how to trade digitally with emphasis on fair access to digital infrastructure and reducing its gap between countries. It promotes multi-lateral collaboration for developing countries to attain the technical and legal support to adopt digital technologies in their economies. The UN human rights framework also cuts across digital governance, which focuses on the protection of privacy, freedom of expression, and the need to stop surveillance and censorship [628, 629]. Apart from UNCTAD, other UN organs dealing with human rights have been vocal about the issues of the need to protect individuals' digital rights, where there is a need to ensure privacy and access to information in terms of the digital domain. The information-carrying nature of the internet, now global, creates complex inter-state problems regarding sovereignty and privacy, which necessitate inter-governmental efforts at regulating such cross-border data flows.

4.2 *The OECD and International Cooperation on Taxation in the Digital Economy*

The development of the digital economy creates a number of challenges for tax authorities, especially for firms that engage in international business in a way that disrupts the traditional forms of taxation [508]. Within the OECD's initiative, a common strategy for taxing digital businesses has been achieved, which aims to curb the income-shifting practices that are commonly used by global firms. The practice of companies transferring profits from high-tax to low-tax regions is the target of the OECD's BEPS project, which guarantees that countries where economic activity is taking place collect the taxes they are entitled to. As part of these, the OECD has introduced the idea of a global minimum tax to ensure that the large technology companies and multinational enterprises contribute their share to the local economies in the form of taxes. This initiative has attracted broad support, especially because big corporations like Google, Amazon, and Facebook have made significant profits at the expense of little tax payment, raising concerns across the world. The OECD's suggested tax structure is likely to ensure that the tax obligations of digital companies are equal to the location of their headquarters, thus promoting equity in tax collection. Moreover, the OECD wants a global consensus on digital taxation to achieve harmonized rules that will not impair digital cross-border transactions.

4.3 *Other Regional and Global Institutions*

Apart from the WTO, UN, and OECD, many regional and global bodies have a substantial impact on setting the regulations of the digital economy [127]. One of the major examples is the EU Digital Single Market initiative, which strives to harmonize digital standards within the EU to make it easier for businesses to trade e-commerce across the European continent. This intervention increases access to e-commerce, data protection, and digital services, simplifying the possibility of doing business and living across countries. In the G7 and G20, representatives discuss crucial digital issues such as digital taxation, cybersecurity, and data governance at the forefront of global discourse [630]. These organizations highlight the importance of collaborating to address difficulties in the digital industry, such as the creation of ethical standards, data privacy, and fair taxation for tech firms. Besides, Brazil, Russia, India, China, and South Africa have played a key role in developing international digital governance frameworks. These nations have presented a radical restructuring of the legal system currently in practice, advocating for guidelines that are more restrictive in proportion to the challenges faced by developing countries.

5 Key Issues in Digital Trade Regulation and International Law

Challenges that come with the shift to digital platforms come with a series of legal and regulatory issues that alter digital economy operations. These problems are directly related to trade restrictions, growth of digital infrastructure, protection of the consumer, and fair competition. Those who regulate digital trade in order to guarantee smooth continuation of digital trade have always to change their procedures to accommodate the fast changing universe of global commerce, data flows, and modern technologies.

5.1 Trade Barriers in the Digital Economy

With increasing trade barriers, digital companies in the world are increasingly facing troubles attempting to transport products and data across the borders. These restrictions are reinventing the way digital world works and non-tariff barriers become a primary issue. differential from conventional trade that is solely based on tariffs and quotas, digital trade countries are often frustrated by set rules that force companies to deposit data within its borders. Countries such as China and Russia, claiming they need to secure their national security and data sovereignty have set severe restrictions that prevent global data transfer [631]. Consequently, global data networks become less easily accessible by multinational companies to use in building abroad operations. Censorship laws present another barrier when users cannot access or share things on the internet. Such forms of restrictions can make the entry of foreign digital business in some markets virtually impossible or highly difficult, as evidenced in platforms such as Amazon and Alibaba. While such policies are usually justified as a safeguard of local industries and culture, in practice, they limit access to the world, they separate people, slowing down innovation and halting development in the global economy. To make the matters worse, countries have significantly varying laws concerning privacy, data protection, and consumer rights. This is like a patchwork of regulations that leaves international businesses puzzling on how to do a complaint. For example, the strict standards of the GDPR are set by the EU, which are dramatically different from areas where rules are weaker of where enforcement has no consistency. The inconsistencies in the world lead to uncertainty and place additional barriers when firms attempt international business in the digital sphere [632].

5.2 The Role of Digital Infrastructure in Global Trade

Digital infrastructure, such as cloud computing, data storage, and cybersecurity, is at the center of the digital economy. It allows businesses to work across borders, store a lot of data, and communicate with both customers and suppliers anywhere in the world. Nevertheless, the regulation of digital infrastructure poses several legal challenges. The cloud burst has enabled such companies to outsource storage and processing of data to third parties (AWS or Microsoft Azure) instead of having their own costly and space-hogging servers. This change has had far-reaching implications on international trade, and companies are now storing essential data in data centers in various countries. Legal implications of cloud computing include questions of data sovereignty, i.e., who holds legal control over data stored in foreign countries, and questions of intellectual property, such as confidentiality of data, which may contain sensitive business or customer information that must be protected [633, 634]. International legal requirements for data storage and cloud services are commonly absent, and thus, there exist legal ambiguities on ownership, access, and protection of data. For instance, when a country implements data protection laws that run contrary to other countries' more significant commercial interests (what then?). One effort to address this issue was the EU-U.S. Privacy Shield, but this had difficulties, especially after the decision of the European Court of Justice that it did not offer sufficient manner, privacy protection to EU citizens. This choice is an example of how the cross-border information regulation is complicated in the digital economy. Cybersecurity is another important feature of the digital infrastructure. Cybersecurity practices are often governed by scattered legal frameworks where each country has its own standards for the protection of digital assets and critical infrastructure [635]. International cooperation is vital to combat cybercrime and data breaches, but the current legal systems have failed to keep pace with the changing nature of threats in cyberspace.

5.3 E-Commerce and Consumer Protection Laws

With billions of dollars of transactions taking place through digital platforms, consumer protection laws have become a key part of the legal environment [636]. Mature international standards of consumer protection are in development, but several countries have enacted elements of legislation aimed at consumers engaged in online transactions. Such problems as digital fraud, fake news, or the safety of online purchasers, for example, are becoming more and more mass. For example, people shopping online are vulnerable to fraud through counterfeit products, identity theft, and data breaches. Even though most countries have enacted e-commerce laws requiring businesses to ensure that their websites are secure and consumers are protected from fraud, the jurisdictional variation in these laws confuses both businesses and consumers. For example, the EU Consumer Protection Cooperation Regulation has specific provisions for how online business needs to return and dispense refunds, but these provisions may vary from the U.S or Asia, therefore, adding regulatory complexity for a global company. The prevalence of fake news and misinformation also presents consumers with several challenges when it comes to consumer protection in digital spaces. Social media such as Facebook and Twitter are common channels for sharing false information of dire implications for individuals and businesses. Governments and international organizations are becoming more interested in learning how to solve this problem through regulation, but balancing free speech with the requirement for accurate information is not an easy task.

5.4 Competition Law and Digital Economy

Competition law (or antitrust law) is crucial in overseeing digital markets and preventing businesses from abusing their leading position in them [637, 638]. The emergence of such digital platforms as Facebook, Amazon, and Google has made antitrust issues to become a high-profile issue for global digital trade regulation. These companies dominate huge swathes of the internet, and their ability to gather data as well as their power over online marketplaces gives these companies important competitive advantages. It is especially difficult to limit monopolies and anti-competitive behavior in the digital economy. Conventional competition law was structured to control industries that had tangible products to trade, but in the digital sphere, many firms exist in a market where the services are free (think of social media), and their earnings come from advertising or the sales of data. This makes it complex to define what qualifies as anti-competitive behavior. For instance, Amazon has been attacked for shrewd competition over the small businesses through unethical use of its market dominance, Google has also been on the receiving end for its superiority in the search engine. Facebook has attracted concerns of leveraging its market share to eliminate the competition in the social media field, especially after acquiring competitors such as Instagram and WhatsApp. International legal systems are finding it difficult to impose the traditional rules of competition that have been used in the operation of previous digital products onto these new forms of digital platforms, hence the call for a change of antitrust law to suit this modern economy.

6 Emerging Legal Issues in the Digital Economy

6.1 Artificial Intelligence and the Legal World

Artificial Intelligence (AI) and machine learning are already changing industries such as trade, labor, and intellectual property (IP) [639]. Nevertheless, the emergence of these technologies has led to discussions of regulations for them in the legal systems of the world. International efforts are currently being made to construct a legal framework for AI, with organizations such as the OECD and EU looking into policy that promotes innovation, but to address the ethical concerns surrounding the same. One of the greatest legal challenges is that AI has effects on trade [640]. In our world economy dominated by AI automation, the roles that men and machines play in trade must change. For instance, manufacturing and logistics industries are now seeing the necessity of AI-driven machines in streamlining the production process, enhancing efficiency, and cutting costs. However, it poses regulatory challenges in affairs like labor rights and fair trade since companies using AI can overtake others that use human labor, thereby negating the workers in certain sectors. In the intellectual property field, AI creates a problem of authorship and innovation. If an AI system comes up with something new in that sense: a piece of art, code, or even a scientific discovery, what then owns the intellectual property? This question remains largely unanswered within the context of international law: some jurisdictions would consider giving developers of AI intellectual property rights, while others are discussing whether the AI itself can be called an inventor or author. The ethical implications of AI also matter a lot [641]; the subject of personal liability and safety is now tackled in autonomous systems such as motor vehicles or robots. Who is responsible for the accident whereby an autonomous car caused, for example? Who was the producer, the writer of the software, or the owner of the car? These questions are being addressed by countries, but the existing laws have not kept pace with autonomous technology. There are also ethical concerns associated with the use of AI in areas such as decision making (in hiring, criminal justice, among others) where there are possibilities of bias and unfair outcomes, which may demand a legal hand of tune just to ensure accountability and fairness in decisions made.

6.2 Fintech and Blockchain Technology

The accelerating trend of fintech (financial technology) and blockchain has made significant contributions to the global economy, making room for innovations in banking, application of payments, and other finance-related services. Nevertheless, these technologies also present considerable regulatory issues. Characteristically, the era of cryptocurrencies such as Bitcoin and Ethereum, and newer variants of decentralized finance (DeFi), has prompted questions regarding the regulatory framework of their use [510]. Cryptocurrencies refer to digital currencies that exist with decentralized digital currencies and operate on blockchain networks, which are secure, transparent, and far less susceptible to control by traditional banking systems. Governments and regulatory bodies have fought hard to regulate these currencies appropriately. While some nations, such as China, have been very firm on hyper in banning them, some other nations, like El Salvador, have accepted hyper by making Bitcoin legal tender [642]. Such regulatory unevenness leads to confusion and risk for users and businesses operating in several jurisdictions. The concern at the center of the matter is an effective regulation across borders of digital currencies. Cryptocurrencies differ from traditional ones because the latter are controlled by national governments and central banks, and are limited by their borders, while the latter are not restricted by borders. This makes it hard to use the conventional regulatory mechanisms, particularly in the case of taxation, the circulation of money laundering, and the protection of consumers. The Financial Action Task Force (FATF) has drafted regulations for cryptocurrency exchanges to suppress illegal activities despite uneven worldwide enforcement of the standards [643]. Also, DeFi, a decentralized system for the conduct of financial transactions on the blockchain, can only lead to regulatory issues concerning the prevention of fraud, protection of investors, and market stability. Because it operates beyond the normal financial institutions, the regulation of DeFi is quite hard, and hence, it becomes easier for fraudulent schemes to proliferate.

6.3 The Future of Work in a Digital Economy

The digital economy has revolutionized the workplace by developing new forms of employment and labor relations. One of the most visible consequences of this transition is the gig economy – jobs with a temporary or freelance, or contract-based nature [644, 645]. Companies such as Uber, Lyft, and TaskRabbit spawned platforms that enable people to get demand jobs, but this model comes with a host of legal issues. First, the legality of gig work provokes a question as to workers' rights, fair pay, job security, health care, and retirement benefits, to name a few. Gig workers are frequently described as independent contractors instead of as workers, and thus, they are not covered by the same protections that full-time employees are under traditional labor laws. This has injected legal uncertainty, particularly when the gig workers are fighting for fair payment and protection from exploitation. In addition, both the field of remote work and digital labor platforms have transformed the nature of work. Though the flexibility provided by the remote work owes benefits to both employees and their employers, it has paved the way for novel challenges about the rights of workers, discrimination, as well as legal protections in various regions. With remote work becoming more widespread, we have started seeing questions arise about the coverage of labor laws for workers located in various countries, especially in cases where companies work across borders.

6.4 Digital Sovereignty and Data Governance

With the further development of the digital economy, digital sovereignty has grown to play a central role in the consciousness of governments of the world. Data sovereignty is the concept that countries should have the power to control the data produced within the borders of their nation, meaning the manipulation of how they are stored, processed, and distributed [534, 646]. This problem has also increased in significance because of extreme cross-border data flows and growing global dependence on digital services. Nations such as China and India enforce rigid data localization laws that force firms to retain data within their boundaries. These laws are frequently rendered in the name of national security or insanity; however, they cause friction with the global tech firms that depend on cloud infrastructure and cross-border data flows. Some will claim that such limitations stifle innovation, as well as the free flow of information; others will regard such limitations as essential if the country should be able to safeguard its national interests. At a broader level, the debate around global data governance is still open. What is the right balance between cross-border data sharing and the protection of individual privacy and sovereignty of the country? There is no standard process for data protection across borders, and although projects such as the EU's GDPR have advanced, most countries remain line with no thorough data protection laws. Privacy rights are also front and center in this debate, with worldwide calls for more transparency and control over personal data. States should not forget to reach a compromise between the interests of the business, which relies on data for innovation and profit, and the right of individuals to protect their data.

7 Reforming International Law to Meet the Demands of the Digital Economy

7.1 Proposals for Reforming Existing Legal Frameworks

The existing legal frameworks that govern the digital economy were not meant to regulate the complexities of the digital world. Though provided by frameworks such as GATS of the WTO (General Agreement on Trade in Services) and the TRIPS (Trade-Related Aspects of Intellectual Property Rights), all these have only labored in the pursuit of digital trade, their role remains limited. One of the major reform proposals is the modernization of international trade laws to better accommodate digitalization better especially in areas of protection and privacy of data. Data protection laws have become the greatest engagement in the governance of the digital economy. With digital technologies that enable massive collection and processing of personal data, current international legal frameworks have not responded with the kind of urgency that seems called for. Suggested reforms include the formulation of global data protection standards, which would harmonize data privacy perspectives across jurisdictions. Today's pioneers include countries such as the

EU with the General Data Protection Regulation (GDPR), but inconsistent national laws around the world confuse business and end consumers. A single internationally agreed framework would make it easier for businesses doing business across borders while providing proper protection of consumers. Besides data protection, there is another issue that requires reforming—cross-border data flows. Even though some regions have improved, such as the EU's framework for free and secure transit of data across its member states, many other countries still lack coherent regulation for cross-border data sharing. One of the proposals for global regulations on data flows will specify how moving data from and to a country should be done properly by moving data securely and respectfully to privacy while nurturing the development of the global digital trade. There is a need for clearer rules in digital trade. Different laws in various countries, like those about online shopping, protecting intellectual property, and consumer rights, create confusion for global digital businesses. Regulatory environment could be simplified and global digital trade encouraged by efforts aimed at harmonizing legal frameworks within countries and regions. For instance international partnership on regulations of e-commerce that would see consistent rules on digital contracts, online payments, and protection of intellectual property would then be able to reach business firms from one country to the other with ease.

7.2 Developing New International Legal Instruments

Whereas reforming the existing frameworks is important, a need to develop new international legal instruments as well is apparent, given the changing nature of the digital economy. A major need is a treaty or convention made on the part of the international community that would address those issues unique to the digital economy, such as inter-border data flows, digital trade regulations, and so on. An important domain where the need exists for new international legal instruments is cross-border flows of data. Data is a valuable asset for the digital economy, but current treaties fail to furnish detailed instructions on the data that should be transferred, protected, and used within the borders. Agreements of this nature, as the ones for the transfer of personal data from the EU to the U.S. (such as the EU-US Privacy Shield), could be enlarged and set on a global scale. Such agreements will create a sounder system of understanding for businesses and governments to use while transferring data across conclusively international boundaries and still guarantee that the data is safe, and the privacy of the individual is maintained. A different proposal could be establishing a global digital trade tribunal or court that is keen on settling disputes relating to digital commerce. As trade in the digital space continues to expand, conflicts on issues of e-commerce, data protection, and intellectual property rights are likely to grow. The establishment of a dedicated digital trade court could ensure impartial dispute resolution with the certainty of uniform judgements that are fair and compliant with global trade standards. This court would be capable of handling issues like intellectual property infringements in online services, regulatory struggles over the flow of data across borders, and privacy concerns in the digital age, creating standardized rules for businesses to follow in the global arena.

7.3 Ensuring Fairness and Equity in the Digital Economy

It is of utmost importance for international legal reform for equity and fairness to all stakeholders, primarily developing countries, to develop with changes in the digital economy. While many opportunities come with digital technologies, many developing countries struggle with engaging in the digital trade. Many developing nations have boundaries caused by the absence of applicable infrastructure, money, and legal systems in the area of utilizing digital technologies. These gaps are vital for international law to close and provide equal access to opportunities provided by the digital economy for all nations. Development of legal frameworks targeting digital inclusion is necessary to promote fairness and the ability of developing countries to gain access to digital market opportunities. For instance, initiatives like encouraging the growth and use of digital technologies in underdeveloped areas, enhancement of capabilities for internet-based commerce, online financial resources, and distance learning may be included in the strategy. It is important to change the intellectual property policies so that the developing countries are not left out and can participate in the digital technology industry. For instance, attempts to make technology transfer easier in such countries so that they could utilize digital innovations without having to pay heavy license fees would close the digital gap. Another major issue is balancing the interests of tech companies, the governments, and consumers. The emergence of digital giants such as Google, Facebook, and Amazon have triggered a wave of concern among the public about the existence of market monopolies and the accumulation of power among a few corporations. The world law should devise some ways of controlling these companies so that they do not use their strong positions to exploit smaller companies or consumers. Practical competitive legislation and anti-trust regulations must evolve to respond to the challenges that digital platforms present, engulfing the markets in their making and manipulating data for their benefit. In addition, as governments try to control the digital economy, they need to figure out how to protect consumers' rights to privacy, security, and freedom of speech. Legal frameworks need to prioritize consumer protection by addressing the "right to be forgotten" while requiring digital platforms to be transparent about how they gather and use data from consumers, thus being able to make clear choices concerning their online interactions.

8 The Future of International Law in a Digital Economy

8.1 *Trends in the World of Digital Trade and Governance*

The increasing importance of international markets of artificial intelligence (AI) and big data promotes digital trade. The impact of AI can be felt in such spheres as finance, healthcare, and retail, and with rapid development in its potential, global trade will only favor AI shortly. To give an example, the application of AI-guided automation in supply chains enables firms to achieve more informed choices and improve consumer profiling using machine learning. However, the advancement in technology also provides complex legal barriers. AI management in cross-border trade is a relatively new issue, and international laws have to change to cover the new scope of AI, especially in the labor and the rights of intellectual property. Legal standards need to be rewritten to address the unique challenges that arise from AI, including ensuring transparency of how AI makes decisions and that it engages ethically to reduce bias and bring about fair results from automated systems. The rising significance of big data will continue to dictate the world's legal frameworks in the future. Data has also become among the most valuable assets in the digital economy, and its cross-border use is key to world trade [647]. But data is also a sensitive commodity, and countries are becoming more concerned about privacy, data protection, and cybersecurity. With the rise of data-driven industries, international law will have to be able to align competing interests of data privacy, national sovereignty, and the flow of data across the world. Legal frameworks would, perhaps, gravitate toward a balancing act between the free movement of data and the need for strict guard against misuse. Digital finance is another area that international law will have to adjust to. The boom of cryptocurrencies and blockchain technology overhauls the global financial system, bringing into question the need for regulation around digital currency, cross-border payments, and financial inclusion. With the advancement of digital finance, there will be a need for more robust international standards of law to prevent fraud, guarantee the security of operations, and reach a fair distribution of digital financial services.

8.2 *The Path Toward a More Inclusive Global Digital Economy*

Though digital technologies are highly promising, they also promote a rapid increase in the digital gap between developed and developing countries. The affordability of access to digital infrastructure, education, and technology is a challenge in many developing nations, making them backward in the digital economy. To build a fairer global digital economy, international law has to deal with these disparities by providing all countries with the opportunity to access technology evenly, especially the ones that are under the Global South. Efforts aimed at bridging the digital rift should center on creating a bridge to digital technologies and bridging the digital literacy gap. This may include international collaborations aimed at providing low-cost internet availability, the assistance of digital education ventures, and the development of infrastructures that will ensure regions that need to be availed of going digital trade can be opened up for participation. Legal frameworks should also be developed with a focus on the protection of intellectual property rights to allow developing countries to innovate and preserve their digital capital in the international marketplace. Simultaneously, closing legal gaps in the digital economy will need cooperation between countries and international organizations to harmonize laws dictating digital transactions, privacy, and the sharing of data. Global treaties or conventions for digital trade may regulate rules internationally, which will ease businesses in developing nations to penetrate the world markets. Inclusive growth in the digital economy is also going to involve dealing with the problem of fair taxation, consumer protection, and regulation of digital platforms, with all countries having a voice in the making of the rules.

8.3 The Role of International Cooperation and Multilateralism

As the digital economy develops, digital trade and governance will become a key factor in the future of the whole world, and international cooperation and multilateralism will be vital in shaping this new economy. Although driven by the private sector, because their influence is global, no one country can regulate them on its own. Countries will have to work with each other in building a legal framework that will give a fair, secure, and efficient digital economy. Multilateralism would be important to tackle global problems such as data governance, cybersecurity, and intellectual property. Global organizations like the WTO, OECD, UNCTAD, and the G20 can assist countries in cooperating to ensure that global digital referees are open and available, but at the same time protecting consumers and workers. Multilateral agreements can also help harmonize digital regulations, thus alleviate trade barriers, and enhance the legal certainty of businesses. Nevertheless, challenges exist in striving for effective international cooperation. Different countries have different economic priorities, cultural norms, and degrees of development in the sphere of the digital world, they may have diverging expectations for such matters as data sovereignty, protection of privacy, and the regulation of the content offered online. To overcome such differences, there would need to be a will to dialogue, compromise, and mutual respect for each nation's regulatory framework. The participation of various global viewpoints in the formulation of digital trade law is essential for the development of a system that is fair and effective [212].

9 Conclusion

The digital economy has resulted in some shifts in international law because of its emergence. With the rise of technologies like AI, e-commerce, blockchain, and big data, international trade and commerce have been impacted fundamentally, although the legal frameworks that are affected have lagged in their adaptation. However, notable accomplishments have been made in such aspects as data privacy, cross-border digital trades, and the protection of consumer information. Through the WTO, OECD, and UN, amongst other institutions, digital taxation, cybersecurity, and protection of intellectual property rights have been effectively addressed. The key insight is that one must have a unified international legal system for effective handling of the different problems that come up in the digital marketplace. Assessment of varied laws, discrepancies in regulation, and inconsistent norms has created significant uncertainty for the entrepreneurs and consumers who are involved in online trade. International law needs to be modernized in such a way that there will be more precise and consistent rules for data sovereignty, intellectual property, and digital privacy for the sake of fair and secure electronic trade. These frameworks are essential for ensuring reliability, protecting legal rights, and maintaining inclusivity in the digital world. Strict and anticipated international rules in the public domain can incentivize innovation, help attract investments, drive an economy forward, and offer solid protection to the public. It is, therefore, pertinent that legal reforms are always reinforced to counteract the rapid changes in technology. The advancement in technology in the form of artificial intelligence, blockchain, and fintech is introducing legal issues that are not being solved by existing laws.

References

1. Boyle, A. and C. Chinkin, *The making of international law*. 2007: OUP Oxford.
2. Weeramantry, C.G., *Universalising international law*. Vol. 48. 2004: Brill.
3. Charney, J.I., *Universal international law*. American Journal of International Law, 1993. **87**(4): p. 529–551.
4. Hoekman, B.M. and P.C. Mavroidis, *World Trade Organization (WTO): law, economics, and politics*. 2015: Routledge.
5. Ramcharan, B.G., *The concept and present status of the international protection of human rights: forty years after the universal declaration*. Vol. 13. 2021: BRILL.
6. Mayer, B., *The international law on climate change*. 2018: Cambridge University Press.
7. Crawford, E. and A. Pert, *International humanitarian law*. 2024: Cambridge University Press.
8. Moens, G. and R. Jones, *International Trade & Business Law Annual Vol I*. 2013: Routledge-Cavendish.
9. Prasad, R., *Cyber borderlines: exploring the interplay between E-commerce and international trade law*. Studies in Law and Justice, 2023. **2**(4): p. 1–9.
10. Singham, S., *A general theory of trade and competition: trade liberalisation and competitive markets*. 2007: Cameron May.
11. Galyna, T., et al., *The role of international law in ensuring international security*. Lex Humana (ISSN 2175–0947), 2023. **15**(4): p. 590–608.
12. Bellamy, A.J., *UN Security Council*. The Oxford handbook of the responsibility to protect, 2016: p. 249–268.
13. Hernández, G., *The International Court of Justice and the judicial function*. 2014: OUP Oxford.
14. Sunga, L.S., *Individual responsibility in international law for serious human rights violations*. Vol. 21. 2021: BRILL.
15. Sadat, L.N., *Crimes against humanity in the modern age*. American Journal of International Law, 2013. **107**(2): p. 334–377.
16. Sands, P., *Environmental protection in the twenty-first century: sustainable development and international law*, in *The global environment*. 2023, Routledge. p. 116–137.
17. Nanda, V. and G.R. Pring, *International environmental law and policy for the 21st century*. Vol. 9. 2012: Martinus Nijhoff Publishers.
18. Tomlinson, J., *Cultural globalization*. The Blackwell companion to globalization, 2007: p. 352–366.
19. Ünay, H. and M. Çemrek, *Globalization and Humanitarian Diplomacy*. Understanding Humanitarian Diplomacy: Principles and Practice, 2024.
20. Moore, K. and D.C. Lewis, *The origins of globalization*. 2009: Routledge.
21. Liu, X., *The Silk Road in world history*. 2010: Oxford University Press.

J. Afzal, *Exploring the New Horizons of International Law Concerning Globalization of Economy*, https://doi.org/10.1007/978-981-95-1312-3

22. Millot, C. and I. Taupier-Letage, *Circulation in the Mediterranean sea.* The Mediterranean Sea, 2005: p. 29–66.
23. Gunn, G.C., *First globalization: The Eurasian exchange, 1500 to 1800.* 2003: Rowman & Littlefield.
24. Mokyr, J., *The enlightened economy: Britain and the industrial revolution, 1700–1850.* 2011: Penguin UK.
25. Mokyr, J. and J.V. Nye, *Distributional coalitions, the industrial revolution, and the origins of economic growth in Britain.* Southern Economic Journal, 2007. **74**(1): p. 50–70.
26. Birol, Ö.H., *Globalization in historical perspective.* International Journal of Business and Social Science, 2012. **3**(8).
27. Manyika, J., et al., *Digital globalization: The new era of global flows.* 2016.
28. Broadman, H.G., *From disintegration to reintegration: Eastern Europe and the former Soviet Union in international trade.* 2006: World Bank Publications.
29. Lardy, N.R., *Trade liberalization and its role in Chinese economic growth*, in *India's and China's recent experience with reform and growth.* 2005, Springer. p. 158–169.
30. Narula, R., *Globalization and technology: Interdependence, innovation systems and industrial policy.* 2014: John Wiley & Sons.
31. Mazumdar, D. and S. Sarkar, *Globalization, labour markets and inequality in India.* 2020: Routledge.
32. Osgerby, B., *Youth culture and the media: Global perspectives.* 2020: Routledge.
33. Taulbee, J.L. and G. Von Glahn, *Law among nations: an introduction to public international law.* 2022: Routledge.
34. Turner, C., *International business: Themes and issues in the modern global economy.* 2024: Routledge.
35. Howse, R., *The World Trade Organization 20 years on: global governance by judiciary.* European Journal of International Law, 2016. **27**(1): p. 9–77.
36. Puslecki, Z.W., *Non-Government Organizations and the Liberalization of Global Trade Policy Under GATT/WTO*, in *The United States and Europe: Policy Imperatives in a Globalizing World.* 2017, Routledge. p. 183–204.
37. Subedi, S.P., *International investment law: reconciling policy and principle.* 2024: Bloomsbury Publishing.
38. Salacuse, J.W., *BIT by BIT: The growth of bilateral investment treaties and their impact on foreign investment in developing countries*, in *Globalization and International Investment.* 2017, Routledge. p. 25–45.
39. Kaldor, M., *Global civil society: An answer to war*, in *The New Social Theory Reader.* 2020, Routledge. p. 252–259.
40. Shaukat, R., et al., *Exploring the Rise of Transnational Issues (such as Pandemics, Terrorism, and Climate Change) and their Impact on State Autonomy.* Review of Applied Management and Social Sciences, 2024. **7**(4): p. 777–789.
41. Heath, J.B., *The new national security challenge to the economic order.* Yale LJ, 2019. **129**: p. 1020.
42. Delbeke, J., et al., *The paris agreement*, in *Towards a climate-neutral Europe.* 2019, Routledge. p. 24–45.
43. Force, F.A.T., *Financial Action Task Force (FATF).* 2015.
44. Inkeles, A., *One world emerging? Convergence and divergence in industrial societies.* 2019: Routledge.
45. Alfredsson, G. and A. Eide, *The Universal Declaration of Human Rights: a common standard of achievement.* 2023: Martinus Nijhoff Publishers.
46. Joseph, S. and M. Castan, *The international covenant on civil and political rights: cases, materials, and commentary.* 2013: Academic.
47. Dhanjee, R. and L.B. De Chazournes, *Trade-Related Aspects of Intellectual Property Rights (TRIPs): Objectives, approaches and basic principles of the GATT and of intellectual property conventions.* Journal of World Trade, 1990. **24**(5).

48. Marcelin, I. and I. Mathur, *Financial development, institutions and banks.* International Review of Financial Analysis, 2014. **31**: p. 25–33.
49. Irwin, D.A., *The GATT in historical perspective*, in *Global Trade.* 2017, Routledge. p. 333–338.
50. Reich, A., *The effectiveness of the WTO dispute settlement system: A statistical analysis.* 2018: Springer.
51. Ilic, M. and A. Jankovic, *The Role of the International Monetary Fund in the International Monetary System.* Facta Universitatis, Series: L. & Pol., 2023. **21**: p. 57.
52. Siegel, D.E., *Legal aspects of the IMF/WTO relationship: the fund's articles of agreement and the WTO agreements.* American Journal of International Law, 2002. **96**(3): p. 561–599.
53. Kapur, D., J.P. Lewis, and R.C. Webb, *The World Bank: its first half century.* Vol. 1. 2011: Brookings Institution Press.
54. Tobin, J.L. and M.L. Busch, *A BIT is better than a lot: Bilateral investment treaties and preferential trade agreements.* World politics, 2010. **62**(1): p. 1–42.
55. Kryvoi, Y., *International centre for settlement of investment disputes (ICSID).* 2023.
56. Ueda, K., *Banking globalization and international business cycles: Cross-border chained credit contracts and financial accelerators.* Journal of international Economics, 2012. **86**(1): p. 1–16.
57. Benjamin, J., *Financial law.* 2007: Oxford University Press.
58. El-Gamal, M.A., *Islamic finance: Law, economics, and practice.* 2006: Cambridge University Press.
59. Ferran, E. and L.C. Ho, *Principles of corporate finance law.* 2014: Oxford University Press.
60. Schott, P.A., *Reference guide to anti-money laundering and combating the financing of terrorism.* 2006: World Bank Publications.
61. Krasner, S.D., *Sovereignty.* Foreign Policy, 2001: p. 20–29.
62. Peters, A., *Humanity as the A and Ω of Sovereignty.* European Journal of International Law, 2009. **20**(3): p. 513–544.
63. Read, R., *The political economy of trade protection: the determinants and welfare impact of the 2002 US emergency steel safeguard measures.* World Economy, 2005. **28**(8): p. 1119–1137.
64. Pinto, M., *International covenant on economic, social and cultural rights.* United Nations Audiovisual Library of International Law, disponível em https://legal.un.org/avl/pdf/ha/icescr/icescr_e.pdf, acesso em, 2022. **11**(01).
65. Ssenyonjo, M., *The influence of the international covenant on economic, social and cultural rights in Africa.* Netherlands International Law Review, 2017. **64**: p. 259–289.
66. MULAT, S.T. and E. Hawassa, *Advantages and drawbacks of globalization in developing countries:(systematic).* 2021.
67. Hamdi, F.M., *The impact of globalization in the developing countries.* Developing Country Studies, 2013. **3**(11): p. 142–144.
68. Barrett, S., *The theory of international environmental agreements.* Handbook of environmental economics, 2005. **3**: p. 1457–1516.
69. Seneviratne, S.I., et al., *The many possible climates from the Paris Agreement's aim of 1.5 C warming.* Nature, 2018. **558**(7708): p. 41–49.
70. Brack, D., *International trade and the Montreal Protocol.* 2017: Routledge.
71. McCormick, J., *The european superpower.* 2017: Bloomsbury Publishing.
72. Abeyratne, R., *Airbus-Boeing Subsidies Dispute-Some Preliminary Legal Issues.* Air & Space L., 2005. **30**: p. 379.
73. Brunet, A. and J.A. Lentini, *Arbitration of international oil, gas, and energy disputes in Latin America.* Nw. J. Int'l L. & Bus., 2006. **27**: p. 591.
74. Salas, C.D. and N. Costábile, *Energy Arbitration in Latin America.* The Arbitration Review of the Americas, 2020: p. 7–17.
75. Boughton, J.M., D. Lombardi, and A. Malkin, *The limits of global economic governance after the 2007–09 international financial crisis.* Global Policy, 2017. **8**: p. 30–41.
76. Erkens, D.H., M. Hung, and P. Matos, *Corporate governance in the 2007–2008 financial crisis: Evidence from financial institutions worldwide.* Journal of corporate finance, 2012. **18**(2): p. 389–411.

77. Ojo, M., *Credit risk measurement, leverage ratios and Basel III: proposed Basel III leverage and supplementary leverage ratios*. 2014.
78. Ibn-Mohammed, T., et al., *A critical analysis of the impacts of COVID-19 on the global economy and ecosystems and opportunities for circular economy strategies*. Resources, Conservation and Recycling, 2021. **164**: p. 105169.
79. Afzal, J., *Implementation of digital law as a legal tool in the current digital Era*. 2024: Springer.
80. Koch, T. and J. Windsperger, *Seeing through the network: Competitive advantage in the digital economy*. Journal of organization design, 2017. **6**: p. 1–30.
81. Fraser, M. and S. Dutta, *Throwing sheep in the boardroom: How online social networking will transform your life, work and world*. 2010: John Wiley & Sons.
82. Matyushok, V., et al., *The global economy in technological transformation conditions: A review of modern trends*. Economic Research-Ekonomska Istraživanja, 2021. **34**(1): p. 1471–1497.
83. Khan, S. and N. Haneklaus, *Sustainable economic development across globe: The dynamics between technology, digital trade and economic performance*. Technology in Society, 2023. **72**: p. 102207.
84. Singh, N. and S. Kundu, *Explaining the growth of e-commerce corporations (ECCs): An extension and application of the eclectic paradigm*. Journal of International Business Studies, 2002. **33**(4): p. 679–697.
85. Chen, M., X. Wang, and Z. Zhang, *How can the digital economy reduce carbon emissions? Empirical evidence from China*. PloS One, 2024. **19**(6): p. e0303582.
86. Graham, M., *Digital economies at global margins*. 2019: MIT Press.
87. Afzal, J., *Legal challenges regarding digital operations*, in *Implementation of Digital Law as a Legal Tool in the Current Digital Era*. 2024, Springer. p. 23–45.
88. Afzal, J., *An Overview of Digital Law*, in *Implementation of Digital Law as a Legal Tool in the Current Digital Era*, J. Afzal, Editor. 2024, Springer Nature Singapore: Singapore. p. 1–21.
89. Narlikar, A., *The World Trade Organization: a very short introduction*. Vol. 135. 2005: Oxford University Press.
90. Banalieva, E.R., G. Gregg, and R. Sarathy, *The impact of regional trade agreements on the global orientation of emerging market multinationals*. Management International Review, 2010. **50**: p. 797–826.
91. Vidigal, G. and K. Claussen, *The Sustainability Revolution in International Trade Agreements*. 2024: Oxford University Press.
92. Khan, A., *E-commerce Regulations in Emerging Era: The Role of WTO for Resolving the Complexities of Electronic Trade*. ASR Chiang Mai University Journal of Social Sciences And Humanities, 2022.
93. Chang, Y., E. Iakovou, and W. Shi, *Blockchain in global supply chains and cross border trade: a critical synthesis of the state-of-the-art, challenges and opportunities*. International Journal of Production Research, 2020. **58**(7): p. 2082–2099.
94. Ernst, D., *Global production networks and the changing geography of innovation systems. Implications for developing countries*. Economics of innovation and new technology, 2002. **11**(6): p. 497–523.
95. Hungerland, F., et al., *The digital economy*. 2015, Strategy 2030-Wealth and Life in the Next Generation.
96. Satyanand, P.N., *Foreign direct investment and the digital economy*. 2021.
97. Titievskaia, J., *United States-Mexico-Canada Agreement (USMCA): Potential Impact on EU Companies*. 2018.
98. Zahniser, S., *United States-Mexico-Canada Agreement (USMCA) Approaches the Starting Block, Offers Growth Opportunities for Agriculture*. USDA Econ. Res. Serv. Amber Waves, 2020. **2020**(1).
99. Ehlermann, C.-D. and L. Ehring, *Decision-making in the World Trade Organization: is the consensus practice of the World Trade Organization adequate for making, revising and implementing rules on international trade?* Journal of International Economic Law, 2005. **8**(1): p. 51–75.

100. Bhattacherjee, A. and A.K. Badhan, *Convergence of data analytics, big data, and machine learning: applications, challenges, and future direction*, in *Data analytics and machine learning: navigating the big data landscape*. 2024, Springer. p. 317–334.
101. Bonkra, A., P. Dhiman, and M.A. Shah, *E-Commerce Data Alchemy: Behind the Picture of Data Collection and Pre-Processing*, in *Strategic Innovations of AI and ML for E-Commerce Data Security*. 2025, IGI Global. p. 185–206.
102. Chin, Y.-C. and J. Zhao, *Governing cross-border data flows: International trade agreements and their limits*. Laws, 2022. **11**(4): p. 63.
103. Burri, M., *A WTO agreement on electronic commerce: an inquiry into its legal substance and viability*. Geo. J. Int'l L., 2021. **53**: p. 565.
104. Panagariya, A. and E. CNUCED, *E-commerce, WTO and developing countries*. 2000: UN.
105. Aydın, A. and T.K. Bensghir. *Digital data sovereignty: towards a conceptual framework*. in *2019 1st International Informatics and Software Engineering Conference (UBMYK)*. 2019. IEEE.
106. Hassan, M., *Africa and the WTO trade facilitation agreement: State of play, implementation challenges, and policy recommendations in the digital era*. Fostering Trade in Africa: Trade Relations, Business Opportunities and Policy Instruments, 2020: p. 5–38.
107. Anderson, M. and J. Mohs, *The information technology agreement: An assessment of world trade in information technology products*. J. Int'l Com. & Econ., 2011. **3**: p. 109.
108. Barrat, J., *Our final invention: Artificial intelligence and the end of the human era*. 2023: Hachette UK.
109. Dneprovskaya, N., A. Urintsov, and M. Afanasev. *Study of the innovative environment of the digital economy*. in *Proceedings of the 15th International Conference on Intellectual Capital, Knowledge Management & Organisational Learning–ICICKM*. 2018.
110. Wang, Y., et al., *Supply chain-based business model innovation: the case of a cross-border E-commerce company*. Sustainability, 2018. **10**(12): p. 4362.
111. Wu, X. and G. Gereffi, *Amazon and Alibaba: Internet governance, business models, and internationalization strategies*, in *International business in the information and digital age*. 2018, Emerald Publishing Limited. p. 327–356.
112. O'Sullivan, C., N. Wise, and P.-P. Mathieu, *The changing landscape of geospatial information markets*. Earth Observation Open Science and Innovation, 2018: p. 3–23.
113. Vermesan, O. and P. Friess, *Digitising the industry Internet of Things connecting the physical, digital and VirtualWorlds*. 2022: CRC Press.
114. Bechara, F.R. and S.B. Schuch, *Cybersecurity and global regulatory challenges*. Journal of Financial Crime, 2021. **28**(2): p. 359–374.
115. Raustiala, K., *Rethinking the sovereignty debate in international economic law*. Journal of International Economic Law, 2003. **6**(4): p. 841–878.
116. Froese, M.D., *Digital trade and dispute settlement in RTAs: An evolving standard?* Journal of World Trade, 2019. **53**(5).
117. Abdelrehim Hammad, A.A., A. Khan, and N.-E. Soomro, *Digital Economy Barriers to Trade Regulation Status, Challenges, and China's Response*. International Journal of Social Sciences Perspectives, 2021. **8**(2): p. 41–49.
118. Glick, L.A., *The United States-Mexico-Canada Agreement (USMCA): Legal and Business Implications*. 2020: Kluwer Law International BV.
119. Słok-Wódkowska, M. and J. Mazur, *Between commodification and data protection: Regulatory models governing cross-border information transfers in regional trade agreements*. Leiden Journal of International Law, 2024. **37**(1): p. 111–138.
120. Anderson, R.D., et al., *Competition policy, trade and the global economy: existing WTO elements, commitments in regional trade agreements, current challenges and issues for reflection*. 2018.
121. Apriliyanti, I.D., et al., *Digital divide in ASEAN member states: analyzing the critical factors for successful e-government programs*. Online Information Review, 2021. **45**(2): p. 440–460.
122. Priharsari, D., et al., *National digital strategy development: Guidelines and lesson learnt from Asia Pacific countries*. Technological Forecasting and Social Change, 2023. **196**: p. 122855.

123. Hoofnagle, C.J., B. Van Der Sloot, and F.Z. Borgesius, *The European Union general data protection regulation: what it is and what it means.* Information & Communications Technology Law, 2019. **28**(1): p. 65–98.
124. Azmeh, S., C. Foster, and J. Echavarri, *The international trade regime and the quest for free digital trade.* International Studies Review, 2020. **22**(3): p. 671–692.
125. Marchetti, J.A. and P.C. Mavroidis, *The genesis of the GATS (General Agreement on Trade in Services).* European Journal of International Law, 2011. **22**(3): p. 689–721.
126. Mavroidis, P.C., *The regulation of international trade, volume 3: The general agreement on trade in services.* 2020: MIT Press.
127. Larionova, M. and A. Shelepov, *Emerging regulation for the digital economy: challenges and opportunities for multilateral global governance.* International Organisations Research Journal, 2021. **16**(1): p. 29–63.
128. Mitchell, A.D. and N. Mishra, *Data at the docks: modernizing international trade law for the digital economy.* Vand. J. Ent. & Tech. L., 2017. **20**: p. 1073.
129. Willemyns, I., *GATS classification of digital services–does 'The Cloud'have a silver lining?* Journal of World Trade, 2019. **53**(1).
130. Ismail, Y., *E-commerce in the World Trade Organization.* International Institute for Systainaable Development and CUTS International, 2020: p. 1–2.
131. Montes, C.G.E., *How Far Beyond the TFA? Trade Facilitation in the WTO and the TPP.* The Comprehensive and Progressive Trans-Pacific Partnership: The Trans-Pacific Partnership, the Comprehensive and Progressive TPP, their Roots in NAFTA and Beyond, 2021: p. 214.
132. Ciuriak, D., *World Trade Organization 2.0: Reforming multilateral trade rules for the digital age.* 2019.
133. Correa, C.M., *Trade related aspects of intellectual property rights: a commentary on the TRIPS agreement.* 2020: Oxford University Press.
134. Wirjo, A., et al., *Assessment of capacity building needs to support WTO negotiation on trade related aspects of e-commerce*, in *Assessment of capacity building needs to support WTO negotiation on trade related aspects of e-commerce.* 2020, Singapore: Asia-Pacific Economic Cooperation Secretariat.
135. Burri, M. and R. Polanco, *Digital trade provisions in preferential trade agreements: introducing a new dataset.* Journal of international economic law, 2020. **23**(1): p. 187–220.
136. Burri, M., *Towards a new treaty on digital trade.* Journal of World Trade, 2021. **55**(1).
137. Heidebrecht, S., *From market liberalism to public intervention: Digital sovereignty and changing European union digital single market governance.* JCMS: Journal of Common Market Studies, 2024. **62**(1): p. 205–223.
138. Schmidt, C. and R. Krimmer, *How to implement the European digital single market: identifying the catalyst for digital transformation.* Journal of European Integration, 2022. **44**(1): p. 59–80.
139. Wu, T. and D. Chadee, *Comprehensive and Progressive Agreement for Trans-Pacific Partnership (CPTPP): Implications for the Asia-Pacific Region.* International Business in the New Asia-Pacific: Strategies, Opportunities and Threats, 2022: p. 53–74.
140. Bobowski, S., I. Cvecic, and P. Dobrzanski. *The Comprehensive and Progressive Agreement for Trans-Pacific Partnership (CPTPP)–Genesis and Challenges of The Trans-Pacific Mega-Regionalism in Trade.* in *37th International Business Information Management Association Conference (IBIMA).* 2021.
141. Gao, H., *Digital or trade? The contrasting approaches of China and US to digital trade.* Journal of International Economic Law, 2018. **21**(2): p. 297–321.
142. Andrews, D.M., *Orderly change: international monetary relations since Bretton Woods.* 2011: Cornell University Press.
143. Gardner, R.N., *The Bretton Woods-GATT System after Fifty Years: A Balance Sheet of Success and Failure*, in *The Bretton Woods-GATT System.* 2015, Routledge. p. 181–209.
144. Güven, A.B., *Defending supremacy: how the IMF and the World Bank navigate the challenge of rising powers.* International Affairs, 2017. **93**(5): p. 1149–1166.

145. Yusuf, S., *Development economics through the decades: A critical look at thirty years of the world development report*. 2008: World Bank Publications.
146. Toniolo, G. and P. Clement, *Central bank cooperation at the Bank for International Settlements, 1930–1973*. 2005: Cambridge University Press.
147. McKenzie, F., *GATT and global order in the postwar era*. 2020: Cambridge University Press.
148. Shukla, S.P., *From GATT to WTO and Beyond*. 2000.
149. Varella, M.D., *The effectiveness of the dispute settlement body of the World Trade Organization*. Journal of International Trade Law and Policy, 2009. **8**(2): p. 100–113.
150. Appleton, A.E. and M.G. Plummer, *The World Trade Organization: legal, economic and political analysis*. 2007: Springer Science & Business Media.
151. Sauvant, K.P., *Appeals mechanism in international investment disputes*. 2008: Oxford University Press.
152. Yannaca-Small, K., *Arbitration under international investment agreements: A guide to the key issues*. 2010: Oxford University Press.
153. Lavdari, F. and X. Lavdari, *Effects of Investor-State Dispute Settlements (ISDS) on Foreign Direct Investment (FDI) Flows*. Policy Perspectives, 2024. **21**(2).
154. Van der Zee, E., *Incorporating the OECD guidelines in international investment agreements: Turning a soft law obligation into hard law?* Legal Issues of Economic Integration, 2013. **40**(1).
155. Rasche, A. and G. Kell, *The United Nations global compact: Achievements, trends and challenges*. 2010.
156. Büthe, T. and H.V. Milner, *Foreign direct investment and institutional diversity in trade agreements: Credibility, commitment, and economic flows in the developing world, 1971–2007*. World Politics, 2014. **66**(1): p. 88–122.
157. Nyekwere, E.H., I. Okogbule, and D.O. Agwor, *Understanding the principles of international environmental law and their reflections in international environmental treaties and non-binding soft law instruments*. JL Pol'y & Globalization, 2022. **123**: p. 73.
158. Koul, A.K., *Guide to the WTO and GATT*. 2005: Springer.
159. Ferdowsi, M.A., *UNCTAD–United Nations conference on trade and development*, in *A Concise Encyclopedia of the United Nations*. 2010, Brill Nijhoff. p. 698–705.
160. Budiana, M., *International Trade Agreement Politics: A Comparative Analysis*. Journal of Law, Social Science and Humanities, 2024. **2**(1): p. 140–152.
161. Thirawat, J., *E-Commerce in ASEAN: An emerging economic superpower and the case for harmonizing consumer protection laws*. South Carolina Journal of International Law and Business, 2022. **18**(2): p. 6.
162. Abbott, R., F. Erixon, and M.F. Ferracane, *Demystifying investor-state dispute settlement (ISDS)*. 2014.
163. Ruggie, J.G. and T. Nelson, *Human rights and the OECD guidelines for multinational enterprises: Normative innovations and implementation challenges*. The Brown Journal of World Affairs, 2015. **22**(1): p. 99–127.
164. Dietrich, A., K. Hess, and G. Wanzenried, *The good and bad news about the new liquidity rules of Basel III in Western European countries*. Journal of Banking & Finance, 2014. **44**: p. 13–25.
165. Bueno, N., et al., *Guiding principles on business and human rights*. 2022.
166. Howse, R., A. Eliason, and M. Trebilcock, *The regulation of international trade*. 2005: Routledge.
167. Shafaeddin, M.S., *Trade liberalization and economic reform in developing countries: structural change or de-industrialization?*, in *The IMF, World Bank and policy reform*. 2012, Routledge. p. 155–182.
168. Rodrik, D., *What do trade agreements really do?* Journal of economic perspectives, 2018. **32**(2): p. 73–90.
169. Hu, J., *The role of international law in the development of WTO law*. Journal of International Economic Law, 2004. **7**(1): p. 143–167.

170. Ojha, S. *The Rise of Exceptions and the Eclipse of the Elemental Principle of Most-Favoured-Nation.* in *Proceedings of the 18th International RAIS Conference on Social Sciences and Humanities.* 2020. Scientia Moralitas Research Institute.
171. Elliott, K.A., *The WTO and regional/bilateral trade agreements*, in *Handbook of International Trade Agreements.* 2018, Routledge. p. 17–28.
172. Trebilcock, M. and M. Fishbein, *International trade: barriers to trade*, in *Research Handbook in International Economic Law.* 2007, Edward Elgar Publishing.
173. Fefer, R.F. and V.C. Jones, *WTO Trade Facilitation Agreement.* 2017: Congressional Research Service.
174. Duval, Y. and C. Utoktham, *Has the WTO trade facilitation agreement helped reduce trade costs?: an ex-post analysis.* 2022.
175. Ingre-Khans, E., et al., *Toxicity studies used in registration, evaluation, authorisation and restriction of chemicals (REACH): How accurately are they reported?* Integrated environmental assessment and management, 2019. **15**(3): p. 458–469.
176. Bieron, B. and U. Ahmed, *Regulating e-commerce through international policy: Understanding the international trade law issues of e-commerce.* Journal of World Trade, 2012. **46**(3).
177. Pavlova, K. and E. Smolina. *Digitalization of tax and customs control of foreign trade operations.* in *Economic systems in the new era: Stable systems in an unstable world.* 2021. Springer.
178. Koenig-Archibugi, M., *Transnational corporations and public accountability.* Government and Opposition, 2004. **39**(2): p. 234–259.
179. Ngwakwe, C.C., *Niger delta oil spill case against the shell company at the Hague: the future of corporate environmental responsibility.* Acta Universitatis Danubius. Juridica, 2021. **17**(2): p. 27–39.
180. Kobrin, S.J., *Private political authority and public responsibility: Transnational politics, transnational firms, and human rights.* Business Ethics Quarterly, 2009. **19**(3): p. 349–374.
181. Fussler, C., A. Cramer, and S. Van der Vegt, *Raising the bar: Creating value with the UN Global Compact.* 2017: Routledge.
182. Bocanegra Soto, F.C., *The impact of Corruption on the withdrawal of companies from the United Nations Global Compact: A Cross-Continental Analysis.* 2024, University of South-Eastern Norway.
183. Luo, Y., *Market-seeking MNEs in an emerging market: How parent–subsidiary links shape overseas success.* Journal of international business studies, 2003. **34**(3): p. 290–309.
184. Mussa, M., *Factors driving global economic integration.* Global economic integration: Opportunities and challenges, 2000: p. 9–55.
185. Bello, W., N. Bullard, and K. Malhotra, *Global finance: New thinking on regulating speculative capital markets.* 2000: Zed Books.
186. Le, C.H.A., *Cross-border financial linkages and international financial contagion: an empirical study of East Asia during the 2007–2011 global financial crisis.* 2013, University of Birmingham.
187. Dorrucci, E. and J. McKay, *The international monetary system after the financial crisis.* ECB Occasional paper, 2010(123).
188. Kendrick, M., *The Legal (Im) possibilities of the EU Implementing the OECD/G20 Inclusive Framework on Base Erosion and Profit Shifting.* Global Trade and Customs Journal, 2022. **17**(1).
189. Nanyun, N.M. and A. Nasiri, *Role of FATF on financial systems of countries: successes and challenges.* Journal of Money Laundering Control, 2021. **24**(2): p. 234–245.
190. Bearpark, N.T., *Deconstructing Money Laundering Risk.* CSR, Sustainability, Ethics & Governance, 2022.
191. Brown, R.P. and T.J. Bulman, *The Clubs: Their Roles in the Management of International Debt.* International Economics, Finance and Trade-Volume I, 2009: p. 272.
192. Wood, P., *Choice of governing law for bonds.* Capital Markets Law Journal, 2020. **15**(1): p. 3–17.

193. White, L.J., *The credit-rating agencies and the subprime debacle.* Critical Review, 2009. **21**(2–3): p. 389–399.
194. Jacklin, N.P., *Addressing collective-action problems in securitized credit.* Law & Contemp. Probs., 2010. **73**: p. 175.
195. Yadav, Y., *Dismantling Bondholder Rights.* Vanderbilt Law Research Paper, 2019(19–37).
196. Shipalana, P. and A. O'Riordan, *Impact of Covid-19 on financial stability in Africa.* 2022: JSTOR.
197. Elkhishin, S. and M. Mohieldin, *External debt vulnerability in emerging markets and developing economies during the COVID-19 shock.* Review of Economics and Political Science, 2021. **6**(1): p. 24–47.
198. Schaeffer, R.K., *Understanding globalization: The social consequences of political, economic, and environmental change.* 2003: Rowman & Littlefield.
199. Plasa, W., *Reconciling international trade and labor protection: why we need to bridge the gap between ILO standards and WTO rules.* 2015: Lexington books.
200. Maji, S.G. and P. Lohia, *Environmental, social and governance (ESG) performance and firm performance in India.* Society and Business Review, 2023. **18**(1): p. 175–194.
201. Chandra, A. and A. Idrisova, *Convention on Biological Diversity: a review of national challenges and opportunities for implementation.* Biodiversity and Conservation, 2011. **20**: p. 3295–3316.
202. Bermann, S., *EC-hormones and the case for an express WTO postretaliation procedure.* Colum. L. Rev., 2007. **107**: p. 131.
203. Mitchell, A.D., A. Taubman, and T. Samlidis, *Intellectual Property and Vaccine Manufacturing: Utilizing Existing TRIPS Agreement Flexibilities for COVID-19 and Other Public Health Crises.* Tul. J. Tech. & Intell. Prop., 2023. **25**: p. 1.
204. Ahmad, I., A. Haider, and J. Afzal, *The Geopolitical and Economic Impact of BRICS on the Middle East.* FWU Journal of Social Sciences, 2024. **18**(4): p. 80–95.
205. Mazenda, A. and R. Ncwadi, *The rise of BRICS development finance institutions: A comprehensive look into the New Development Bank and the Contingency Reserve Arrangement.* African East-Asian Affairs, 2016(3).
206. Xu, Z., et al., *China-Pakistan Cultural Exchanges and Cooperation under Belt & Road Initiative.* Siazga Research Journal, 2023. **2**(3): p. 186–191.
207. Huo, Z. and M. Yip, *Comparing the international commercial courts of China with the Singapore international commercial court.* International & Comparative Law Quarterly, 2019. **68**(4): p. 903–942.
208. Afzal, J., *Implementation of Digital Law as a Legal Tool in the Current Digital Era.* Springer.
209. Howell, K.B., *Prosecutorial discretion and the duty to seek justice in an overburdened criminal justice system.* Geo. J. Legal Ethics, 2014. **27**: p. 285.
210. Afzal, J., *Execution of Bilateral Digital Law*, in *Implementation of Digital Law as a Legal Tool in the Current Digital Era.* 2024, Springer. p. 79–93.
211. Karake-Shalhoub, Z. and L. Al Qasimi, *Cyber law and cyber security in developing and emerging economies.* 2010: Edward Elgar Publishing.
212. Afzal, J., *Development of Legal Framework of Digital Laws*, in *Implementation of Digital Law as a Legal Tool in the Current Digital Era.* 2024, Springer. p. 139–154.
213. Afzal, J., et al., *Review of Various Aspects of Digital Violence.* Journal of Engineering, Science and Technological Trends, 2024. **1**(2): p. 76–86.
214. Ajayi, E.F.G., *Challenges to enforcement of cyber-crimes laws and policy.* Journal of Internet and Information Systems, 2016. **6**(1): p. 1–12.
215. Brown, C.S., *Investigating and prosecuting cyber crime: Forensic dependencies and barriers to justice.* International Journal of Cyber Criminology, 2015. **9**(1): p. 55.
216. Afzal, J., *Digital Evidence and Permissibility in Court of Law*, in *Implementation of Digital Law as a Legal Tool in the Current Digital Era.* 2024, Springer. p. 121–137.
217. Cole, D. and J.X. Dempsey, *Terrorism and the constitution: Sacrificing civil liberties in the name of national security.* 2006: The New Press.

218. Afzal, J., *Future of Legal Tools and Justice*, in *Implementation of Digital Law as a Legal Tool in the Current Digital Era*. 2024, Springer. p. 155–177.
219. NJOROGE, E.W., *Effect of Cyber Crime Related Costs On Development of Financial Innovation Products and Services*. 2018, JKUAT-COHRED.
220. Lenong, J., *State Cybersecurity Governance in the Fourth Industrial Revolution: An International Law Perspective*. The Disruptive Fourth Industrial Revolution: Technology, Society and Beyond, 2020: p. 69–93.
221. Menon, S. and T. Guan Siew, *Key challenges in tackling economic and cyber crimes: Creating a multilateral platform for international co-operation*. Journal of Money Laundering Control, 2012. **15**(3): p. 243–256.
222. Mphatheni, M.R. and W. Maluleke, *Cybersecurity as a response to combating cybercrime: Demystifying the prevailing threats and offering recommendations to the African regions*. International Journal of Research in Business and Social Science (2147–4478), 2022. **11**(4): p. 384–396.
223. Mugarura, N. and E. Ssali, *Intricacies of anti-money laundering and cyber-crimes regulation in a fluid global system*. Journal of Money Laundering Control, 2021. **24**(1): p. 10–28.
224. Franjić, S., *Cybercrime is very dangerous form of criminal behavior and cybersecurity*. Emerging Science Journal, 2020. **4**(18): p. 18–26.
225. Afzal, J., *Best Practice of Digital Laws and Digital Justice*, in *Implementation of Digital Law as a Legal Tool in the Current Digital Era*. 2024, Springer. p. 95–120.
226. Yongmei, C. and J. Afzal, *Impact of enactment of 'the prevention of electronic crimes act, 2016'as legal support in Pakistan*. Academy of Education and Social Sciences Review, 2023. **3**(2): p. 203–212.
227. Farsaris, A.E., *Jurisdiction Over the Realms Unlocked by Technology: Outer Space and Cyberspace*. Outer Space and Cyber Space: Similarities, Interrelations and Legal Perspectives, 2021: p. 1–13.
228. Wall, D., *Insecurity and the policing of cyberspace*, in *Crime and insecurity*. 2013, Willan. p. 198–222.
229. Ulsch, M., *Cyber threat!: how to manage the growing risk of cyber attacks*. 2014: Wiley Online Library.
230. Tarrad, K.M., et al., *Cybercrime challenges in Iraqi Academia: creating digital awareness for preventing cybercrimes*. International Journal of Cyber Criminology, 2022. **16**(2): p. 15–31.
231. Bendiek, A., *European cyber security policy*. 2012, SWP Research Paper.
232. Saini, H., Y.S. Rao, and T.C. Panda, *Cyber-crimes and their impacts: A review*. International Journal of Engineering Research and Applications, 2012. **2**(2): p. 202–209.
233. Finnie, T., T. Petee, and J. Jarvis, *Future challenges of cybercrime*. Proceedings of the Futures Working Group, 2010. **5**.
234. Manulis, M., et al., *Cyber security in new space: analysis of threats, key enabling technologies and challenges*. International Journal of Information Security, 2021. **20**: p. 287–311.
235. Andress, J. and S. Winterfeld, *Cyber warfare: techniques, tactics and tools for security practitioners*. 2013: Elsevier.
236. Broadhurst, R., *Developments in the global law enforcement of cyber-crime*. Policing: An International Journal of Police Strategies & Management, 2006. **29**(3): p. 408–433.
237. Zaid, T. and S. Garai, *Emerging Trends in Cybersecurity: A Holistic View on Current Threats, Assessing Solutions, and Pioneering New Frontiers*. Blockchain in Healthcare Today, 2024. **7**.
238. Olukoya, O., *Assessing frameworks for eliciting privacy & security requirements from laws and regulations*. Computers & Security, 2022. **117**: p. 102697.
239. Hagemann, R., J. Huddleston Skees, and A. Thierer, *Soft law for hard problems: The governance of emerging technologies in an uncertain future*. Colo. Tech. LJ, 2018. **17**: p. 37.
240. Henriksen, A., *The end of the road for the UN GGE process: The future regulation of cyberspace*. Journal of Cybersecurity, 2019. **5**(1): p. tyy009.
241. Carr, J., *Inside cyber warfare: Mapping the cyber underworld*. 2012: "O'Reilly Media, Inc.".

242. Tsakalidis, G. and K. Vergidis, *A systematic approach toward description and classification of cybercrime incidents.* IEEE Transactions on Systems, Man, and Cybernetics: Systems, 2017. **49**(4): p. 710–729.
243. Viano, E.C., *Cybercrime: Definition, typology, and criminalization.* Cybercrime, Organized Crime, and Societal Responses: International Approaches, 2017: p. 3–22.
244. McGinnis, J.O. and R.G. Pearce, *The great disruption: How machine intelligence will transform the role of lawyers in the delivery of legal services.* Fordham L. Rev., 2013. **82**: p. 3041.
245. Liska, A. and T. Gallo, *Ransomware: Defending against digital extortion.* 2016: "O'Reilly Media, Inc.".
246. Phillips, K., et al., *Conceptualizing cybercrime: Definitions, typologies and taxonomies.* Forensic sciences, 2022. **2**(2): p. 379–398.
247. Ramírez, J.M. and J. Biziewski, *Security and defence in Europe.* 2020: Springer.
248. Ziegeldorf, J.H., O.G. Morchon, and K. Wehrle, *Privacy in the Internet of Things: threats and challenges.* Security and Communication Networks, 2014. **7**(12): p. 2728–2742.
249. Benvenisti, E., *Upholding democracy amid the challenges of new technology: what role for the law of global governance?* European Journal of International Law, 2018. **29**(1): p. 9–82.
250. Bagley, C.E., *What's Law Got to Do with It: Integrating Law and Strategy.* Am. Bus. LJ, 2010. **47**: p. 587.
251. Holt, T.J., *The human factor of cybercrime.* 2019: Routledge.
252. Wall, D.S., *Cybercrime: The transformation of crime in the information age.* 2024: John Wiley & Sons.
253. Shinder, D.L. and M. Cross, *Scene of the Cybercrime.* 2008: Elsevier.
254. Chimni, B., *The international law of jurisdiction: A TWAIL perspective.* Leiden Journal of International Law, 2022. **35**(1): p. 29–54.
255. Shaffer, G., *Transnational legal process and state change.* Law & Social Inquiry, 2012. **37**(2): p. 229–264.
256. Bernstein, S. and E. Hannah, *Non-state global standard setting and the WTO: legitimacy and the need for regulatory space.* Journal of International Economic Law, 2008. **11**(3): p. 575–608.
257. Bonucci, N., *The Organisation for Economic Co-operation and Development (OECD) and its General Counsel: An evolving role in an evolving organization*, in *Legal Advisers in International Organizations.* 2023, Edward Elgar Publishing. p. 315–336.
258. Guild, E. and R. Weiland, *The UN global compact for safe, orderly and regular migration: what does it mean in international law?* Global Community: Yearbook of International Law and Jurisprudence, 2020.
259. Blank, Y., *Localism in the new global legal order.* Harv. Int'l LJ, 2006. **47**: p. 263.
260. Li, X., *Regulation of cyber space: An analysis of Chinese law on cyber crime.* International Journal of Cyber Criminology, 2015. **9**(2): p. 185.
261. Tropina, T., *Cybercrime: Setting international standards*, in *Routledge Handbook of International Cybersecurity.* 2020, Routledge. p. 148–160.
262. Kobia, R., *International Inter-Agency Coordination of State and Non-State Actors in Combating Global Cyber threat: Case Study of Kenya and Zambia.* 2021, University of Nairobi.
263. Alshamrani, A., et al., *A survey on advanced persistent threats: Techniques, solutions, challenges, and research opportunities.* IEEE Communications Surveys & Tutorials, 2019. **21**(2): p. 1851–1877.
264. Sonko, S., et al., *Quantum cryptography and US digital security: a comprehensive review: investigating the potential of quantum technologies in creating unbreakable encryption and their future in national security.* Computer Science & IT Research Journal, 2024. **5**(2): p. 390–414.
265. Gambín, Á.F., et al., *Deepfakes: current and future trends.* Artificial Intelligence Review, 2024. **57**(3): p. 64.

266. Buchanan, B., *The cybersecurity dilemma: Hacking, trust, and fear between nations.* 2016: Oxford University Press.
267. Kshetri, N., *The global cybercrime industry: economic, institutional and strategic perspectives.* 2010: Springer Science & Business Media.
268. Shukurov, E. and U.U. Jafarov, *Legal Professionals' Perspectives on the Challenges of Cybercrime Legislation Enforcement.* Interdisciplinary Studies in Society, Law, and Politics, 2023. **2**(4): p. 25–31.
269. AllahRakha, N., *Global perspectives on cybercrime legislation.* Journal of Infrastructure, Policy and Development, 2024. **8**(10): p. 6007.
270. Tikk, E. and M. Kerttunen, *Routledge handbook of international cybersecurity.* 2020: Routledge London.
271. Sumadinata, W.S., *Cybercrime And Global Security Threats: A Challenge In International Law.* Russian Law Journal, 2023. **11**(3): p. 438–444.
272. Singh, T., *Cybercrime And International Law: Jurisdictional Challenges And Enforcement Mechanisms.* African Journal of Biomedical Research, 2024. **27**(3S): p. 697–708.
273. Balarabe, K., *Digital Borders and Beyond: Establishing Normative Grounds for Cybersecurity and Sovereignty in International Law.* Available at SSRN 4876617.
274. Casino, F., et al., *SoK: Cross-border criminal investigations and digital evidence.* Journal of Cybersecurity, 2022. **8**(1): p. tyac014.
275. Williams, L.D., *Concepts of Digital Economy and Industry 4.0 in Intelligent and information systems.* International Journal of Intelligent Networks, 2021. **2**: p. 122–129.
276. Kovalchyk, O. and I. Kovalchyk, *Analysis of the main global trends for e-commerce.* Електронне наукове фахове видання" Соціально-економічні проблеми і держава", 2021(2 (25)): p. 541–549.
277. Denysenko, Y., *Development trends of the global e-commerce market.* 2021.
278. Faccini, M., *Digital innovation and Cross-border e-commerce in China.* 2018, Politecnico di Torino.
279. Stalmachova, K., R. Chinoracky, and M. Strenitzerova, *Changes in business models caused by digital transformation and the COVID-19 pandemic and possibilities of their measurement—case study.* Sustainability, 2021. **14**(1): p. 127.
280. Xue, N., *Research on Issues and Strategies of International Trade Law under the Background of the Rapid Development of Cross-Border E-Commerce.* Science of Law Journal, 2024. **3**(8): p. 32–41.
281. Filippov, V.M., et al., *The Cyber Economy.* 2019: Springer.
282. Afzal, J., *Digital Law Enforcement Challenges and Improvement*, in *Implementation of Digital Law as a Legal Tool in the Current Digital Era*, J. Afzal, Editor. 2024, Springer Nature Singapore: Singapore. p. 47–78.
283. Wirtz, B.W., *Digital business models.* 2019: Springer.
284. Schmuck, R., *The use of online business models.* Procedia Manufacturing, 2021. **54**: p. 45–51.
285. Sakız, B. and A.H. Gencer. *Blockchain technology and its impact on the global economy.* in *International Conference on Eurasian Economies.* 2019.
286. Ertz, M. and É. Boily, *The rise of the digital economy: Thoughts on blockchain technology and cryptocurrencies for the collaborative economy.* International Journal of Innovation Studies, 2019. **3**(4): p. 84–93.
287. Tredinnick, L., *Cryptocurrencies and the blockchain.* Business Information Review, 2019. **36**(1): p. 39–44.
288. Yuan, Y. and F.-Y. Wang, *Blockchain and cryptocurrencies: Model, techniques, and applications.* IEEE Transactions on Systems, Man, and Cybernetics: Systems, 2018. **48**(9): p. 1421–1428.
289. Hashemi Joo, M., Y. Nishikawa, and K. Dandapani, *Cryptocurrency, a successful application of blockchain technology.* Managerial Finance, 2020. **46**(6): p. 715–733.
290. Viriyasitavat, W. and D. Hoonsopon, *Blockchain characteristics and consensus in modern business processes.* Journal of Industrial Information Integration, 2019. **13**: p. 32–39.

291. Milosevic, D., D. Ilic, and J. Popovic, *Trends analysis in Gig economy.* Journal of Economic Development, Environment and People, 2021. **10**(3): p. 50.
292. Ticona, J., *Left to our own devices: Coping with insecure work in a digital age.* 2022: Oxford University Press.
293. Bolatbekkyzy, G., *Legal Issues of Cross-Border Data Transfer in the Era of Digital Government.* Journal of Digital Technologies and Law, 2024. **2**(2): p. 286–307.
294. Palmieri III, N.F., *Who should regulate data: An analysis of the california consumer privacy act and its effects on nationwide data protection laws.* Hastings Sci. & Tech. LJ, 2020. **11**: p. 37.
295. Afzal, J., et al., *Review of Various Aspects of Digital Violence.* Journal of Engineering, Science and Technological Trends, 2024. **1**(2).
296. Maskus, K.E., *Private rights and public problems: The global economics of intellectual property in the 21st century.* 2012: Peterson Institute.
297. Schroeder, D. and J.C. Lucas, *Benefit sharing.* Encyclopedia of applied ethics, 2014: p. 237–245.
298. Cottier, T., *The agreement on trade-related aspects of intellectual property rights*, in *The World Trade Organization: legal, economic and political analysis.* 2005, Springer. p. 1041–1120.
299. Kuhlmann, K., *Handbook on provisions and options for trade in times of crisis and pandemic.* 2021.
300. Woodward, R., *The organisation for economic co-operation and development (OECD).* 2009: Routledge.
301. Kim, Y.R. *Digital Services Tax.* in *Proceedings. Annual Conference on Taxation and Minutes of the Annual Meeting of the National Tax Association.* 2019. JSTOR.
302. DeNardis, L., *The global war for internet governance.* 2014: Yale University Press.
303. Yakovleva, S., *Should Fundamental Rights to Privacy and Data Protection be a Part of the EU's International Trade 'Deals'?* World Trade Review, 2018. **17**(3): p. 477–508.
304. Cumming, D.J., S. Johan, and A. Pant, *Regulation of the crypto-economy: Managing risks, challenges, and regulatory uncertainty.* Journal of Risk and Financial Management, 2019. **12**(3): p. 126.
305. Xie, R., *Why China had to ban cryptocurrency but the US did not: A comparative analysis of regulations on crypto-markets between the US and China.* Wash. U. Global Stud. L. Rev., 2019. **18**: p. 457.
306. Lindsay, M.G., *International Rise of Cryptocurrency: A Comparative Review of the United States, Mexico, Singapore, and Switzerland's Anti-Money Laundering (AML) Regulation.* SCJ Int'l L. & Bus., 2022. **19**: p. 161.
307. Ahmad, J., A. Haider, and A. khalid, *Firewall Technology Testing in Pakistan: The Fine Line Between National Security and Freedom of Expression.* Journal of Engineering, Science and Technological Trends, 2025. **2**(1).
308. Cramer, B.W., *Entity of the State: The Transparency of Restricting Telecommunications Firms as Threats to America's National Security.* Notre Dame J. on Emerging Tech., 2023. **4**: p. 56.
309. Trautman, L.J., *Bitcoin, virtual currencies, and the struggle of law and regulation to keep peace.* Marq. L. Rev., 2018. **102**: p. 447.
310. Abbas Khan, M., et al., *Impact of artificial intelligence on the global economy and technology advancements*, in *Artificial General Intelligence (AGI) Security: Smart Applications and Sustainable Technologies.* 2024, Springer. p. 147–180.
311. Cihon, P., *Standards for AI governance: international standards to enable global coordination in AI research & development.* Future of Humanity Institute. University of Oxford, 2019. **40**(3): p. 340–342.
312. Avila Pinto, R., *Digital sovereignty or digital colonialsim.* SUR-Int'l J. on Hum Rts., 2018. **15**: p. 15.
313. Meltzer, J.P., *Governing digital trade.* World Trade Review, 2019. **18**(S1): p. S23-S48.
314. Posner, E.A. and A.O. Sykes, *Economic foundations of international law.* 2012: Harvard University Press.

315. Epstein, R.A. and R.A. Epstein, *Simple rules for a complex world*. 2009: Harvard University Press.
316. Barbieri, K., *Geopolitics and international trade*, in *The Palgrave Handbook of Contemporary Geopolitics*. 2024, Springer. p. 957–979.
317. Park, J., J. Sarkis, and Z. Wu, *Creating integrated business and environmental value within the context of China's circular economy and ecological modernization*. Journal of Cleaner Production, 2010. **18**(15): p. 1494–1501.
318. Solodan, K., *Legal regulation of cryptocurrency taxation in European countries*. European Journal of Law and Public Administration, 2019. **6**(1): p. 64–74.
319. Goldman, M., *Imperial nature: The World Bank and struggles for social justice in the age of globalization*. 2005: Yale University Press.
320. Rofe, J.S., *Global perspectives on the Bretton Woods conference and the post-war world order*. 2017: Springer.
321. Lekkas, S.-I. and A. Tzanakopoulos, *Pacta sunt servanda versus Flexibility in the Suspension and Termination of Treaties*, in *Research Handbook on the Law of Treaties*. 2014, Edward Elgar Publishing. p. 312–340.
322. Mantese, C., *The Most-Favored-Nation Treatment Standard*. Trento Student Law Review, 2024. **6**(1): p. 125–163.
323. Hoekman, B.M. and M.M. Kostecki, *The political economy of the world trading system: the WTO and beyond*. 2009: Oxford University Press.
324. Yeoh, P., *Causes of the global financial crisis: Learning from the competing insights*. International journal of disclosure and governance, 2010. **7**(1): p. 42–69.
325. Cerruti, C. and A. Valeri, *AI-Powered Platforms: automated transactions in digital marketplaces*. PhD diss., Dissertation, Master of Science in Business Administration, Università degli Studi di Roma" Tor Vergata" Department of Management and Law, 2022.
326. Allali, F. and Z. Allali, *The impact of the COVID-19 pandemic on the development of e-commerce in word*. World, 2020. **1**.
327. Yang, Y., *Digital Economy and the Sustainable Development of ASEAN and China*. Vol. 9. 2022: World Scientific.
328. Avi-Yonah, R., Y.R. Kim, and K. Sam, *A new framework for digital taxation*. Harv. Int'l LJ, 2022. **63**: p. 279.
329. Cockfield, A.J., *Designing tax policy for the digital biosphere: How the internet is changing tax laws*. Conn. L. Rev., 2001. **34**: p. 333.
330. Ajayi, M., *Taxation of the Digital Economy: An Appraisal of the Effectiveness of the OECD Tax Deal on Low-and-Middle Income Countries*. Available at SSRN 4925227, 2024.
331. Iqbal, N., N. Khan, and L. Khan, *The Impact of Global Tax Reforms on Multinational Corporations: A Study of Base Erosion and Profit Shifting (BEPS)*. The Critical Review of Social Sciences Studies, 2025. **3**(1): p. 3412–3425.
332. Bodo, B. and P. De Filippi, *Trust in context: the impact of regulation on blockchain and DeFi*. Regulation & Governance, 2022.
333. Agarwal, J., et al., *Economics of cryptocurrencies: Artificial intelligence, blockchain, and digital currency*, in *Information for efficient decision making: big data, blockchain and relevance*. 2021, World Scientific. p. 331–430.
334. Masiha, R.Y., *Effects of cryptocurrencies on global economics: a review study*. Qubahan Academic Journal, 2022. **2**(2): p. 9–15.
335. Jaatinen, I., *Global Financial Risks of Cryptocurrencies: a Case Study of El Salvador*. 2022.
336. Chiarella, M.L., *Digital Markets Act (DMA) and Digital Services Act (DSA): New Rules for the EU Digital Environment*. Athens JL, 2023. **9**: p. 33.
337. Novelli, C., et al., *Taking AI risks seriously: a new assessment model for the AI Act*. AI & SOCIETY, 2024. **39**(5): p. 2493–2497.
338. Group, W.B., *World development report 2016: Digital dividends*. 2016: World Bank Publications.
339. Chawla, N. and B. Kumar, *E-commerce and consumer protection in India: the emerging trend*. Journal of Business Ethics, 2022. **180**(2): p. 581–604.

340. Hill, R., *The New International Telecommunications Regulations and the Internet*. 2013: Springer.
341. Bacchus, J., *Trade links: new rules for a new world*. 2022: Cambridge University Press.
342. Armstrong, S. and P. Drysdale, *The economic cooperation potential of East Asia's RCEP agreement*. East Asian Economic Review, 2022. **26**(1): p. 3–25.
343. Ajibo, C.C., et al., *RCEP, CPTPP and the changing dynamics in international trade standard-setting*. Manchester J. Int'l Econ. L., 2019. **16**: p. 425.
344. Petersmann, E.-U., *How should the EU and other WTO members react to their WTO governance and WTO Appellate Body crises?* Robert Schuman Centre for Advanced Studies Research Paper No. RSCAS, 2018. **71**.
345. Kalantzakos, S., *China and the geopolitics of rare earths*. 2017: Oxford University Press.
346. Van den Bossche, P. and S. Akpofure, *The Use and Abuse of the National Security Exception under Article XXI (b)(iii) of the GATT 1994*. 2020: World Trade Institute, Universität Bern.
347. Group, U.N.I.L.C.S. and M. Koskenniemi, *Fragmentation of international law: difficulties arising from the diversification and expansion of international law*. 2007: Erik Castrén Institute of International Law and Human Rights.
348. Streck, C., P. Keenlyside, and M. Von Unger, *The Paris Agreement: a new beginning*. Journal for European Environmental & Planning Law, 2016. **13**(1): p. 3–29.
349. Klein, D., et al., *The Paris Agreement on climate change: Analysis and commentary*. 2017: Oxford University Press.
350. Espa, I., J. Francois, and H. van Asselt, *The EU proposal for a carbon border adjustment mechanism (CBAM): an analysis under WTO and climate change law*. 2022.
351. Dmuchowski, P., et al., *Environmental, social, and governance (ESG) model; impacts and sustainable investment–Global trends and Poland's perspective*. Journal of Environmental Management, 2023. **329**: p. 117023.
352. Cremasco, C. and L. Boni, *Is the European Union (EU) Sustainable Finance Disclosure Regulation (SFDR) effective in shaping sustainability objectives? An analysis of investment funds' behaviour*. Journal of Sustainable Finance & Investment, 2024. **14**(4): p. 1018–1036.
353. Board, F.S., *Task force on climate-related financial disclosures*. Final Report: Recommendations of the Task Force on Climate-Related Financial Disclosures, 2017.
354. Osmanski, E., *Investor-state dispute settlement: is there a better alternative*. Brook. J. Int'l L., 2017. **43**: p. 639.
355. Jacur, F.R., *The Vattenfall v. Germany disputes: Finding a balance between energy investments and public concerns*. Bridging the Gap between International Investment Law and the Environment. Den Haag: Legal Perspectives on Global Challenges Series Eleven Legal Publishing, 2015: p. 339–356.
356. Sjostedt, B., *The Role of Multilateral Environmental Agreements*. 2020.
357. Shrader-Frechette, K., *Environmental justice: Creating equality, reclaiming democracy*. 2002: Oxford university press.
358. Muhumed, M.M. and S.A. Gaas, *The World Bank and IMF in developing countries: Helping or hindering?* World, 2016. **28**(4): p. 237–249.
359. Franceschini, M., *Economics of Independence: Import Substitution Industrialization in sub-Saharan Africa*. 2023.
360. Helleiner, E. and H. Wang, *Limits to the BRICS'challenge: credit rating reform and institutional innovation in global finance*. Review of International Political Economy, 2018. **25**(5): p. 573–595.
361. Morris, S., et al., *Chinese and World Bank lending terms: A systematic comparison across 157 countries and 15 years*. 2020, Center for Global Development Washington, DC.
362. Acker, K., D. Brautigam, and Y. Huang, *Debt relief with Chinese characteristics*. Acker, Kevin, Deborah Brautigam, and Yufan Huang, 2020.
363. Wang, H., *The new development Bank and the Asian infrastructure investment Bank: China's ambiguous approach to global financial governance*. Development and Change, 2019. **50**(1): p. 221–244.

364. Humphrey, C., *From drawing board to reality: the first four years of operations at the Asian Infrastructure Investment Bank and New Development Bank.* 2020.
365. Mauro, M.R., *Sovereign Default and Litigation: NML Capital v. Argentina.* The Italian Yearbook of International Law Online, 2015. **24**(1): p. 249–268.
366. Horas, Y., F. Morra, and A. Wiedenbrüg, *Debt Relief for Resilience.* 2025.
367. Soutar, N., *The Political Economy of the African Continental Free Trade Area (AfCFTA): A Policy Analysis of the Prospects and Challenges.* 2021.
368. Beyleveld, A. and F. Sucker, *Regulating Cross-Border Data Flows under the AfCFTA Protocol on Digital Trade: The What, Why, How, Where and When.* Manchester J. Int'l Econ. L., 2023. **20**: p. 299.
369. Hulkó, G., J. Kálmán, and A. Lapsánszky, *The politics of digital sovereignty and the European Union's legislation: navigating crises.* Frontiers in Political Science, 2025. **7**: p. 1548562.
370. Laux, J., S. Wachter, and B. Mittelstadt, *Taming the few: Platform regulation, independent audits, and the risks of capture created by the DMA and DSA.* Computer law & Security review, 2021. **43**: p. 105613.
371. Apiko, P., S. Woolfrey, and B. Byiers, *The promise of the African Continental Free Trade Area (AfCFTA).* Political Economy Dynamics of Regional Organizations in Africa, 2020.
372. Ajewumi, O.E., J.A. Afolabi, and I. Joe-Akunne, *Regional trade agreements and economic integration in Africa: assessing the impact of the African Continental Free Trade Area (AFCFTA).* 2024.
373. Nazmul, I.M. and C.E. Eymen, *Strategic competition, economic diplomacy and trade warfare: Re-conceptualizing the 'Cold War'in the case of recent US-China Trade War.* Journal of Globalization Studies, 2021. **12**(2): p. 119–142.
374. Haskan, S., *Trade Wars Between the United States of America (USA) and the People's Republic of China (PRC) in the Trump Era (2018–2020).* 2021, Marmara Universitesi (Turkey).
375. Wang, X., *The Impact and Response of Trade Sanctions.* Asia Pacific Journal of Society and Law, 2024. **1**(1).
376. Mawdsley, E., *South–South Cooperation 3.0? Managing the consequences of success in the decade ahead.* Oxford Development Studies, 2019. **47**(3): p. 259–274.
377. 세비아, *Mainstreaming South-South and Triangular Cooperation in Peace and Democracy: A Case Study of Indonesia.* 2017, 서울대학교 국제대학원.
378. Tschorsch, F. and B. Scheuermann, *Bitcoin and beyond: A technical survey on decentralized digital currencies.* IEEE Communications Surveys & Tutorials, 2016. **18**(3): p. 2084–2123.
379. Howell, S.T., M. Niessner, and D. Yermack, *Initial coin offerings: Financing growth with cryptocurrency token sales.* The Review of Financial Studies, 2020. **33**(9): p. 3925–3974.
380. Hrytsai, S., *The place of virtual assets in the structure of digital financial technology.* International Science Journal of Management, Economics & Finance, 2022. **1**(3): p. 34–48.
381. Zhang, D., *Security Tokens: Complying with Security Laws and Regulations Provides More than Token Rewards.* UMKC L. Rev., 2019. **88**: p. 323.
382. Maume, P. and M. Fromberger, *Regulations of initial coin offerings: reconciling US and EU securities laws.* Chi. J. Int'l L., 2018. **19**: p. 548.
383. Joireman, S.F., *Where there is no government: Enforcing property rights in common law Africa.* 2011: Oxford University Press.
384. Schwarz, N., et al., *Virtual assets and anti-money laundering and combating the financing of terrorism (1): Some legal and practical considerations.* 2021: International Monetary Fund.
385. De Koker, L., T. Ocal, and P. Casanovas, *Where's Wally? FATF, virtual asset service providers, and the regulatory jurisdictional challenge*, in *Financial technology and the law: combating financial crime.* 2022, Springer. p. 151–183.
386. Wronka, C., *Crypto-asset activities and markets in the European Union: issues, challenges and considerations for regulation, supervision and oversight.* Journal of Banking Regulation, 2024. **25**(1): p. 84–93.
387. Oleg, S. and P. Denis, *Legal view on the introduction of new technologies.* Russian Law Journal, 2018. **6**(3): p. 149–171.

388. Yereli, A.B. and I.F. Orkunoğlu-Şahin. *Cryptocurrencies and taxation.* in *Proceedings of the 5th International Annual Meeting of Sosyoekonomi Society.* 2018.
389. Izhar, H. and A.S. Gundogdu, *Characterizing cryptocurrencies and why it matters.* Halal Cryptocurrency Management, 2019: p. 107–116.
390. Forgang, G., *Money laundering through cryptocurrencies.* Economic Crime Forensics Capstones, 2019. **40**.
391. Carroll, J.M. and V. Bellotti. *Creating value together: The emerging design space of peer-to-peer currency and exchange.* in *Proceedings of the 18th ACM conference on computer supported cooperative work & social computing.* 2015.
392. Ward, O. and S. Rochemont, *Understanding central bank digital currencies (CBDC).* Institute and Faculty of Actuaries, 2019. **13**(2): p. 263–268.
393. Chen, J. and I.O. Nesterov, *Central bank digital currencies: Digital Yuan and its role in Chinese digital economy development.* RUDN Journal of Economics, 2023. **31**(1): p. 120–133.
394. Passacantando, F., *The digital euro: Challenges and opportunities.* The (Near) Future of Central Bank Digital Currencies, 2021. **113**.
395. Islam, S. and K.U. Apu, *Decentralized vs. Centralized database solutions in blockchain: advantages, challenges, and use cases.* Global Mainstream Journal of Innovation, Engineering & Emerging Technology, 2024. **3**(4): p. 58–68.
396. Tasca, P., *Digital currencies: Principles, trends, opportunities, and risks.* 2015.
397. Irina, C., *Cryptocurrencies legal regulation.* BRICS law journal, 2018. **5**(2): p. 128–153.
398. Matsuura, J.H., *Digital Currency: An International Legal and Regulatory Compliance Guide.* 2016: Bentham Science Publishers.
399. Caudevilla, O. and H.M. Kim, *The Digital Yuan and Cross-Border Payments: China's Rollout of Its Central Bank Digital Currency.* University of Hong Kong Faculty of Law Research Paper, 2022(2023/30).
400. Faux, Z., *Number go up: Inside Crypto's wild rise and staggering fall.* 2024: Random House.
401. Kallianiotis, J.N., *Central Banks, Monetary Policy, and their Efficiency.* Chapter in Monetary Policy: Perspectives, Strategies and Challenges, Harriet Ward (editor), New York: Nova Science Publishers, 2017.
402. Viñuela, C., J. Sapena, and G. Wandosell, *The future of money and the central bank digital currency dilemma.* Sustainability, 2020. **12**(22): p. 9697.
403. Sater, S., *Do we need KYC/AML: The bank secrecy act and virtual currency exchanges.* Ark. L. Rev., 2020. **73**: p. 397.
404. Carata, C. and W.J. Knottenbelt. *Towards a harmonized global regulation: an analysis of the MiCA regulation and its implications for the European crypto-asset market.* in *2024 IEEE International Conference on Blockchain and Cryptocurrency (ICBC).* 2024. IEEE.
405. Hofmann, J., C. Katzenbach, and K. Gollatz, *Between coordination and regulation: Finding the governance in Internet governance.* New Media & Society, 2017. **19**(9): p. 1406–1423.
406. Woebbeking, F., *Cryptocurrency volatility markets.* Digital finance, 2021. **3**(3): p. 273–298.
407. Gurdgiev, C., D. O'Loughlin, and B. Chlebowski, *Behavioral basis of cryptocurrencies markets: Examining effects of public sentiment, fear, and uncertainty on price formation.* Journal of Financial Transformation, 2019. **49**: p. 110–121.
408. Thielen, M., *Crypto Titans: How trillions were made and billions lost in the cryptocurrency markets.* 2023: Markus Thielen.
409. Hughes, S.D., *Cryptocurrency Regulations and Enforcement in the US.* W. St. UL Rev., 2017. **45**: p. 1.
410. Schär, F., *Decentralized finance: on blockchain and smart contract-based financial markets.* Review of the Federal Reserve Bank of St Louis, 2021. **103**(2): p. 153–174.
411. Raskin, M. and D. Yermack, *Digital currencies, decentralized ledgers and the future of central banking*, in *Research handbook on central banking.* 2018, Edward Elgar Publishing. p. 474–486.
412. Baldwin, J., *In digital we trust: Bitcoin discourse, digital currencies, and decentralized network fetishism.* Palgrave Communications, 2018. **4**(1).

413. Fry, J. and E.-T. Cheah, *Negative bubbles and shocks in cryptocurrency markets.* International Review of Financial Analysis, 2016. **47**: p. 343–352.
414. Pocher, N., *Distributed ledger technologies between anonymity and transparency: AML/CFT regulation of cryptocurrency ecosystems in the EU.* 2023.
415. Khalilov, M.C.K. and A. Levi, *A survey on anonymity and privacy in bitcoin-like digital cash systems.* IEEE Communications Surveys & Tutorials, 2018. **20**(3): p. 2543–2585.
416. Le Nguyen, C., *Preventing the use of financial institutions for money laundering and the implications for financial privacy.* Journal of money laundering control, 2018. **21**(1): p. 47–58.
417. Khan, A., et al., *Regulatory strategies for combatting money laundering in the era of digital trade.* Journal of Money Laundering Control, 2025. **28**(2): p. 408–423.
418. Jani, S., *An overview of ripple technology & its comparison with bitcoin technology.* Retrieved from ResearchGate: https://www.researchgate.net/publication, 2018.
419. Woodley, D., *Globalization and capitalist geopolitics: Sovereignty and state power in a multipolar world.* 2015: Taylor & Francis.
420. Serfati, C., *The transatlantic bloc of states and the political economy of the Transatlantic Trade and Investment Partnership (TTIP).* Work Organisation, Labour and Globalisation, 2015. **9**(1): p. 7–37.
421. Scott, J.W., *Bordering, border politics and cross-border cooperation in Europe.* Neighbourhood policy and the construction of the European external borders, 2015: p. 27–44.
422. Sohn, C. and R. Giffinger, *A policy network approach to cross-border metropolitan governance: The cases of Vienna and Bratislava.* European planning studies, 2015. **23**(6): p. 1187–1208.
423. Mau, S., et al., *The global mobility divide: How visa policies have evolved over time.* Journal of Ethnic and Migration Studies, 2015. **41**(8): p. 1192–1213.
424. Pinto, É.G., *Budgetary-financial erosion of social rights in the constitution of 1988.* Ciência & Saúde Coletiva, 2019. **24**: p. 4473–4478.
425. Rubin, I.S., *The politics of public budgeting: Getting and spending, borrowing and balancing.* 2019: CQ Press.
426. Ladeur, K.-H., *Public governance in the age of globalization.* 2017: Routledge.
427. Sassen, S., *De-nationalized state agendas and privatized norm-making*, in *Public governance in the age of globalization.* 2017, Routledge. p. 51–67.
428. Voszka, E., *Nationalization or privatization? The fragmentation of the mainstream.* Annals of Public and Cooperative Economics, 2017. **88**(1): p. 91–120.
429. Wallace, C.D., *The multinational enterprise and legal control: host state sovereignty in an era of economic globalization.* 2021: BRILL.
430. Perlas, N., *Shaping globalization.* 2019: Temple Lodge Publishing.
431. Goldthau, A. and N. Sitter, *A liberal actor in a realist world: The European Union regulatory state and the global political economy of energy.* 2015: OUP Oxford.
432. Addo, M.K., *Human rights standards and the responsibility of transnational corporations.* 2024: Brill.
433. Niemeyer, G. and M. Henry, *Law without force: the function of politics in international law.* 2018: Routledge.
434. Verger, A., C. Fontdevila, and A. Zancajo, *The privatization of education: A political economy of global education reform.* 2016: Teachers College Press.
435. Starr, P., *The new life of the liberal state: Privatization and the restructuring of state-society relations*, in *The political economy of public sector reform and privatization.* 2019, Routledge. p. 22–54.
436. Brunnermeier, M.K. and I. Schnabel, *Bubbles and central banks: Historical perspectives.* 2015: Centre for Economic Policy Research.
437. Hunter, D., *Moving beyond State-Centrism in International Environmental Law.* Environmental Policy and Law, 2022. **52**(3–4): p. 201–212.
438. Jacobsson, B., J. Pierre, and G. Sundström, *Governing the embedded state: The organizational dimension of governance.* 2015: OUP Oxford.

439. Jovanović, M.N., *The economics of international integration*, in *The Economics of International Integration, Second Edition.* 2015, Edward Elgar Publishing.
440. Lake, D.A. and M. Kahler, *Governance in a global economy: Political authority in transition.* 2021.
441. Brunet-Jailly, E., *Cross-border cooperation: a global overview.* Alternatives, 2022. **47**(1): p. 3–17.
442. Neuwirth, R.J., *Global market integration and the creative economy: The paradox of industry convergence and regulatory divergence.* Journal of International Economic Law, 2015. **18**(1): p. 21–50.
443. Mügge, D., *Widen the market, narrow the competition: banker interests and the making of a European capital market.* 2024: ECPR press.
444. Riekhof, M.-C., E. Regnier, and M.F. Quaas, *Economic growth, international trade, and the depletion or conservation of renewable natural resources.* Journal of Environmental Economics and Management, 2019. **97**: p. 116–133.
445. Canton, H., *Organisation for economic co-operation and development—OECD*, in *The Europa Directory of International Organizations 2021.* 2021, Routledge. p. 677–687.
446. Woo, K.-Y., et al., *Review on efficiency and anomalies in stock markets.* Economies, 2020. **8**(1): p. 20.
447. Cavalcante, R.C., et al., *Computational intelligence and financial markets: A survey and future directions.* Expert Systems with Applications, 2016. **55**: p. 194–211.
448. Hart, K., *The idea of economy: six modern dissenters*, in *Beyond the Marketplace.* 2019, Routledge. p. 137–160.
449. Weber, M., *General economic history.* 2017: Routledge.
450. Eisner, M.A., *Antitrust and the triumph of economics: Institutions, expertise, and policy change.* 2017: UNC Press Books.
451. Freeman, J.R., *Democracy and markets: The politics of mixed economies.* 2018: Cornell University Press.
452. Tanzi, V., *Monitoring the state or the market: From Laissez Faire to market fundamentalism.* 2023: Cambridge University Press.
453. Howells, G., H.-W. Micklitz, and T. Wilhelmsson, *European fair trading law: the unfair commercial practices directive.* 2016: Routledge.
454. Toye, J., *The International Monetary Fund and the World Bank*, in *The Handbook of Globalisation, Third Edition.* 2019, Edward Elgar Publishing. p. 368–379.
455. Voutsa, M.E. and G. Borovas, *The operation of the Bretton Woods institutions in the modern globalized environment: problems and challenges.* Procedia Economics and Finance, 2015. **33**: p. 168–180.
456. Klimiuk, Z., *The principles and operation of the Bretton Woods international monetary system in the years 1944–1971. The reasons for its collapse.* Internal Security, 2016. **8**(2): p. 225–257.
457. Villareal, M. and I.F. Fergusson, *The North American Free Trade Agreement (NAFTA).* 2017.
458. Mao, J., *The Plausibility Check of Governmental and Legal Intervention to the Free Market System.* Advances in Economics, Management and Political Sciences, 2024. **69**: p. 213–219.
459. Graafland, J. and H. Verbruggen, *Free-market, perfect market and welfare state perspectives on "good" markets: An empirical test.* Applied Research in Quality of Life, 2022. **17**(2): p. 1113–1136.
460. Duvanova, D., *Thieves, Opportunists, and Autocrats: Building Regulatory States in Russia and Kazakhstan.* 2023: Oxford University Press.
461. Babb, S.L. and A.E. Kentikelenis, *International financial institutions as agents of neoliberalism.* The SAGE handbook of neoliberalism, 2018. **1**: p. 16–27.
462. Kranke, M., *The politics of collaborative global governance: organisational positioning in IMF-World Bank collaboration.* 2017, University of Warwick.
463. Bond, P., *Bretton Woods Institution narratives about inequality and economic vulnerability on the eve of South African austerity.* International Journal of Health Services, 2015. **45**(3): p. 415–442.

464. Jackson, K., *Asian contagion: the causes and consequences of a financial crisis*. 2018: Routledge.
465. Basri, M.C., *Twenty years after the Asian financial crisis*. Realizing Indonesia's economic potential, 2018: p. 21–45.
466. Carroll, T., J. Clifton, and D.S. Jarvis, *Power, leverage and marketization: The diffusion of neoliberalism from North to South and back again*. Globalizations, 2019. **16**(6): p. 771–777.
467. Naseemullah, A., *The political economy of national development: A research agenda after neoliberal reform?* World Development, 2023. **168**: p. 106269.
468. Lindblad, J.T., *Foreign direct investment in Indonesia: Fifty years of discourse*. Bulletin of Indonesian Economic Studies, 2015. **51**(2): p. 217–237.
469. Shaxson, N., *The finance curse: How global finance is making us all poorer*. 2018: Random House.
470. Dagan, T., *The Global Market for Tax and Legal Rules*. Fla. Tax Rev., 2017. **21**: p. 148.
471. Helpman, E., *Globalization and inequality*. 2018: Harvard University Press.
472. Peters, G.W., A. Chapelle, and E. Panayi, *Opening discussion on banking sector risk exposures and vulnerabilities from virtual currencies: An operational risk perspective*. Journal of banking regulation, 2016. **17**: p. 239–272.
473. Ajayi, A.J., et al., *The impact of artificial intelligence on cyber security in digital currency transactions*. Available at SSRN 5137847, 2025.
474. Nimma, S., *Money laundering in the cyberworld: emerging trends*. Part 1 Indian J. Integrated Rsch. L., 2022. **2**: p. 1.
475. Mercurio, B. and R. Yu, *Regulating Cross-Border Data Flows: Issues, Challenges and Impact*. 2022: Anthem Press.
476. Chuen, D.L.K. and R.H. Deng, *Handbook of blockchain, digital finance, and inclusion: cryptocurrency, fintech, insurtech, regulation, Chinatech, mobile security, and distributed ledger*. 2017: Academic Press.
477. Halaburda, H., M. Sarvary, and G. Haeringer, *Beyond bitcoin*. 2022: Springer.
478. Cohen, L. and S. Chen, *Blockchain 2022*. 2022.
479. MANUAL, G., *Virtual assets and virtual asset service providers ml/tf risk assessment tool*.
480. Hardjono, T., A. Lipton, and A. Pentland, *13. Exchange Networks for Virtual Assets*. Building the New Economy, 2020.
481. Westermeier, C., *The Bank of International Settlements as a think tank for financial policy-making*. Policy and Society, 2018. **37**(2): p. 170–187.
482. Huertas, T., *How to deal with the Resolution of Financial Market Infrastructures. 2nd interim report of the ceps task force on implementing financial sector resolution. October 2016*. 2016.
483. Huber, J., *CBDC system design principles*, in *The Monetary Turning Point: From Bank Money to Central Bank Digital Currency (CBDC)*. 2023, Springer. p. 117–150.
484. Li, D., et al., *Design principles and best practices of central bank digital currency*. International Journal of Performability Engineering, 2021. **17**(5): p. 411.
485. Zagaris, B. and E. Hong, *Money Laundering, Bank Secrecy and Financial Crime*. IELR, 2024. **40**: p. 459.
486. Boot, P.J., *OCC Opens the Door for Banks to Offer Cryptocurrency Services*. Banking LJ, 2020. **137**: p. 457.
487. Ferreira, A. and P. Sandner, *Eu search for regulatory answers to crypto assets and their place in the financial markets' infrastructure*. Computer Law & Security Review, 2021. **43**: p. 105632.
488. Bansal, R. and S. Singh, *China's digital yuan: An alternative to the dollar-dominated financial system*. 2022: Carnegie Endowment for International Peace.
489. Peretolchin, A.P., *Genesis and Prospects of Development of Legal Regulation of Digital Financial Assets in the Russian Federation*. Journal of Digital Technologies and Law, 2023. **1**(3).
490. Muradyan, S.V., *Digital assets: Legal regulation and estimation of risks*. Journal of Digital Technologies and Law, 2023. **1**(1).

491. Kashina, E., *Current Challenges and Possible Solutions for Anti-Money Laundering Regulation of Virtual Currencies in the EU and the UK*. 2019, University of London.
492. Campbell-Verduyn, M., *Bitcoin, crypto-coins, and global anti-money laundering governance.* Crime, Law and Social Change, 2018. **69**: p. 283–305.
493. Ostern, N.K. and J. Riedel, *Know-your-customer (KYC) requirements for initial coin offerings.* Business & Information Systems Engineering, 2021. **63**(5): p. 551–567.
494. Trautman, L.J., B. Elzweig, and N.F. Newman, *The SEC, Fraud, and Crypto Currencies.* 2024.
495. Scharfman, J., *The Cryptocurrency and Digital Asset Fraud Casebook, Volume II.* Springer Books, 2024.
496. GULIYEV, R., *Rethinking Boundaries: The Ftx Fiasco and The Imperative of Regulating Cryptocurrency Exchanges.* Annals of Spiru Haret University. Economic Series, 2024. **24**(1): p. 149–158.
497. Trautman, L.J. and L.D. Foster, *The FTX Crypto Debacle: Largest Fraud Since Madoff?* U. Mem. L. Rev., 2023. **54**: p. 289.
498. Tiwari, M., et al., *Crypto Crashes: An examination of the Binance and FTX scandals and associated accounting challenges.* The British Accounting Review, 2025: p. 101584.
499. Xia, L., S. Baghaie, and S.M. Sajadi, *The digital economy: Challenges and opportunities in the new era of technology and electronic communications.* Ain Shams Engineering Journal, 2024. **15**(2): p. 102411.
500. Shi, Y. and F. Wei, *Comparative analysis of digital economy-driven innovation development in China: An international perspective.* Journal of the Knowledge Economy, 2024: p. 1–43.
501. Javaid, M., et al., *Digital economy to improve the culture of industry 4.0: A study on features, implementation and challenges.* Green Technologies and Sustainability, 2024: p. 100083.
502. Carlaw, K., et al., *Beyond the hype: Intellectual property and the knowledge society/knowledge economy.* Journal of Economic Surveys, 2006. **20**(4): p. 633–690.
503. Bell, A. and G. Parchomovsky, *A theory of property.* Cornell L. Rev., 2004. **90**: p. 531.
504. Parker, G.G., M.W. Van Alstyne, and S.P. Choudary, *Platform revolution: How networked markets are transforming the economy and how to make them work for you.* 2016: WW Norton & Company.
505. Muldoon, J., et al., *Platforming equality: Policy challenges for the digital economy.* 2020.
506. Belleflamme, P. and M. Peitz, *Platforms and network effects.* 2018: Edward Elgar Publishing.
507. Decker, C., *Modern economic regulation: An introduction to theory and practice.* 2023: Cambridge University Press.
508. Olbert, M. and C. Spengel, *International taxation in the digital economy: Challenge accepted?* World Tax J., 2017: p. 3.
509. Schäfer, H.-B., *Current Legal and Economic Problems of Privacy Protection, Data Sharing, and Market-Opening in the Digital Economy.* The Antitrust Bulletin, 2023. **68**(4): p. 641–656.
510. Makarov, I. and A. Schoar, *Cryptocurrencies and decentralized finance (DeFi).* Brookings Papers on Economic Activity, 2022. **2022**(1): p. 141–215.
511. Zhuk, A., *Crypto-anarchy: a paradigm shift for society and the legal system.* Journal of Computer Virology and Hacking Techniques, 2024. **20**(4): p. 697–723.
512. Aziz, A., N.A.M. Noor, and O. Mashhour, *The money of the future: A study of the legal challenges facing cryptocurrencies.* BiLD Law Journal, 2022. **7**(1): p. 21–33.
513. Gaviyau, W. and A.B. Sibindi, *Global anti-money laundering and combating terrorism financing regulatory framework: A critique.* Journal of Risk and Financial Management, 2023. **16**(7): p. 313.
514. Pavlidis, G., *International regulation of virtual assets under FATF's new standards.* Journal of Investment Compliance, 2020. **21**(1): p. 1–8.
515. Pocher, N., *Traceability of crypto-asset transfers under the new EU AML/CFT regime: the crypto travel rule between challenges and open issues*, in *A Research Agenda for Financial Law and Regulation.* 2025, Edward Elgar Publishing. p. 197–220.
516. Andersson, E., *A comparative analysis of the taxation of crypto currencies.* 2022.

517. Stanford, J., *The resurgence of gig work: Historical and theoretical perspectives.* The Economic and Labour Relations Review, 2017. **28**(3): p. 382–401.
518. Mäntymäki, M., A. Baiyere, and A.N. Islam, *Digital platforms and the changing nature of physical work: Insights from ride-hailing.* International Journal of Information Management, 2019. **49**: p. 452–460.
519. Donovan, S.A., D.H. Bradley, and J.O. Shimabukuru, *What does the gig economy mean for workers?* 2016.
520. Lobel, O., *The gig economy & the future of employment and labor law.* USFL Rev., 2017. **51**: p. 51.
521. Manyika, J., et al., *Independent-Work-Choice-necessity-and-the-gig-economy.* 2016, McKinsey Global Institute.
522. Upex, R., *Workers and the gig economy: an appraisal of the Supreme Court's Decision in the Uber case.* Coventry Law Journal, 2021. **26**(1).
523. Adams-Prassl, A., J. Adams-Prassl, and D. Coyle, *Uber and beyond: Policy Implications for the UK.* Available at SSRN 3823829, 2021.
524. Thomas, K.D., *Taxing the gig economy.* University of Pennsylvania Law Review, 2018: p. 1415–1473.
525. Marcus, A.J., *Financial intelligence units (FIUs): effective institutional design, mandate and powers.* 2022: JSTOR.
526. Simchenko, N.A., N.V. Apatova, and O.L. Korolev, *System analysis of digital economy virtualization processes.* Перспективы науки и образования, 2021(2): p. 23–39.
527. Mikołajewicz-Woźniak, A. and A. Scheibe, *Virtual currency schemes–the future of financial services.* Foresight, 2015. **17**(4): p. 365–377.
528. Milskaya, E. and O. Seeleva. *Main directions of development of infrastructure in digital economy.* in *IOP Conference Series: Materials Science and Engineering.* 2019. IOP Publishing.
529. Tara, A.-Y., *Introduction to Tactile Internet.* The Tactile Internet, 2022: p. 1.
530. Hui, L. and Y. Xin, *Co-governed sovereignty network: legal basis and its prototype & applications with MIN architecture.* 2021: Springer Nature.
531. Lewis, T.G., *Critical infrastructure protection in homeland security: defending a networked nation.* 2019: John Wiley & Sons.
532. Bailey, L.E. and N. Nyabola, *Digital equity as an enabling platform for equality and inclusion.* Pathfinders for Peaceful, Just, and Inclusive Societies/NYU Center on International Cooperation, June 2021, https://cic.nyu.edu/resources/digital-equityas-an-enabling-platform-for-equality-and-inclusion, 2021.
533. Alessandrini, D., *Progressive taxation and economic stability.* The Scandinavian Journal of Economics, 2021. **123**(2): p. 422–452.
534. Hummel, P., et al., *Data sovereignty: A review.* Big Data & Society, 2021. **8**(1): p. 2053951720982012.
535. Henningsson, S. and B.D. Eaton, *Governmental regulation and digital infrastructure innovation: The mediating role of modular architecture.* Journal of Information Technology, 2023. **38**(2): p. 126–143.
536. Verdecchia, R., P. Lago, and C. De Vries, *The future of sustainable digital infrastructures: A landscape of solutions, adoption factors, impediments, open problems, and scenarios.* Sustainable Computing: Informatics and Systems, 2022. **35**: p. 100767.
537. Forge, S. and K. Vu, *Forming a 5G strategy for developing countries: A note for policy makers.* Telecommunications Policy, 2020. **44**(7): p. 101975.
538. Van Loo, R., *Rise of the digital regulator.* Duke LJ, 2016. **66**: p. 1267.
539. Schneier, B., *Secrets and lies: digital security in a networked world.* 2015: John Wiley & Sons.
540. De Lucca, N., G.M. Martins, and R.C.Z. Queiroz, *Brazilian General Data Protection Law (LGPD) and California Consumer Privacy Act (CCPA): a critical analysis of consumer personal data protection in Brazil and the State of California (USA).* Brazilian Journal of Law, Technology and Innovation, 2023. **1**(1): p. 38–57.

541. de Magalhães, M.A., *Data protection regulation: a comparative law approach: Proteção de dados: Estudo comparado de normas nacionais.* International Journal of Digital Law, 2021. **2**(2): p. 33–53.
542. Pennell, D., et al., *Should Australia have a law against cyberbullying? Problematising the murky legal environment of cyberbullying from perspectives within schools.* The Australian Educational Researcher, 2022. **49**(4): p. 827–844.
543. Özdan, S., *The right to freedom of expression versus legal actions against fake news: A case study of singapore.* The Epistemology of Deceit in a Postdigital Era: Dupery by Design, 2021: p. 77–94.
544. Hacker, P., *Teaching fairness to artificial intelligence: existing and novel strategies against algorithmic discrimination under EU law.* Common market law review, 2018. **55**(4).
545. Girasa, R., *Regulation of cryptocurrencies and blockchain technologies.* National and International Perspectives. Suiza: Palgrave Macmillan, 2018.
546. Régnier, P. and P. Wild, *Recent Trends in First-Class World Competitiveness: Singapore and Switzerland in Global Entrepreneurship Rankings.* Singapore and Switzerland: secrets to small state success, 2016: p. 137–164.
547. Gostin, L.O., *The Americans with Disabilities Act at 25: the highest expression of American values.* Jama, 2015. **313**(22): p. 2231–2235.
548. Perzanowski, A. and J. Schultz, *The end of ownership: Personal property in the digital economy.* 2016: MIT Press.
549. Marinotti, J., *Possessing intangibles.* Nw. UL Rev., 2021. **116**: p. 1227.
550. Siren, A. and S.G. Knudsen, *Older adults and emerging digital service delivery: A mixed methods study on information and communications technology use, skills, and attitudes.* Journal of aging & social policy, 2017. **29**(1): p. 35–50.
551. Athanassiou, P.L., *Digital innovation in financial services: legal challenges and regulatory policy issues.* 2016: Kluwer Law International BV.
552. Andriychuk, O., *Shaping the new modality of the digital markets: The impact of the DSA/DMA proposals on inter-platform competition.* World Competition, 2021. **44**(3).
553. Turcios, E.M., *Regulation of Digital Platforms under EU Competition Law.* Economic Review of the European Union, 2025. **8**(1): p. 70–91.
554. Ruan, K., *Digital asset valuation and cyber risk measurement: Principles of cybernomics.* 2019: Academic Press.
555. Alessandro, M., *Non-fungible tokens: An argument for the ownership of digital property?* Int'l JL Changing World, 2023. **2**: p. 171.
556. Bartoli, C., et al., *Opportunities and challenges in the metaverse and NFTs for business model innovation: a managerial point of view.* IEEE Transactions on Engineering Management, 2025.
557. Pavlidis, G., *The digital transformation of the global green bonds market: New-fashioned international standards for a new generation of financial instruments*, in *Data Governance in AI, FinTech and LegalTech.* 2022, Edward Elgar Publishing. p. 263–278.
558. Dombalagian, O.H., *Bond Trading at the Digital Frontier.* J. Corp. L., 2023. **49**: p. 489.
559. Collomb, A. and K. Sok, *Blockchain/distributed ledger technology (DLT): What impact on the financial sector?* Digiworld Economic Journal, 2016(103).
560. Dönbekci, K., *Navigating The Future of Finance and Instruments Through the Regulation of Digital Bonds and Challenges (Preprint).* 2024.
561. Loader, D., *Clearing, settlement and custody.* 2019: Butterworth-Heinemann.
562. Lemieux, V., et al., *Blockchain technology & recordkeeping.* ARMA International Educational Foundation, 2019.
563. Soner, S., R. Litoriya, and P. Pandey, *Exploring blockchain and smart contract technology for reliable and secure land registration and record management.* Wireless Personal Communications, 2021. **121**(4): p. 2495–2509.
564. Ducrée, J., et al., *Unchaining collective intelligence for science, research, and technology development by blockchain-boosted community participation.* Frontiers in Blockchain, 2021. **4**: p. 631648.

565. Panagiotidis, P., *Blockchain in Education--The Case of Language Learning.* European Journal of Education (EJED), 2022. **5**(1): p. 66–83.
566. Brown, B. and B. Brown, *Digitalization, Camouflage, and Monetary Inflation.* The Case Against 2 Per Cent Inflation: From Negative Interest Rates to a 21st Century Gold Standard, 2018: p. 75–93.
567. Iuga, I.C. and S.R. Jafri, *Digitalization and future money supply dynamics.* Macroeconomics and Finance in Emerging Market Economies, 2025: p. 1–22.
568. Rayna, T., *Understanding the challenges of the digital economy: The nature of digital goods.* Communications & Strategies, 2008(71): p. 13–16.
569. Kaur Nagpal, G. and L. Renneboog, *Valuing Digital Art: On Non-fungible Tokens, Blockchain Hypes, and the Creation of Scarcity.* Blockchain Hypes, and the Creation of Scarcity (November 3, 2023), 2023.
570. Ozili, P.K., *Decentralized finance research and developments around the world.* Journal of Banking and Financial Technology, 2022. **6**(2): p. 117–133.
571. Yim, S.T., J.C. Son, and J. Lee, *Spread of E-commerce, prices and inflation dynamics: Evidence from online price big data in Korea.* Journal of Asian Economics, 2022. **80**: p. 101475.
572. Chouliaraki, L. and M. Georgiou, *The digital border: Migration, technology, power.* Vol. 44. 2022: NYU Press.
573. Taylor, R.D., *"Data localization": The internet in the balance.* Telecommunications Policy, 2020. **44**(8): p. 102003.
574. Mishra, N., *Data localization laws in a digital world: Data protection or data protectionism?* The Public Sphere (2016), NUS Centre for International Law Research Paper, 2015(19/05).
575. Pohle, J. and T. Thiel, *Digital sovereignty.* Pohle, J. & Thiel, 2020.
576. Couture, S. and S. Toupin, *What does the notion of "sovereignty" mean when referring to the digital?* New media & society, 2019. **21**(10): p. 2305–2322.
577. Hoffmann, S., D. Lazanski, and E. Taylor, *Standardising the splinternet: how China's technical standards could fragment the internet.* Journal of Cyber Policy, 2020. **5**(2): p. 239–264.
578. Mueller, M., *Will the internet fragment?: Sovereignty, globalization and cyberspace.* 2017: John Wiley & Sons.
579. Steingartner, W., D. Galinec, and A. Kozina, *Threat defense: Cyber deception approach and education for resilience in hybrid threats model.* Symmetry, 2021. **13**(4): p. 597.
580. Jacobs, B., *A comparative study of EU and US regulatory approaches to cybersecurity in space.* Air and Space Law, 2023. **48**(4/5).
581. Markopoulou, D., V. Papakonstantinou, and P. De Hert, *The new EU cybersecurity framework: The NIS Directive, ENISA's role and the General Data Protection Regulation.* Computer Law & Security Review, 2019. **35**(6): p. 105336.
582. Paterson, T. and L. Hanley, *Political warfare in the digital age: cyber subversion, information operations and 'deep fakes'.* Australian Journal of International Affairs, 2020. **74**(4): p. 439–454.
583. Ivan, C., I. Chiru, and R. Arcos, *A whole of society intelligence approach: critical reassessment of the tools and means used to counter information warfare in the digital age.* Intelligence and National Security, 2021. **36**(4): p. 495–511.
584. Jaquet-Chiffelle, D.-O., et al., *Virtual persons and identities*, in *The Future of identity in the Information Society.* 2009, Springer. p. 75–122.
585. Cover, R., *Digital identities: Creating and communicating the online self.* 2015: Academic Press.
586. Magnusson Sjöberg, C., *The Digital Person—A New Legal Entity? On the Role of Law in an AI-Based Society.* Legal tech and the new sharing economy, 2020: p. 81–91.
587. Vazquez, M.L., *Neither Matter Nor Spirit: The Ambivalent Substance of Digital Legal Personhood and Its Theological Antecedents.* International Journal for the Semiotics of Law-Revue internationale de Sémiotique juridique, 2024. **37**(4): p. 1223–1258.

588. Teubner, G., *Digital personhood? The status of autonomous software agents in private law.* The Status of Autonomous Software Agents in Private Law (May 11, 2018), 2018.
589. Karaboga, M., et al., *Is There a Right to Offline Alternatives in a Digital World?* Data Protection and Privacy:(In) visibilities and Infrastructures, 2017: p. 31–57.
590. Taylor, L., *What is data justice? The case for connecting digital rights and freedoms globally.* Big Data & Society, 2017. **4**(2): p. 2053951717736335.
591. Custers, B., *New digital rights: Imagining additional fundamental rights for the digital era.* Computer Law & Security Review, 2022. **44**: p. 105636.
592. March, J., *The technology of foolishness*, in *Shaping Entrepreneurship Research.* 2020, Routledge. p. 120–130.
593. Darioshi, R. and E. Lahav, *The impact of technology on the human decision-making process.* Human Behavior and Emerging Technologies, 2021. **3**(3): p. 391–400.
594. Flyverbom, M., R. Deibert, and D. Matten, *The governance of digital technology, big data, and the internet: New roles and responsibilities for business.* Business & Society, 2019. **58**(1): p. 3–19.
595. Hanna, N., *A role for the state in the digital age.* Journal of Innovation and Entrepreneurship, 2018. **7**(1): p. 5.
596. Dapp, T., et al., *Fintech reloaded–Traditional banks as digital ecosystems.* Publication of the German original, 2015: p. 261–274.
597. Evdokimova, Y., O. Shinkareva, and A. Bondarenko. *Digital banks: development trends.* in *2nd International Scientific conference on New Industrialization: Global, national, regional dimension (SICNI 2018).* 2019. Atlantis Press.
598. Dauda, S.Y. and J. Lee, *Technology adoption: A conjoint analysis of consumers' preference on future online banking services.* Information Systems, 2015. **53**: p. 1–15.
599. Salem, M.Z., S. Baidoun, and G. Walsh, *Factors affecting Palestinian customers' use of online banking services.* International Journal of Bank Marketing, 2019. **37**(2): p. 426–451.
600. Chen, P.-W., B.-S. Jiang, and C.-H. Wang. *Blockchain-based payment collection supervision system using pervasive Bitcoin digital wallet.* In *2017 IEEE 13th international conference on wireless and mobile computing, networking and communications (WiMob).* 2017. IEEE.
601. Raghavendra, R., et al., *An emphasis of digital wallets for E-commerce transactions.* Journal of Computational and Theoretical Nanoscience, 2019. **16**(9): p. 3748–3753.
602. POLICY, A.M.L.A., *Know your customer ("KYC") and anti-money laundering ("AML") policy.* Policy, 2019.
603. Dekho, P.H., *Know Your Customer & Anti-Money Laundering Policy (KYC and AML Policy).* Policy, 2015.
604. Inozemtsev, M. *Digital assets in the United States: Legal aspects.* In *Engineering Economics: Decisions and Solutions from Eurasian Perspective.* 2021. Springer.
605. van der Merwe, A., *Cryptocurrencies and other digital asset investments.* The Palgrave Handbook of FinTech and Blockchain, 2021: p. 445–471.
606. Schwarz, N., et al., *Virtual assets and anti-money laundering and combating the financing of terrorism (2): Effective anti-money laundering and combating the financing of terrorism regulatory and supervisory framework—Some legal and practical considerations.* 2021: International Monetary Fund.
607. Szirmai, A., *Manufacturing and economic development.* Pathways to industrialization in the twenty-first century: New challenges and emerging paradigms, 2013: p. 53–75.
608. Kumar, V., D. Ramachandran, and B. Kumar, *Influence of new-age technologies on marketing: A research agenda.* Journal of Business Research, 2021. **125**: p. 864–877.
609. Ayres, R.U. and E. Williams, *The digital economy: Where do we stand?* Technological Forecasting and Social Change, 2004. **71**(4): p. 315–339.
610. Lehmacher, W., *Digitizing and automating processes in logistics.* Disrupting Logistics: Startups, Technologies, and Investors Building Future Supply Chains, 2021: p. 9–27.
611. Shrier, D., G. Canale, and A. Pentland, *Mobile money & payments: Technology trends.* Massachusetts Inst. Technol, 2016. **27**.
612. Emmanuella Tracy Eyram, A., *International payment systems in international business.* 2023.

613. Richter, C., et al., *Digital entrepreneurship: Innovative business models for the sharing economy.* Creativity and innovation management, 2017. **26**(3): p. 300–310.
614. Kaine, S. and E. Josserand, *The organisation and experience of work in the gig economy.* Journal of Industrial Relations, 2019. **61**(4): p. 479–501.
615. Huang, J., et al., *Design Tensions in Online Freelancing Platforms: Using Speculative Participatory Design to Support Freelancers' Relationships with Clients.* Proceedings of the ACM on Human-Computer Interaction, 2024. **8**(CSCW1): p. 1–28.
616. Bănică, C.-F., A. Sover, and D.-C. Anghel, *Printing the future layer by layer: A comprehensive exploration of additive manufacturing in the era of Industry 4.0.* Applied Sciences, 2024. **14**(21): p. 9919.
617. Komandla, V. and S. PERUMALLA, *Transforming traditional banking: Strategies, challenges, and the impact of fintech innovations.* Educational Research (IJMCER), 2017. **1**(6): p. 01–09.
618. Nylén, D. and J. Holmström, *Digital innovation strategy: A framework for diagnosing and improving digital product and service innovation.* Business horizons, 2015. **58**(1): p. 57–67.
619. Zhai, D., *RCEP Rules on Cross-Border Data Flows: asian characteristics and implications for developing countries.* Asia Pacific Law Review, 2025. **33**(1): p. 24–45.
620. Illman, E. and P. Temple, *California consumer privacy act.* The Business Lawyer, 2019. **75**(1): p. 1637–1646.
621. Teoh, C.S. and A.K. Mahmood. *National cyber security strategies for digital economy.* in *2017 International Conference on Research and Innovation in Information Systems (ICRIIS).* 2017. IEEE.
622. Glenn, H.P., *n'the Transsystemic: Legal Systems and Legal Traditions.* McGill LJ, 2005. **50**: p. 863.
623. Khan, M.N.I., *Cross-border data privacy and legal support: a systematic review of international compliance standards and cyber law practices.* American Journal of Scholarly Research and Innovation, 2025. **4**(01): p. 138–174.
624. Ryan, P., *Trust and distrust in digital economies.* 2019: Routledge.
625. Zeynalova, Y., *The law on recognition and enforcement of foreign judgments: is it broken and how do we fix it.* Berkeley J. Int'l L., 2013. **31**: p. 150.
626. Cannataci, J.A., et al., *Privacy, free expression and transparency: redefining their new boundaries in the digital age.* 2016: Unesco Publishing.
627. Walters, R., *The Digital Economy and International Trade: Transnational Data Flows Regulation.* 2022.
628. Ziccardi, G. and G. Ziccardi, *Digital activism, Internet control, transparency, censorship, surveillance and human rights: An international perspective.* Resistance, liberation technology and human rights in the digital age, 2013: p. 187–307.
629. Veerabhadraiah, C., *Human Rights in the Digital Age: Balancing Privacy, Freedom, and Security.* International Journal of Commerce, Management, Leadership, and Law, 2024. **1**(1): p. 77–89.
630. Shelepov, A., *The Influence of the G20's digitalization leadership on development conditions and governance of the digital economy.* International Organisations Research Journal, 2022. **17**(1).
631. Yun, H., *China's data sovereignty and security: Implications for global digital borders and governance.* Chinese Political Science Review, 2024: p. 1–26.
632. Volberda, H.W., et al., *Strategizing in a digital world: Overcoming cognitive barriers, reconfiguring routines and introducing new organizational forms.* Long Range Planning, 2021. **54**(5): p. 102110.
633. Irion, K., *Government cloud computing and national data sovereignty.* Policy & Internet, 2012. **4**(3–4): p. 40–71.
634. Mahida, A., *A Comprehensive Review on Ethical Considerations in Cloud Computing-Privacy Data Sovereignty, and Compliance.* Journal of Artificial Intelligence & Cloud Computing. SRC/JAICC-248. https://doi.org/10.47363/JAICC/2022 (1), 2022. **231**: p. 2–4.

635. AllahRakha, N., *Cybersecurity Regulations for Protection and Safeguarding Digital Assets (Data) in Today's Worlds.* Lex Scientia Law Review, 2024. **8**(1): p. 405–432.
636. Fletcher, A., et al., *Consumer protection for online markets and large digital platforms.* Yale J. on Reg., 2023. **40**: p. 875.
637. Newman, J.M., *Antitrust in digital markets.* Vand. L. Rev., 2019. **72**: p. 1497.
638. Haucap, J. and T. Stühmeier, *Competition and antitrust in internet markets.* 2015: Düsseldorf Institute for Competition Economics (DICE).
639. Aristodemou, L. and F. Tietze, *The state-of-the-art on Intellectual Property Analytics (IPA): A literature review on artificial intelligence, machine learning and deep learning methods for analysing intellectual property (IP) data.* World Patent Information, 2018. **55**: p. 37–51.
640. Khan, A., *The Intersection Of Artificial Intelligence And International Trade Laws: Challenges And Opportunities.* IIUMLJ, 2024. **32**: p. 103.
641. Bankins, S. and P. Formosa, *The ethical implications of artificial intelligence (AI) for meaningful work.* Journal of Business Ethics, 2023. **185**(4): p. 725–740.
642. Angwald, A., *The Illumination of Money: An Ethnography of Bitcoin in El Salvador.* 2023.
643. Al-Tawil, T.N.e., *Anti-money laundering regulation of cryptocurrency: UAE and global approaches.* Journal of Money Laundering Control, 2023. **26**(6): p. 1150–1164.
644. Oranburg, S. and L. Palagashvili, *The gig economy, smart contracts, and disruption of traditional work arrangements.* Smart Contracts, and Disruption of Traditional Work Arrangements (October 22, 2018), 2018.
645. Guest, D. and K. Isaksson, *Is there a future for research on job insecurity and the psychological contract in a changing world of work?*, in *Job Insecurity, Precarious Employment and Burnout.* 2023, Edward Elgar Publishing. p. 87–104.
646. Woods, A.K., *Litigating data sovereignty.* The Yale Law Journal, 2018: p. 328–406.
647. Ahmedov, I., *The impact of digital economy on international trade.* European Journal of Business and Management Research, 2020. **5**(4).

MIX
Papier aus verantwortungsvollen Quellen
Paper from responsible sources
FSC® C105338

If you have any concerns about our products,
you can contact us on
ProductSafety@springernature.com

In case Publisher is established outside the EU,
the EU authorized representative is:
Springer Nature Customer Service Center GmbH
Europaplatz 3, 69115 Heidelberg, Germany

Printed by Libri Plureos GmbH
in Hamburg, Germany